THE CONSISTENT
CONSUMER

PRAISE FOR *THE CONSISTENT CONSUMER*

I believe in this book. The Consistent Consumer *synthesizes politics, the arts, history, economics, and philosophy and reaches valuable conclusions. It is immensely entertaining, but most importantly to me, it is a valuable business tool. We are excited about applying its wisdom to our sales presentations.*

Neil S. Cumsky, CEO, Princeton Resorts Group, LLC

There are no limits to where you can take the information you gather from this book in improving your understanding of today's consumers. Open your briefcase and find a permanent place for this great read.

John A. Pryor, President and COO, Cousins Subs

The Consistent Consumer*'s exciting definition of generations holds together far better than the broader categories we are all used to using (such as "boomers"). The lively descriptors bring them to life in ways we can all relate to, and so in turn determine appropriate actions, as well.*

Chris Shipp, Sr. Vice President, Investment Advice and Products, Charles Schwab and Company, Inc.

An insightful and long overdue book! Finally someone has explained clearly how to predict future behavior based on generational values. A must-read for any businessperson. Our marketing department is all over this book.

Therese Thilgen, President and Chief Content Officer, Franchise UPDATE, Inc.

Precise, witty . . . observations that are so dead-on that they hit you in the head like a well-aimed hammer. The Consistent Consumer *doesn't just identify what people do and how they behave, but it uncovers the* why *people do what they do. It's one of the smartest books you'll ever meet.*

Dan Fogarty, Keeper of the Faith, Chipotle Mexican Grill

This is the book all executives need to have on their shelves if they want to understand the real issues that enable them to enhance the power of their brand, develop a viable, long-term relationship with their customers, and increase bottom-line results. Most importantly, The Consistent Consumer *can be readily implemented . . . it makes sense!*

Florence Stone, Editorial Director, American Management Association

Beller, Weiss, and Patler introduce a fresh perspective on five "generations" of American consumers. Their value-centered approach defines what really drives employee and buyer behavior and delivers a strategic and hands-on guide for 21st-century business managers and marketers.

Michael Bartlett, former Editor-in-Chief, *Restaurants & Institutions* **Magazine**

THE CONSISTENT
CONSUMER

PREDICTING FUTURE BEHAVIOR
THROUGH LASTING VALUES

**KEN
BELLER**

**STEVE
WEISS**

**LOUIS
PATLER**

Dearborn™
Trade Publishing
A **Kaplan Professional** Company

This publication is designed to provide accurate and authoritative information in regard to the subject matter covered. It is sold with the understanding that the publisher is not engaged in rendering legal, accounting, or other professional service. If legal advice or other expert assistance is required, the services of a competent professional should be sought.

President, Dearborn Publishing: Roy Lipner
Vice President and Publisher: Cynthia A. Zigmund
Acquisitions Editor: Michael Cunningham
Senior Project Editor: Trey Thoelcke
Interior Design: Lucy Jenkins
Cover Design: Design Solutions
Typesetting: the dotted i

Published by Dearborn Trade Publishing
A Kaplan Professional Company

Printed in the United States of America

05   06   07   10   9   8   7   6   5   4   3   2   1

Library of Congress Cataloging-in-Publication Data

Beller, Ken.
    The consistent consumer : predicting future behavior through lasting values / Ken Beller, Steve Weiss, and Louis Patler.
        p.   cm.
    Includes index.
    ISBN 1-4195-0273-5
    1. Consumer behavior. I. Patler, Louis. II. Weiss, Steve M. III. Title.
HF5415.32.B45 2005
658.8′342—dc22

2004026173

Dearborn Trade books are available at special quantity discounts to use for sales promotions, employee premiums, or educational purposes. Please call our Special Sales Department to order or for more information at 800-621-9621 ext. 4444, e-mail trade@dearborn.com, or write to Dearborn Trade Publishing, 30 South Wacker Drive, Suite 2500, Chicago, IL 60606-7481.

$25.00

DEDICATION

To the Patriots, Performers, Techticians, Believers, and Transformers . . .

May we all come to better understand each other and work in unison toward creating a more compassionate and peaceful world—for us and for all future Value Populations.

Contents

A book is always the result of many more people than its authors. We would like to especially thank our agent, John Willig, for bringing the opportunity to us. Michael Cunningham and the editors and staff at Dearborn Trade Publishing proved to be a wonderful matching of the minds, and made this project proceed smoothly. This book benefited greatly from the excellent research and data gathering skills of Near Bridge, Inc.'s, Ernie Baillargeon, Melinda Haseth, Laurie Masters, and Jesse Weiss.

We would also like to thank our friends and colleagues Betsy Gullickson, John Reynolds, Mike Moser, John Darling, Bob Steinbaugh, Craig Allen, Bill Daniels, Kitty Forseth, Bill Hoppin, Susan Freund, Jim Kennedy, Michael Knight, Linda Larkey, Jay Conrad Levinson, David Mills, Pat Lynch, Amy Robinson, Frank DiChristofano, Florence Stone, John Raphael, Lynn Ware, Tim Wasserman, Nancy White, Jason Saeler, Frank Chance, Jennifer Robinson, Darryl Sink, Roger Watson, Chris Shipp, Marion McGovern, Paula Reynolds, and Claire McAuliffe, who supported us early on in our efforts.

Being able to report both our research and its use in selected business settings in Part 3 of the book requires special thanks be given to our clients, who believed in the application and usefulness of our data early on: Anthony Vidergauz, CEO, California Closets; Edward Leaman, CEO, Growers & Nomads; Eric Woolworth, President, and Kim Stone, Vice President, The Miami Heat; Bernie Mullin, Vice President, The National Basketball Association; Matt Levine, President, Source USA; Dan Leese, CEO, Beringer Wineries; Linda Hudson, President, General Dynamics ATP; Craig Dewald, Global Vice President, American Express; Steve Ells, President/Founder, Jim Adams, Director of Marketing, and Dan Fogarty, Keeper of the Faith, Chipotle Mexican Grill; Phil Friedman, President, McAlister's Deli; Matt Ball and Jack Norris, Founders, Vegan Outreach; Michael Burke, Executive Director, and Lynn Rosseth, Director of Market Development, The Foodservice Packaging Institute; the Members of the United States Potato Board; Webb Howell, Publisher, Greg Sanders, Editorial Director, and Margaret Gayle, Director, Foodservice Programmes, *QSR Magazine.*

Lastly, a very special thank you to our wives—Heather, Ann, and Catherine—whose patient and endless support made this all possible.

This book has its roots in the search for consumer trends—not just any trends, mind you, but big important trends, the sort of trends that marketers, business leaders, and futurists can use to make vast pronouncements at conferences, board meetings, and cocktail parties; trends embracing really significant insights, such as, "Marketing to women is increasingly important." and "People expect to have choices."

On our quest to uncover such trends, however, we discovered that the road to understanding often was muddy with inconsistent information. As we searched for ways to free ourselves from the quagmire, it became increasingly clear that the old way of trend prediction, based on continually shifting behavioral data, was essentially washed out and that the era of the multigenerational macrotrend was, in all likelihood, gone forever. Yet, as we took the time to examine the true nature of our journey, we realized that an entirely new path on the road to understanding mass consumer behavior had opened itself up to us.

It was this realization that led us to the research and the title for this book. Simply put, mass consumer behavior, however apparently random it might seem, is best understood when built on a base of lasting values.

Like many who have preceded us, we could not resist the glimmer of truth that lurks in the apparent consistencies of demography. After exhaustive research into the most commonly accepted demographic attributes, including factors such as gender, ethnicity, education, income, and age, we concluded that age is the most fruitful attribute to focus on when searching for trends. It also eventually became clear that the identification of shared formative experiences of similarly aged consumers was an effective way to uncover common values—the drivers that create trends.

Having established this understanding, we began trying to catalog the currently accepted aged-based "generational" groups including: The Greatest Generation, Baby Boomers, Gen Xers, Millennials, and so forth. What became readily apparent was that there was little consistency or scientific reasoning behind how the beginning and ending date boundaries for each group were chosen. The clearest beginning and ending dates we found for any group were those of the Baby Boom generation, whose boundaries were based on a boom and bust in the birth rate just after World War II (1946–1964). In general, though, we found so many discrepancies in the defining dates and descriptions of the other aforementioned generations that we began calling the existing age classifications "demographic dislocation!" (A more detailed discussion of this can be found in Chapter 3, "Understanding the Ages.")

While a boom and bust in the birth rate might define a group that behaves consistently throughout its lifetime, it is unlikely. Rather, it is reasonable to assume that a group who grew up during a boom in the birth rate would experience a considerably different environment (politically, economically, socially, etc.) than one experiencing a decline in a birth rate. With the Baby Boomers, this seems to be the case, as marketers now consistently divide this generation into Early and Late Boomers—clearly showing that this classification does not work well.

This was very apparent to us on a personal level as well. Although all three authors of this book fall into the traditionally defined Baby Boom generation, two of the authors, Steve Weiss and Louis Patler, who were born in the first half of this generation, felt they were somewhat well represented by the traditional Baby Boomer profile. On the other hand, Ken Beller, the youngest of the three, who was born at the tail end of the Boomer generation, felt that he and his age-based brethren were nothing like the Boomers—nor were they aptly described by the "Slacker" profile that is typically associated with Gen Xers. So the quest to find consistency in contemporary generational profiling began.

This posed a challenge to us. If there was such inconsistency in this field of study, what age ranges and what factors would we then consider acceptable criteria for defining useful groups? How would we identify the driving forces that consistently affect consumer behavior through a group's entire life? What factors consistently shape consumer choices? Where could we look for predictive information about groups of people as they grow and mature and pass through the time honored and inevitable "phases of life?"

During our investigation, we were drawn to a body of sociological research that suggests that broad sociocultural adaptation, which begins as early as infancy, is a strong platform for lifelong group value formation. Armed with this insight, we began the rigorous project of examining American culture with a particular eye toward those people, places, things, and events—*icons* as it were—that reflect and capture the zeitgeist of society at particular and clearly defined periods in history. We postulated that groups who share the same formative iconic experiences could be identified, and once identified, would constitute very powerful and consistent target markets—whose lifelong values, preoccupations, and predispositions would be ingrained by cultural happenings and would reveal insights into likely and consistent future behaviors.

The specific research for this book spanned a three-year period, and it began by compiling an enormous database of tens-of-thousands of events and artifacts occurring since the turn of the twentieth century. This time frame was chosen because it coincided with the beginning of the era of mass communication—a period marking the ascension of universal sociocultural influences (radio, movies, television, and the Internet) over local and "tribal" influences (family tradition) as the chief catalysts of value formation in America.

Ultimately, this database of historical icons grew to include artifacts from all areas of social influence, ranging from life-altering events such as world wars and the incredible transformations of technology, to more "everyday" occurrences and artifacts culled from the realm of sports, music, television, radio, commercials, movies, books, comics, etc. In short, we tried to collect as much data on the parade of American contemporary history as possible—everything from the Great Depression to the Golden Arches, from VJ-day to Veg-O-Matics.

Our research utilized both primary and secondary information sources. The primary information came from focus groups and interviews while much of the secondary research came together in great part thanks to the significant amount of information that is now readily available on the Internet. Particularly rich veins of information are available through the many publicly available U.S. government databases, such as those of the Census Bureau and the Bureau or Labor Statistics, as well as thousands of business and private Web sites. It is amazing what one can find by "Googling" anything from "women's history in America" to "commercials of the 1930s" to the "top rated movies of the 1970s and 1980s."

Once we realized that values created by sociocultural, rather than biological, forces play such an important and increasing role in defining consistently behaving cohort groups, we could no longer rely on the term "generation" to accurately define them, so we coined a new term, Value Populations™.

In order to clearly define these Value Populations, our team began mining our database for common social and cultural themes. During this analysis process, we began discovering some significant starting and stopping points in those themes in American history. As we continued through this process, lines of differentiation began to emerge and groups having strong cultural coherence and integrity began to coalesce. Ultimately, clear demarcation points emerged, and within those periods we found a coherent set of lasting values.

Our research also revealed something unanticipated. Because the speed of societal change and the maturing of today's youth have both been increasing steadily since the beginning of the twentieth century, a Value Population no longer spans the tidy 20-year interval of a traditional generation and is, in fact, continually diminishing in length. Furthermore, it also became clear that value formation in later Value Populations becomes increasingly influenced by the multiple and very different Value Populations acting out in society at any one time.

In summary, sociocultural value formation suitably lends itself to effective consumer profiling, making it possible to not only define and understand values-based cohort groups, but to *anticipate* how they are likely to behave in future human-made and naturally occurring environments and situations. Further, because shared, common values of each Value Population last a lifetime, to the observant business leader, the benefits gained by understanding these values is significant—and can be highly profitable. From this revelation comes our perspective on *the consistent consumer.*

This book is divided into four main parts. Part 1 is intended to give the reader a better sense of the research and reasoning behind values-based demographic profiling and the method used to identify values-based cohort groups. Part 2 introduces the reader to the Value Populations and outlines the significant events, cultural artifacts, and lasting icons of the eras during their formation period. Part 3 demonstrates the application of this research within real businesses that have successfully used our Value Population research findings to increase their marketing impact and business profitability. Finally, Part 4 illustrates how values can and should be an important part of any business strategy from organizational structure, to operational excellence, to product development, to trend identification and creation.

That this material has already proven to be an aid to marketers in helping to anticipate and satisfy customers' wants and needs is something of which we are particularly proud. However, while we believe that this book offers a wealth of benefits for business leaders, it also offers a plethora of understanding that is extremely useful to teachers, parents, public policy makers—actually anyone who can derive benefit from understanding the consistent values held within large age groups, their own, and others.

With greater insight into Value Populations, we can all better understand who we are and, in doing so, increase our understanding, mutual appreciation, and consideration for each other's perspectives. That will always be a path worth taking.

THE VALUES OF
A NATION

1

THE VALUE OF VALUES

The aim of education is the knowledge, not of facts, but of values.
—William S. Burroughs, American Writer

In the past 30 years, much has changed in the field of demographic and behavioral marketing. Significant advances in technology, coupled with easy access to data and an ever-increasing array of software tools, allow marketers to access and analyze customer transaction data in vast quantities and at an amazing rate of speed. But, it seems reasonable to ask the question, "Are we getting too much measurement and not enough meaning?"

In order to help balance out this quantitative approach to measuring consumers' past behaviors and increase their understanding of "why" consumers behave the way they do, marketers regularly employ age-based generational demographics in their marketing strategies. This approach is intended to help marketers gain a better understanding of the attitudes and beliefs held by consumers, because if these attitudes and beliefs can be understood, future behavior can be better predicted and marketing strategies and advertising campaigns can be made more effective.

Interestingly, when the current methods used for this approach are closely examined, what resonates consistently throughout them is an unstated assumption that consumers' attitudes are best understood by their past behaviors. However, because behaviors are the results of deep-seated and often unconscious values, our research strongly suggests that these methods are flawed.

For marketers to be able to predict future behavior and spot future trends, a clear understanding of consumers' consistent shared values is

3

required. Values drive behavior and can act as motivational filters through which the mass of past behavioral data becomes comprehensible and future actions predictable. For marketers, predictable behavior is what dreams are made of because it allows them to effectively and accurately communicate with target audiences and sell more products at higher profit margins.

So, if shared values are the Holy Grail for marketers, how can values-based groups be uncovered? We think it's best done by analyzing significant historical events and cultural icons and defining their impact on the formation of group values. This analysis method yields a qualitative, yet data-driven approach to understanding major and newly defined age-based demographic markets and offers an effective way to uncover common tastes and behavioral consistencies within consumer groups.

What is important to clearly understand is that these new age-based groupings, or Value Populations, are not based on randomly chosen periods of time nor are they based on the extrapolation of past and current behaviors—as are those of the traditionally defined generational groups (Baby Boomers, Gen X, Gen Y, etc.). Value Populations, as their name implies, are groups whose consistent connection is shared values—values that were created by experiencing shared events in the cultural environment. We have identified five such groups: Patriots, Performers, Techticians™, Believers, and Transformers.

While the second section of this book is devoted entirely to understanding the Value Populations, a brief introduction to their formative periods and a comparison of them to the traditional and generally accepted generational cohort groups is made in Figure 1.1.

During their formative years, each Value Population is presented with unique thematic issues that they will be associated with throughout their collective lifetime. In other words, whatever a Value Population's collective and seemingly inconsistent behaviors might be, there are underlying values that will resonate consistently and continually with them throughout their lifetimes and that explain these seeming inconsistencies. Because values drive behaviors, consistent values allow astute marketers to predict behaviors and increase marketing effectiveness. It is this consistency of values that lead us to the title, *The Consistent Consumer: Predicting Future Behavior through Lasting Values.*

The foundation of this book is that experiences in our formative years create lasting values that remain constant over time. It is the recognition that every cultural time period produces art, artifacts, people, places, and things—in a word, *icons*—that seal the meaning of a moment in history. Icons embody all of the values, cross trends, and cultural cur-

FIGURE 1.1
Value Populations—A Redefinition of Generations

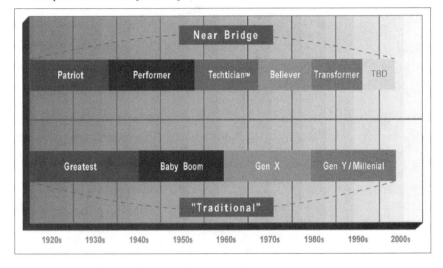

rents of the time—the essence of the moment. When these icons are recognized and analyzed, they allow researchers to clearly identify the values that people carry with them—throughout a lifetime. Icons offer an amazing plethora of understanding and meaning, and as will be shown in the next chapter, can be as seemingly inconsequential, or as surprising, as a child's toy.

2

THE POWER OF ICONS
Mr. Potato Head

*For we don't just look at icons—we resonate with them. To really take one in,
some part of us must say: it is me. The more of us who do that,
the more universal its acceptance.*

—Douglas Rushkoff, Cultural Writer

In the history of the United States
of America, it is difficult to find a more economically upbeat year than
1952. Basic American industry definitively turns a corner away from an
emphasis on military goods and a shortage-stressed war economy toward
an emphasis on all the things a peacetime consumer economy may desire in terms of creature comforts and corporate profits. With only 7 percent of the world's population, the United States finds itself producing
65 percent of the world's manufactured goods; the Gross National Product and disposable income soar to unprecedented levels; and the nation's 3.3 percent unemployment rate is the lowest in peacetime history.

Nearly four million new automobiles roll off assembly lines in 1952
and, even more importantly, the nation's parents produce just about the
same amount of new passengers. This new peak in the birth rate, which
has been growing since the end of World War II in 1945, and which will
be superseded every year for the next six years, is the true backbone of
the nation's economic optimism about the future. Nothing, after all, sup-
ports a consumer economy like a large number of consumers.

On a more somber note, it must be appreciated that these relatively
affluent 1952 babies are born into what are still hellaciously dangerous
and stressful times. This is the dawn of the Cold War and atom bomb
era, which some cultural commentators believe first viscerally hits home
with the general American public during the 1952 Summer Olympics—
the first Olympics participated in by the Soviet Union in 40 years and in

which they very nearly top the victorious Americans point total—with the outcome in doubt until late on the last day. More urgently, war with Communist forces still rages in Korea and an enormous cloud over all future prospects is cast by America's testing of the first hydrogen bomb on the Eniwetok Atoll on November 1, 1952—30 times more powerful than the Hiroshima bomb and more powerful than all of the munitions fired in World War II combined.

It is against this backdrop of material prosperity and global anxiety that Mr. Potato Head is born. Brought to the marketplace by a pair of brothers whose company would soon come to be known as Hasbro, the original toy consists of a spike-topped plastic body where a real potato is placed and then stuck with an assortment of

plastic pin-inserted eyes, ears, noses, mouths, hats, and so forth, that make a variety of whimsical faces. Reputedly the first toy ever advertised on television, Mr. Potato Head is an immediate success and sells about four million units in its first year.

In the study of generational values, what makes Mr. Potato Head such an interesting toy at the starting point of his still-illustrious career is his role as an icon of consumption for two different generations, or more specifically, Value Populations. For the parents in 1952, all of whom were touched by the privations of world war and the material want of a global depression, what greater taboo could be broken than the injunction against *playing* with one's food? Yet here they are in 1952, apparently flush with the relief of war's end and rapidly growing material abundance, encouraging their offspring to waste food by sticking brightly colored plastic noses on real potatoes!

What does this say about this group's long-term *values?*

Also, what of the recipients of these toys? In 1952 we find them playing, endlessly playing, while the governments of hostile nations sponsor the development of new ways to eradicate the human species. Many decades later, will the values of these erstwhile tots still center around self-expression, material entitlement and, one might argue, bravery as expressed as child's play in the face of possible annihilation?

By 1964, America comes to the realization that not all of its citizens have been invited to the prosperity party. While affluence mounts for the great majority of Americans, the nation acknowledges that 20 percent of its population, situated primarily in rural areas such as Appalachia and in the ghettos of major cities abandoned by a suburbia-bound middle class, lives at or below the poverty level. Lyndon Johnson, as the focal point of his first State of the Union address, declares a War on Poverty.

Mirroring the nation's growing faith in the economic power and benefits of technology, there is a clear sense in 1964 that the solutions to vast social problems can be engineered through a combination of scientific approach and well-intentioned legislation. In addition to the aid programs of the War on Poverty, including a massive tax cut, the year witnesses the passage of the Civil Rights Act, the most comprehensive piece of antidiscrimination legislation of the twentieth century. In the public health arena, 1964 is the year of the first surgeon general's report on smoking that establishes the link between cigarette smoking and cancer.

Despite good intentions, however, 1964 is a year in which cracks are just beginning to show in the nation's faith in its capability to outthink the future. The country is still in deep shock and mourning over the loss of its visionary president, John F. Kennedy, assassinated in November 1963. Furthermore, in response to a Vietnamese gunboat attack, the Gulf of Tonkin Resolution is passed and the Vietnam War formally begins.

The craziness that is coming to American cultural discourse is also foreshadowed by a much-noted television event. The appearance of The Beatles on *The Ed Sullivan Show* is the symbolic start of what most cultural observers mean when they talk about "the 60s." In 1964, American society is right on the verge of going a little nuts.

It is deeply consonant with the times that government regulatory agencies have a go at Mr. Potato Head. After a determination that the sharp points of the Mr. Potato Head appendages are dangerous to children, Hasbro is instructed to round off the points, which means that they no longer easily pierce a real potato. Thus, in 1964, Mr. Potato Head undergoes technological reformation, becoming a plastic potato with predrilled holes.

So what will become of the children who play with this iteration of Mr. Potato Head? Decades later will they be inclined to some sacrifice of variety, creativity, and personal expression for the sake of safety and technological efficiency? Will they become a generation of pragmatists, a little cynical perhaps, but, in the face of the enormously disruptive and capricious forces of actual life, still be convinced of the value of a rational approach to social problem solving?

In 1973, the economic fortunes of the United States of America take a turn for the worse. This is particularly unfortunate because the United States accomplishes a much-coveted social objective in this year. Although it smacks of flat out retreat, the enormously divisive war in Vietnam ends and all American ground troops are at last brought home.

It is not unexpected that a figurative sort of cultural exhaustion might set in after the conclusion of such a prolonged society-wrenching event. But the universal energy depletion that transpires during 1973 is anything but figurative or metaphorical. In retaliation for America's support of Israel in the so-called Yom Kippur War, the member nations of OPEC induce a world-wide oil shortage that causes the price of a barrel of oil to soar from $1.50 a barrel to $11.50 a barrel in the course of just a few months.

The economic and cultural impact of this oil embargo is stamped all over American life in 1973. Not only do significant directional changes occur in the macrotrends of the previously dynamic American economy, but everyday life is impacted by such factors as long lines at gas stations and the legislation of a national speed limit set at 55 miles per hour. It is a year when, as an energy conservation measure, no electric ornaments are placed on the national Christmas tree.

Sadly, the growing sense of powerlessness is compounded by a very real leadership crisis. The Vice President of the United States, Spiro Agnew, resigns in disgrace after pleading guilty to tax evasion charges. More memorably, the Watergate investigation is in full bloom, with President Richard Nixon doing little to calm the national angst when he famously tells a group of reporters, "I am not a crook."

It is against this backdrop that Mr. Potato Head is inflated, enervated, and emasculated. In 1973, the plastic Mr. Potato Head body suddenly swells to twice its original size and the pre-drilled holes are replaced with slots so that the various appendages can now only be fastened in a single physiologically "accurate" manner. Most  telling, however, is that Mr. Potato Head's body and arms simply disappear (although he has had them in all product iterations to this time).

What will become of the generation subjected to such a plaything? Will they retain a lifelong fear of personal impotence seasoned with a mistrust of the clueless maneuverings of patriarchal authority? Or will they inevitably rise above it through the very experience of coping with down times, putting their hearts into empathic friendships, and believing with patient faith that things just "have to get better" in the future?

As Ronald Reagan begins his second term as President in 1985, the United States is once again feeling its collective oats. The country is in the third year of a broad economic, political, and cultural rebound that will last with few interruptions through most of the 1980s and 1990s. As the President remarks in his second inaugural address, fully capturing the mood of the moment: "In this blessed land, there is always a better tomorrow."

Arguably, it is a foreign event, the accession of Mikhail Gorbachev to the top governmental post in the Soviet Union, that best demarcates the wondrous possibilities of the era. Gorbachev's place as the last President of the Soviet Union ushers in an age of reformation and liberalization that ultimately results in the doctrinal and political dissolution of America's most feared and powerful adversary. By the end of the year, Presidents Reagan and Gorbachev are meeting face to face, earnestly discussing cultural exchange and nuclear disarmament.

Along with the sense of potential that pervades the economic and geopolitical scene, the year ushers in an important new window on tomorrow when Microsoft Windows 1.0 is introduced into the personal computer marketplace. Along with the graphical interface of the Apple McIntosh, introduced the previous year, the world embarks on a potent new era of perception, thought organization, and knowledge creation. The children of 1985, the year in which the Nintendo Entertainment System is also first brought to market, will be citizens of the interactive computer age, virtually from birth.

As with every other time in the history, 1985 does have its share of truly negative news stories. Terrorist acts and airplane hijackings are liberally sprinkled across the year's front pages. The existence of crack cocaine and the hole in the ozone layer are formally established. Rock Hudson's death from AIDS makes a high profile point about the seriousness of the news that is to come on that front.

Yet, most significantly and unlike the reaction just a decade earlier, the times just seem to be characterized by their optimistic focus. Nowhere is this more apparent than in society's return of children to a place of prominence, protection, and concern in the national agenda. Typified by the creation of the National Children's Advocacy Center to combat child abuse, by Tipper Gore's appearances before Congress to warn against the alarming trends in rock music, and, for that matter, by famous rock musicians singing about taking care of the world's children in the year's noteworthy foreign aid anthem, "We Are the World," it is clear that kids are back in the cultural limelight.

While 1985 is note-
worthy as the year that
Mr. Potato Head enters
the computer age by
fronting a children's
software program de-
veloped for Apple, the
year's really big news is

that Mr. and Mrs. Potato Head become parents. Baby Potato Head, an
adorable freckle-faced plastic spud, is introduced as the feature item in
the Mr. Potato Head family kit, and, quite appealingly, the whole family
has bendable, permanently attached arms!

Who are the children to play with such a toy? Surely they are blessed
by the simple fact that society welcomes them into the social fold. Might
not such a group grow into a generation of confident can-doers? Might
they not employ the nascent power of technology and their belief in the
irresistibility of the collective social will to not only bend their arms in
effort, but to ultimately even bend reality itself?

3

UNDERSTANDING
THE AGES

Where is the knowledge that is lost in information?

—T.S. Eliot, American Poet

While the Mr. Potato Head example
was selected to tickle the imagination, it is also intended to make the point
that significant social meaning and cultural understanding can be contained in cultural icons—even the permutations of a simple toy. As marketers, whom do we trust for insight? Is Mr. Potato Head telling us something
much more important than quantitative analysis? Is he a legitimate symbol of the collective generational consciousness and values of an era, or
is the real truth about attitudinal marketing to be revealed from our
spreadsheets and computer projections? This chapter will explore these
questions through critical examination of current thinking and methods
related to demographic, behavioral, and attitudinal information and
analysis.

In an era when customer transaction data is easily and continually
gathered and analyzed—from supermarket club cards that are scanned
and analyzed at every register to radio frequency identification (RFID)
microchips being used to identify our pets—why shouldn't marketers
capitalize on the burgeoning amount of computer power at their fin-
gertips and rely heavily on expert systems to predict future behaviors?

First, transactional data only deals with the behaviors or end results
of consumers' decisions, not their motivational drivers—the personal,
unconscious, emotional, and underlying reasons "why" they behave the
way they do. As was stated earlier in this book, past behavior does not drive
or consistently predict future behavior. A previous flip of a coin has no

bearing on the outcome of a future toss. Behaviors are driven by values—not previous behaviors.

Second, behavioral correlation does not necessarily equate to behavioral cause. Does a 75 percent increase in storks and a 75 percent increase in babies prove that storks bring babies? Statistically, a strong correlation can be observed—but does this correlation accurately define the cause of the increased population growth? No. Complex problems often have simple, easy to understand, but incorrect answers.

Third, expert systems are best understood as "idiot geniuses." They are very adept within a narrow range of problem solving, but they are "stone stupid" at everything else. Why? Because machines cannot think, reason, or gather information on their own and are therefore only as intelligent as the information that is input into them. Trying to capture and control the millions of variables, both dependent and independent, as well as the historical, social, biological, emotional, and environmental factors that go into every decision each of us makes is impossible.

To completely understand human behavior on a purely scientific basis misses the power, the thrusts, and the essence of human behavior.

So, is behavioral data useless? No, it can and should play a part in marketing and business decision making, but a clear understanding of people's lasting values is significantly more valuable when attempting to predict future actions than is extrapolating from past behaviors. While data analysis is a powerful tool, that gives marketers a way of measuring the outcomes of their assumptions and predictions, it is important to remember that it is only a tool—and one that is always looking in the rear view mirror.

What is interesting, and will be addressed in greater detail later in this book, is that the current Value Population responsible for this data analysis charge, the Techticians, (see Part 2, Chapters 10, 11, and 12) is clearly drawn to this way of looking at the world—one where everything is scientifically collected and measured. This is not to say that the Techticians and their data-crunching methods have not added many new and important ways of looking at consumer actions, it is just that their strength is also their Achilles heal—in that sometimes one can get too much measurement and not enough meaning.

So if a purely quantitative analysis of behavioral data is not the silver bullet to finding the driving forces behind behaviors, what *causes* consumer behavior and deeply motivates choices?

For years, marketers have been looking at demographic profiling to help answer this question. Today one would have a hard time finding even a small company that lacks insight into the age segmentation of its customers. While gender, income, ethnicity, and a host of other factors also enter into the picture, target markets are now almost invariably first referenced with regard to age and typically take one of two forms—life phase or generational.

Life phase is the term used for dividing populations into age-based groups that behave similarly at each phase of life, regardless of when they were born. Categories that are frequently used include terms such as infancy, childhood, adolescence, teens, adulthood, old age, etc.

Upon examination of these life-phase classifications, it becomes clear that there are useful, valid, and consistent "marker" events often linked to certain biological truths that lead to some consistent behaviors. For example, American teens have a voracious appetite, are obsessed with looking good, don't like to hang out with their parents, and have raging hormones. Young adults, as they begin to "find themselves," often behave erratically when they "try on" new identities or "fall in love." Then there is menopause and the midlife crisis in the "middle age" group, and the loss of hearing, eyesight, and taste in the elderly.

While all generations go through the same life phases, there is a significant difference between a generation and a life phase. For example, a teenager today and a teenager in the 1930s might both fight similar problems with acne, but their values and behaviors as a whole are significantly different—same life phase, different generation. So, while life phase has a place in understanding behaviors, there has to be more to capturing the lasting drivers of behavior that remain consistent with a group as it ages.

Traditionally, social scientists have used a so-called psychobiological approach in defining generational cohort groups. This approach is based upon a regularly structured and repeating pattern of human psychological and biological development, typically 20 years in duration.

But, are all 20-year generations the same? According to Strauss and Howe, in their best selling book, *Generations: The History of America's Future, 1584 to 2069*, they are—kind of. Their theory is that every generation belongs to one of four types of generations that repeat sequentially in a fixed pattern. They claim that understanding this pattern of generational repetition allows for the prediction of the future. However, with the exponential gains in technology and the ever-increasing complexity of cultural changes that have occurred over the last 500 years, it seems reasonable to question the validity of this assumption. Societies and people's values change and evolve, and to think that social behaviors will follow a consistent pattern every fourth generation for 500 years seems unreasonable.

In 1946, the great "Baby Boom" of the post World War II era "began" and "lasted" until 1964. The naming of this group in and of itself sparked a new interest and way of looking at consumers by marketers and social scientists. The thrust of consumer profiling had new life breathed into it, and consumers were now being grouped and analyzed based on specific birth periods. After the Baby Boom generation was defined, a new cottage industry was created by those laying claim to a new name for yet another "generation"—all emphasizing behavioral-based trend prediction.

Oddly enough, since the defining of the Baby Boom generation, there has been very little consensus among demographers as to the starting point and duration of future generations. The basic methodology used is to choose a time frame, give it a name, review the current and past behaviors of the group, and attempt to extrapolate past behavior into predicting future behavior.

The problem with this methodology is that human behavior is complex, nonlinear, and ever changing. For instance, take a look at the so-called "Baby Boomers." In the 1960s, they were the most "antiestablishment" generation America had ever seen, but in the 1990s Boomers became voracious capitalists. Where is the consistency in this behavior and what can account for it?

Values are like the hub of a wheel and behaviors are like the spokes. Just as all spokes originate from a hub, behaviors originate from values. In practical terms, the behavior/value connection of the Baby Boomers, illustrated by such icons as soap operas, cowboy movies, and Disneyland, yields a cohort group characterized by its dramatic and theatrical response to situations—the mining of any event for its drama, fun, and adventure—whether at a campus protest or in a corporate boardroom.

Figure 3.1 outlines some of the different generational names used by marketers to define age-based cohort groups and the range of their beginning and ending dates. Upon examination of this chart, it becomes apparent that there are some significant differences in even supposedly "consistent" cohort groupings like the Baby Boomers who traditionally began in 1946 and lasted until 1964, but who now are often classified based on a four-year range for the beginning date and a six-year range for the ending date. That does not even take into account the splitting up of the generation up into "Early" and "Late" Boomers.

So, why is there all of this difference in beginning and ending date definition? Because, unlike Value Populations, where a clear set of shared experiences and values-based criteria was used to define the demarcation dates of each group, the time frames for most generally accepted generational groupings were chosen somewhat at random based on past behavior instead of on lasting and consistent criteria. In Value Populations "speak," that lasting criteria is shared values.

FIGURE 3.1
Demographic Dislocations

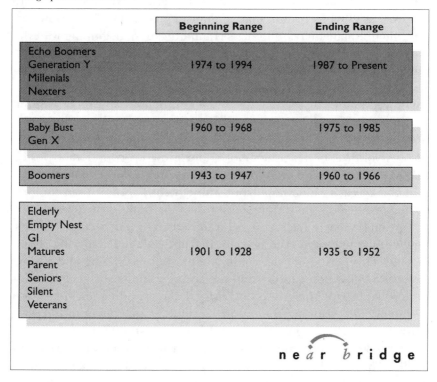

	Beginning Range	Ending Range
Echo Boomers Generation Y Millenials Nexters	1974 to 1994	1987 to Present
Baby Bust Gen X	1960 to 1968	1975 to 1985
Boomers	1943 to 1947	1960 to 1966
Elderly Empty Nest GI Matures Parent Seniors Silent Veterans	1901 to 1928	1935 to 1952

ne*a*r *b*ridge

So, what forms shared values? Before analyzing value formation, it is important to first define a value. *A* value *is a thematically shared and culturally based orientation, derived from significant events primarily instilled in youth and often linked to external events occurring as early as gestation.*

As was stated in Chapter 1, values are the filters through which the mass of behavioral data becomes comprehensible. In order to identify these value filters, a unique and proprietary sociocultural approach to age-based demographic analysis has been used to define consistent and lasting cohort groups. This sociocultural approach is based on the assumption that generational consciousness is created by the social and cultural environment of the time and that this in turn creates lasting values within the generation being formed. What causes behaviors in a sociological model is not past behavior, but a values response to emotions that are activated by the external forces or events occurring in a group's environment in the early years of life.

Prior to the twentieth century, youth experienced events and environments that were similar to those experienced by their parents and grandparents, so a fairly homogenous society and value-set existed. In this context, local cultural and family conditions played a more significant role in value formation than did outside social influence. However, with the dramatic increase in mass communication, beginning with the radio in the 1920s, value formation became increasingly driven by cultural conditions that were broader and more complex—coming from across the country and around the world.

Interestingly, the increased volume and quickened rate of cultural information flow and change due to new avenues of communication such as the TV and the Internet is shortening value formation periods. Today's youth experience far more, and grow up considerably faster, than their parents and grandparents did at their same age, making the duration of each Value Population subsequently shorter than the preceding one—and significantly shorter than the traditional 20-year cycle.

When society is analyzed from a shared-event perspective, a consistent set of lasting values can be identified and linked to a specific period in time. This period of time is what defines the beginning and ending dates of a Value Population—and the lasting values associated with this time period shape the group's behavioral and spending decisions for a lifetime. Understanding these value sets allows marketers to focus on consistent and lifelong branding and marketing strategies.

So, how are these values captured and made useful by savvy marketers? Through the use of historical icons. Icons are valuable because, among other things, they encapsulate cultural attributes and attitudes of the time. When a Value Population encounters these icons again, they emotionally resonate with them. For marketers, recognizing these emotionally consistent triggers within a target audience is crucial in creating an effective and lasting marketing campaign. An excellent example of this is McDonald's Happy Meal and its notion that a brand can be your "friend." A marketing icon that still resonates strongly with the generation that was formed during the period of the Happy Meal's introduction, the Believers, see Part 2, Chapters 13, 14, and 15.

History tells many stories that define how social interactions and shared experiences play a fundamental role in the development of consistent and lifelong values. As distinguished Pulitzer prize winning author and social commentator Ellen Goodman said, "Values are not trendy items that are casually traded in." This sociocultural approach not only facilitates broad yet precise trend prediction but, by emphasizing history, opens a treasure trove of associations that can be used by the astute marketer to understand consumers' needs, wants, and desires at a core level—making it possible to elicit behavior, not just sell to it.

GETTING TO KNOW THE VALUE POPULATIONS

Part Two of *The Consistent Consumer* presents our research findings. It outlines the general characteristics of each Value Population, highlights the significant events associated with each value formation period, and draws conclusions concerning lasting values.

Each Value Population has three chapters dedicated to its discussion. The first chapter is intended to give the reader a cursory understanding of the broad demographic and value characteristics of the Value Population under discussion; the second chapter provides a high-level overview, or "event matrix," of the historic events that played a significant role in the value formation of the period; and the third chapter uses an analysis of contemporary cinema (the only medium that spans all of the Value Population periods—making it a strong source for comparison) as a focal point for capturing and understanding the essence of the Value Population under discussion.

The five Value Populations and their associated chapters are:

Patriots   (born 1920–1937)   —   Chapters 4, 5, and 6,

Performers   (born 1938–1957)   —   Chapters 7, 8, and 9,

Techticians   (born 1958–1971)   —   Chapters 10, 11, and 12

Believers   (born 1972–1983)   —   Chapters 13, 14, and 15

Transformers   (born 1984–1995)   —   Chapters 16, 17, and 18

It is important to note that while the first chapter of each Value Population gives the reader an overall understanding of the Value Population's general characteristics, it is the authors' strong belief that the second and third chapters of each section are critical reading for those who truly want to understand the Value Population and put their power and their wealth of historical icon associations to work.

The last chapter of Part Two, Chapter 19, "'Who's' Next?," briefly discusses the authors' current views on the Value Population that is currently being formed. While the authors are not certain about when this Value Population's formation period will end, there is a clear line of debarkation from the events and cultural spirit of the Transformer value-formation period to that of a new Value Population.

While Part Two contains a significant amount of information about the fundamental characteristics and makeup of each Value Population, it also offers a wonderful trip down the corridors of our collective national history and our individual memory lanes. We hope you enjoy the journey.

4

THE PATRIOTS
An Overview

POPULATION OVERVIEW

Age:	Born 1920–1937
Size:	12% of the U.S. Population
Spending:	$580 Billion Annually
Themes:	Freedom/Fear
Values:	Comfort/Virtue

Summary

It would be naïve to assume that life was easy prior to the Patriot value-formation period. On the other hand, it can be argued that life experiences were somehow more consistent, measured, local, and familiar prior to the advent of mass communication, industrialization, global depression, and world war. With the Patriots, one encounters a Value Population "forced" to collectively accept a complex, unknown, and seemingly dangerous future. While mass prosperity and cultural freedom beckon in this new age, it is the collective pain that fate inflicts on this group, primarily via economic disappointment, but also through significant changes in the established social fabric, that most clearly leaves a lasting mark on their values. For this group there is a strong sense that life-changing decisions are made on their behalf—ones that they do not fully participate in making, that they do not necessarily want, and that at times hurt them badly. Throughout the social commentary of the Patriot period, there is a deserved litany of suspicion regarding bankers, businessmen, brokers, and most politicians. Subjected to the grim residue of war, disease, and want, Patriots, more than any other Value Population, are about exercising caution, mistrusting the motives of others, keeping their hands on their wallets, and most of all, attending to the rules and rituals of the families, friends, and social equals who validate and protect their own stash of valuables and values.

PATRIOT HISTORICAL EVENT MATRIX

Anxiety/Boom and Bust/Anxiety

Anxiety

The end of World War I (1914–1919) was largely positive for the United States in terms of its international, economic, and geopolitical standing. Yet, the postwar period, with a final wartime death toll of 5,500 fatalities per day, and a worldwide influenza epidemic in 1919, which killed 20 to 40 million additional people, including more than a half-million Americans, caused great post-traumatic stress to society.

Marked by enormous xenophobia and a clamor for cultural fundamentalism, the suddenly industrializing, immigrant-absorbing, globally ensnared, and socially/sexually liberated American society (women gain universal suffrage in 1920) breeds enormous cultural disorientation and elicits fierce counter pressure to take things back to a more simple, familiar, and orderly time.

Boom and Bust

WW I marks the U.S. turn from a debtor to a creditor nation. The 1920s are a time of enormous economic and industrial expansion, with assembly-line manufacturing, easy credit, and rising stock prices bringing significant material prosperity into the life of the common citizen.

The Jazz Age, with its flappers and speakeasies, is perhaps the most memorable icon of the Roaring Twenties—but the real news is the introduction of socially liberating automobile travel, broadcast radio, handset telephones, and movies into the cultural fabric of modern America life.

The stock market collapse from 1929 to 1932 erases 91 percent of the value of stocks. Most of this damage is done in less than a single week during the "Great Crash" of 1929. Everything economic suddenly and desperately changes for the worse.

Anxiety

The Great Depression, which is not entirely dispelled until America's involvement as an arms seller in the early years of WW II, begins with the Wall Street crash and peaks in 1932, with 12.5 percent of the U.S. adult population out of work—and painful economic dislocation apparent in every aspect of American life. Franklin Delano Roosevelt's New Deal programs (1932–1937) play an important part in acknowledging and addressing the relief and reform challenges facing the U.S. economy. Nevertheless, there is much conservative political opposition to FDR's "welfare" programs, and a thorough watering down of the New Deal initiatives leads to another painful recessionary period in 1937.

PATRIOT POPULATION VALUES

Familiarity

- *Historical drivers.* Global conflict emerges; worldwide influenza pandemic; ethnic immigration; assembly line mechanization replacing natural agrarian rhythms.
- *Value manifestation.* Strange, disruptive, and dangerous forces in the macroenvironment lead to a high valuation of the familiar.

Creature Comfort

- *Historical drivers.* The downside of modernization balanced by an emerging consumer goods economy—first widespread availability of creature comforts, such as autos, radios, refrigerators, etc.
- *Value manifestation.* Material things take the edge off of heightened anxiety.

Wealth

- *Historical drivers.* Real ruin and deprivation after a period of enormous economic optimism (the "Roaring 20s" followed by Great Depression) pushes wealth to a primary position in the value matrix.

- *Value manifestation.* While wealth always makes the good times better, lack of it makes the bad times worse—and one should always have a little put away for the inevitable rainy day.

Affection

- *Historical drivers.* Disruption of sedentary and localized lifestyles; greater exposure to impersonal culture of mass industrialization, poverty extremes, and threatening foreign influences; the battle between the sexes as reflected in suffrage issues.
- *Value manifestation.* Being liked can often provide a better psychological buffer and sense of security than being loved.

A Place in the Collective

- *Historical drivers.* War and poverty followed by the advent of social recovery programs during the FDR administration
- *Value manifestation.* The world is too dangerous for individualists, but working together we can each find our unique place while contributing to the general good of all.

Loyalty

- *Historical drivers.* The opening round in the battle between previously existing social domination and isolationist tendencies and the threats posed by multiculturalism and forces outside the system.
- *Value manifestation.* In a world of suddenly conflicting and potentially dangerous ideologies, allegiance to the belief system of the collective is more than a pledge—it is sacred duty.

Virtue

- *Historical drivers.* The conflict over modern cultural evolution entails a debate over what constitutes moral integrity, especially about fundamentalist issues and events such as Prohibition.
- *Value manifestation.* A rapidly changing environment creates a strong drive to claim the moral high ground and the resultant support of an "absolute" for one's own beliefs-driven sect.

Courage

- *Historical drivers.* The difficulty in adapting to a world that is faster, more locally diverse, and more remotely dangerous than ever before.
- *Value manifestation.* With so much to be truly fearful of, there is hardly a greater virtue than personal courage—particularly on behalf of the clan.

Defense and Security Systems

- *Historical drivers.* The fear of aggression from outside forces ranging from foreign armies to germs to threatening cultures to the displacement of modern mechanized society to catastrophic financial reversals.
- *Value manifestation.* A strong military presence, a vigilant police force, a tall wall around the city, good locks, some money in the bank, and a resolute belief system help to neutralize the bad guys— and there are always bad guys.

PATRIOT MACRO INTERESTS

(Life-phase considerations projected through 2010)

Public Health and Welfare Policy

It is harder to think of anything that aging Patriots are more passionate about than what they feel is a firm government promise to help support them in their old age. As children of the Depression, they witnessed the creation of a Social Security system, which they then supported all their working lives. It is now payoff time.

Loss of Partners

Possible heartbreak aside, what matters most to a Patriot is how loss of a partner will impact personal security. Insurance, a decent bank balance, and a close-knit support group are all great comforts.

Death

Generally fearful of the unknown all their lives, Patriots are wary regarding what may await them on the other side. They'd feel better if they could talk to someone dear who has already been there, and they would probably like to take a few dollars and a sack lunch along with them.

Legacies

Much of the economic future of the nation is tied into the inevitable reallocation of wealth that has been amassed by the Patriot Value Population. But this is a group that has no problem with putting a price on relationships. Beware the proudly displayed bumper sticker that declares, "We are spending our children's inheritance."

Grandchildren

Surely there is sentimental attachment here, but to fully understand the Patriots is to appreciate that they are always grooming members of the tribe. What's particularly interesting is that some of the grandchildren are, unlike the members of most of the in-between Value Populations, being value-formed in ways that are quite resonant with their grandparents' values.

All Things Medical

Patriots' concern with all things medical is of course obvious, but not so obvious is the Patriots' most deep-seated, and most often frustrated, expectation of the medical community. This is a group that is sold miracle pills, prognostications, and processes. Yet what they crave most is empathy and "high touch."

Military Affairs

One misses the full picture here if all one sees are grizzled veterans celebrating their own courageous survival of past wars. Yes, this group can be fierce and unquestioning in protection of the homeland, but by the same token, no group better understands that wars are political and economic enterprises whose costs and sacrifices (and profits if it comes to that) are rarely shared equally.

Comfort Food—Not Nutrition and Dietetics

Influencing the diet of the Patriots is not going to be an easy matter. This is the group that invented comfort food, and there is very little of a scientific nature that will convince them that food exists for a more important clinical purpose.

Retail Function and Adaptation

Yes, more and more Patriots are likely to be persuaded to the ease and personal safety of shopping on the Internet. It is nevertheless still important for retailers to understand that this is a highly social group that finds human interaction an important part of commerce.

Better Safe than Sorry

Patriots are especially motivated by safety concerns. Conspicuous signs that a parking lot is under surveillance and the presence of uniformed guards, etc., are very appealing to this group.

Relaxation for Patriots

Family gatherings (although these are so vital to personal definition, they also have heavier overtones of responsibility and conflict), picnics, block parties and other local celebrations, rooting for the home team, dining out in the neighborhood with friends, homespun humor, music, dancing, and alcoholic beverages.

5

THE PATRIOTS
History Creating Values

The Patriot value formation period begins at the end of World War I (1914–1919). Although largely a European event, it is an enormous and sobering historical watershed for all life on the planet. The sheer carnage of the war (8.5 million dead— 600,000 at the battle of Verdun alone), facilitated by such "modern" armaments as the machine gun and poison gas, puts a chill into global human affairs that will never again fully abate. Coupled with a worldwide influenza pandemic that strikes during the final years of the war and causes the death of another 20 to 40 million people (the worst plague in recorded history until the advent of AIDS), the wartime legacy is one of deep mistrust of both "progress" and foreign involvement. See Figure 5.1.

THE ANXIOUS AFTERMATH OF WW I (1920+)

As the war ends, the United States has fewer casualties than other war participants, and the nation benefits from increased economic and political authority in the postwar period. Yet the comprehension of what has taken place overseas, and the taste of death at home (50,000 combat fatalities; more than a quarter of the entire nation afflicted with influenza, resulting in more than a half-million deaths), impact upon both the external and internal affairs of the nation throughout the Patriot period.

FIGURE 5.1
Casualties of World War I

Allied Powers		Central Powers	
Russia	9,150,000	Germany	7,142,558
France	6,160,800	Austria-Hungary	7,020,000
British Empire	3,190,235	Turkey	975,000
Italy	2,197,000	Bulgaria	266,919
Romania	535,706		
United States	364,800	**Total Allied Power Casualties**	
Serbia	331,106	22,104,209	
Belgium	93,061		
Portugal	33,291	**Total Central Power Casualties**	
Montenegro	20,000	15,404,477	
Greece	17,000	**Total Casualties of World War I**	
Japan	1,210	37,508,686	

Source: Spartacus Education

To characterize the tone of the Patriot value-formation era as "cautious," especially regarding the acceptance of outsiders, is an understatement.

Isolationism

By the end of WW I, the United States is well on its way to becoming the world's most powerful and influential nation. American president Woodrow Wilson is particularly prominent in driving a global policy of national self-determination that radically alters the maps of Europe and the Middle East. The crown of his conception is the League of Nations, a forerunner of the United Nations, established in 1919 under the Treaty of Versailles "to promote international cooperation and to achieve peace and security." In many ways, the Patriot era officially starts in 1920 when the U.S. Senate votes *against* ratification of the League of Nations Covenant (in the same year, Congress also passes legislation to sharply curtail immigration via a national quota system). Through the next four presidential administrations, a formal government policy of noninvolvement and neutrality in international affairs prevails. Even during the early years of the FDR administration, which would eventually lead the nation's effort in WW II, separate neutrality acts are passed in 1935, 1936, and 1937.

Cultural Fundamentalism

Far more immediate and dramatic than the isolationist tone of geo-politics is the sense of extremely conservative cultural fundamentalism that dominates domestic affairs, particularly among the nation's vested Anglo-Saxon population. If death and disease are derived from foreign sources, "true" Americans must be vigilant in monitoring all that is foreign, including immigrants and homegrown defenders of exotic social beliefs. While much of this is born of an understandable fear of current events and a reasonable nostalgic longing for order, safety, and conformity, there is still much real pain and repression in the course of events. Some of the representative developments of the period in this regard include:

- *The Red Scare (1920).* Nearly 3,000 communists, anarchists, and other radicals are arrested without due cause in government raids.
- *Sacco-Vanzetti Trial (1920–1927).* Two immigrant anarchist fish peddlers are tried and convicted of murders they likely have not committed and are subsequently executed. Massachusetts's governor Michael Dukakais reverses the controversial verdict 50 years later.
- *Scopes Trial (1925).* Clarence Darrow faces off against William Jennings Bryan in a battle of science versus religious fundamentalism. Defendant John Scopes is found guilty of teaching evolution in a Tennessee school and is "symbolically" fined $100.
- *Ku Klux Klan.* Advocating biblical fundamentalism, less government interference, labor pacifism, racial and ethnic purity, and a return to the values of small-town life, KKK membership grows from 100,000 in 1920 to more than 2 million in 1925. Not just a southern or rural phenomenon, the KKK has a significant presence on the city councils of Chicago, Denver, Dallas, and Indianapolis.
- *Prohibition (1920–1933).* Prohibition is a complex issue, but it is apparent that the staunchest advocates of an alcohol-free America are largely the same group that empathizes with the cultural fundamentalist agenda. Historical observers have amply demonstrated that in the postwar climate most alcoholic beverages (German beer, Italian wine, Russian vodka, etc.) are identified as immigrant products and therefore suspect on those grounds alone. Cynical political observers point out that the prohibition of liquor also particularly undermines the tax revenue and power base of politicians in industrial and ethnic-based big cities.

Boom and Bust

There is a counterpoint to the generally apprehensive tone of the Patriot value formation period—to be found in rapidly growing prospects for economic prosperity and social liberation in the mid- and late 1920s. What is often overlooked in analyses that dwell upon such factors, however, is that this state of economic and social opportunity hardly equates to a richer, more meaningful, or more secure life for all American citizens—for although the 1920s certainly do "roar" for a time, hardly anyone makes it through the Great Depression of the 1930s unscathed or unchastened.

Economic Growth

A number of factors converge to establish the United States as a great economic force during most of the 1920s. WW I leaves the competitive economies of Europe in disarray. The development of assembly-line production principles and the wide availability of cheap urban labor allow for the mushrooming of factories. Increasing availability of electricity and communications technology facilitates the growth of production and the range of available consumer goods. A rapidly rising stock market, fueled by margin-buying and a prevailing government bias toward nonregulation of business, makes investment capital extremely cheap and most industrial expansion plans extremely practicable.

For the average American consumer, it is a time when telephones, vacuum cleaners, washing machines, refrigerators, and radios (often bought on installment plans) become part of ordinary household life. Ford's Model Ts and Model As begin to roll off assembly lines and by 1930, 77 percent of American households own a car (versus 2 percent in 1910). Indicative of the times is the rise in magazine advertising revenues, which more than triple from $58.5 million in 1918 to $200 million in 1929.

The Jazz Age

The great social icons of the 1920s include the speakeasy, the flapper, and the gangster, all generationally symbolic of new wealth, new social mores, and a youthful urge to escape the darker social and psychological repressions of the period. While the "Gatsby" life is hardly a cultural condition for most Americans, its very existence represents a prevailing desire to evade the grimness of the times. It is certainly interesting to note that many of the great heroes of the 1920s—Babe Ruth, Charles Lindbergh, Amelia Earhart, Will Rogers, and even Al Capone (an antihero, but arguably more admired than reviled by a majority of ordinary citizens)—are neither political nor military heroes and are celebrated for testing the social limits of the times as well as for their noteworthy achievements.

More important than heroic icons, perhaps, is the emergence of a mass media that allows for the proliferation of new social trends. Radio storms onto the American scene, with the first commercial broadcasts taking place in 1922, and it rapidly becomes a powerful political and entertainment platform thereafter. Although the first "talkie" doesn't appear in movie theatres until 1927 *(The Jazz Singer)*, the movie industry is selling $100 million in tickets per week by 1929, making it one of the largest industries in the United States.

Coupled with such factors as women's suffrage, the proliferation of handset telephones, and the rising number of automobiles (even as early as the 1920s, parents of teenagers are clucking about these "bedrooms on wheels"), American society seems ready to open up and embrace an affluent and high-spirited future.

Then, and it is this fact that must be embraced to truly appreciate the Patriot value-formation period, everything economic slams into a wall.

The Crash of 1929

Hindsight is 20/20, and there is now an ample body of scholarship that explains why the crash of the stock market in 1929 was inevitable. Too much margin buying of stocks, an overproduction of durable goods, and a laissez-faire approach toward market regulation are among the most frequently cited culprits. To fully appreciate the impact of the event is, however, to acknowledge that for the vast majority of Americans, who in 1929 are still being encouraged to invest in stocks by everyone from the President of General Motors to the President of the United States. The devastation to come is swift and largely unexpected.

It is generally agreed that the loss value of the stock market in the first few weeks of the panic is roughly two-thirds, or in 1929 dollars, $30 billion. The figure grows to $50 billion by 1932. As devastating as the economic news is, the crash is also a crippling blow to the American spirit, as the rise in stock-market value has largely become the key symbolic indicator of the nation's improving emotional well-being. See Figure 5.2. In short, the national mood is devastated and suddenly, all those previous anxieties about modern life seem quite validated.

FIGURE 5.2

Dow Jones Industrial Average

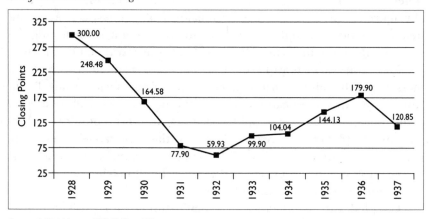

Source: MSN Money (CSNBC)—CSI

THE GREAT DEPRESSION (1929–1939)

It is hard to capture a decade-long period of abject suffering and misery in just a few sentences. Suffice it to say that the 1930s are a time never to be forgotten by those who lived through them. The raw numbers—12 million unemployed adults in 1932, representing about 12.5 percent of the American workforce—can't paint the picture harshly enough. Nor do they immediately convey images of bread lines, soup kitchens, communities of makeshift shacks, the roving unemployed, the institutionally displaced, or the thousands of farm families unable to sell (and because of mercilessly bitter climate patterns, often unable to grow) their crops.

Even for those who manage to survive this fierce period, there is an erosion of confidence in institutions that stamps the Patriot value-formation period forever. The common man becomes aware that most of the wealth of the nation is concentrated in the hands of the very rich (in 1929 the top 1 percent of Americans have a combined wealth 650 times greater than the bottom 11 percent), who have little intention of recovery spending or investing during unpromising economic times. Further, politicians, especially those who advocate a hands-off policy toward domestic financial regulation, are *de facto* tools of the relatively small pool of very rich capitalists, whose companies control the wealth of the nation (in 1929, the 200 largest American corporations controlled 50 percent of the nation's business wealth). The politics of the era are laced with far more political scandal than dedicated public service.

Ultimately, the Great Depression leaves its mark on a Value Population that grows up suspicious of authority that represents its motives as anything other than financial. Yet even the resentment of such authority pales in the wake of the devastation of the period. The real value lesson of the Great Depression is that being among the haves is a great gift of grace. Ethical questions may be raised regarding the acquisition of fortune, but the glitter of gold is nothing less than the light of salvation.

PREWAR ANXIETY (1933–1937)

The New Deal

Running on a promise to deal with the problems of the Depression and to repeal Prohibition (it is worth noting that to the Patriot generation, alcoholic beverage consumption is a symbolic political act as well as a form of escapist behavior), Franklin Delano Roosevelt is elected to the first of four presidential terms in 1932. The massively aggressive social agenda of Roosevelt's pre-WW II terms in office includes a host of "New Deal" public relief measures such as the Civilian Conservation Corps and the Works Progress Administration (programs that put 8.5 million Americans to work building the nation's infrastructure of roads, bridges, public facilities, and airports). Additionally, there is far-reaching fiscal policy legislation, such as banking reform (including the establishment of the FDIC), a variety of measures to rein in "excessive corporate profits," agricultural commodities support, an aggressively graduated income tax (1934), prolabor legislation (the Wagner Act of 1935 protects the rights of unions to organize and strike), and the institution of Social Security (1935).

Championing the cause of the "forgotten common man," the FDR administration once and for all establishes the principle that government has a broadly proactive, and perhaps even paternalistic, obligation to the welfare of the masses.

The fly in the ointment is that much of this progressive initiative and outlook, not to mention the high taxes and deficit spending in their wake, is bitterly opposed by the "economic royalists," FDR's term for the wealthy capitalists who control the finances, and therefore wield much of the political power of the nation. Using the considerable means at their disposal to mitigate FDR's initiatives, the New Deal programs are significantly compromised by 1937—a year that ushers in a painful new recession. Ultimately, while FDR's programs cannot be underestimated in their salutary effect on the morale of the nation, the real death of the Great Depression comes only as a result of a new global war.

The Age of Dictatorship

It is essential to keep in mind that however desperate the conditions in the United States become during the Patriot value-formation period, they are consistently much worse in economically devastated Europe and Asia. With promises of salvation to their politically disenfranchised, psychologically scarred, and economically desperate countrymen, Italy's Mussolini (assumes dictatorial power in 1922), Russia's Stalin (1924), Japan's Hirohito (1926), and Germany's Hitler (1933) offer radical plans for economic recovery and renewed national pride. Tragically, these visions are entwined with some of the most unspeakable acts of mass terrorism ever perpetrated upon humanity and are the forerunner of a military expansionism that will lead to a second global war.

As mentioned earlier in this analysis, the prevailing American response to these ominous rumblings is largely a policy of foreign neutrality and isolationism (although it is interesting to note that American membership in the communist party, reflecting an infatuation with socialist economic theory, peaks in 1935). American economic policy, particularly with regard to international trade tariffs, is particularly restrictive and in fact helps to fuel the breakdown of world trade and the resultant global financial crisis. As late as 1937, FDR is promising the nation that American boys will never again be sent to fight in a foreign war.

Americans are still dragging their heels and digging in as the Second World War in Europe begins. Unavoidable confrontation is massing on the horizon but with it will come a new Value Population, the Performers, who, unlike their immediate predecessors, the Patriots, will be as outward looking and universally involved as any generation in history.

6

THE PATRIOTS
Cultural Expressions of an Era

I can't help what I do! I can't help it. I can't.
—Peter Lorre as M (1931)

MONSTERS AND MADMEN

The movie industry, in any modern sense, begins during the Patriot era—and perhaps with no other Value Population does cinema provide such an unguarded look into an era's very soul. Even a casual observer will readily note how many of the earliest commercial films are extremely dark and humorless "horror" movies. In terms of the era's guilt, doubt, pain, and fear of the unknown, it is not a very far leap from Hollywood to the headlines.

A heartbeat removed from full-out psychological confession, the films of the period swarm with truly evil and scary monsters dwelling in terribly creepy and surreal habitats. From Dracula's first appearance in *Nosferatu* (1922) through *Dr. Jekyll and Mr. Hyde* (1931), *Dracula* (1931), *Frankenstein* (1931), *Freaks* (1932), *King Kong* (1933), and *The Bride of Frankenstein* (1935), to name just few well-known films, one gets a suggestion that the protagonist of the Patriot value-formation period is a very uncomfortable resident of a nightmarish land just brimming with secret terrors, noxious spirits, and unhealthy impulses. "Demonic urge" movies like *M* (1931) and *The Invisible Man* (1933) are similarly full of uncontrollable dementia; the former featuring a child-murderer so possessed by evil that other criminals pitch in to help catch him; the latter portraying a victim of a rash experiment whose side effect is an evil desire to take over the world. See Figure 6.1.

FIGURE 6.1
Top Ten Horror Films of the Patriot Era

---

1. *Nosferatu* (1922)
2. *Bride of Frankenstein* (1935)
3. *Kabinett des Doktor Caligari, Das* (1920)
4. *King Kong* (1933)
5. *Frankenstein* (1931)
6. *Freaks* (1932)
7. *The Invisible Man* (1933)
8. *The Phantom of the Opera* (1925)
9. *Dracula* (1931)
10. *M* (1931)

Source: As voted on by the members of Internet Movie Database, Inc.

With little subtlety, the message is delivered that God has abandoned the world and that the devil has indeed taken up residence within the flock. It is worth noting that in some of the era's films, *King Kong* and *The Bride of Frankenstein* come to mind, the title monsters are portrayed with a modicum of sympathy, seen as somewhat innocent victims of a foul human manipulation, rather than as perpetrators of original sin. Indicative of the era's tone is the fact that the single most popular box-office star of the 1930s is Boris Karloff, who as Frankenstein in *The Bride of Frankenstein* mutters to his would-be spouse one of the era's most revealing and poignant closing lines, "we belong dead."

Privilege and Pain (It Hurts Only When I'm Hungry . . .)

> *The state's promise did not mean anything. It was all lies! They just wanted to get me back so they can have their revenge. Why, their crimes are worse than mine, worse than anybody's here. They're the ones who should be in chains, not we!*
>
> **—James Allen, *I Am a Fugitive from a Chain Gang* (1932)**

> *You know, the Parkes were never educated to face life. We'd been puppets for ten generations. Boy, did I feel sorry for myself. I wandered down to the East River one night thinking I'd just slide in and get it over with. But I met some fellas living there on a city dump. Here were people fighting it out and not complaining.*
> *I never got as far as the river.*
>
> **—William Powell, *My Man Godfrey* (1936)**

Patriots do not come into the world looking to be preoccupied by trouble and sorrow—they are too busy looking for work or attempting to hold on to what they have. Revolutionary economic and political fervor, stirred up by charismatic military dictators, might be on the menu elsewhere in the world, but the temptations and tribulations foisted upon foreign populations are hardly the focus of the American culture (or perhaps they represent a showdown too painful to contemplate).

Much of this period's cinematic portrayal of the rich and powerful, at least of the domestic variety, is as bemused as it is critical—a fact that likely says something important about the Patriot value-formation period. In blockbuster flicks of the era such as *Platinum Blonde* (1931), *Dinner at Eight* (1933), *The Thin Man* (1934), *Top Hat* (1935), and *My Man Godfrey* (1936), one gets the clear impression that the primary function of the upper class is to preserve the social spirit of the Roaring 20s by hosting parties, imbibing alcohol, dancing, and exchanging witty banter. Even when the rich are portrayed as elaborately egotistical and are raked over the coals for their personal duplicity and social pretentiousness, it is somehow also clear that it wouldn't be such a terrible thing to have one's place among them.

Despite the prevailing mellow tone, however, it would be wrong to dismiss the abject want and frustration that does come across in some of the period's popular art. In movies such as *Metropolis* (1927), *All Quiet on the Western Front* (1930), *I Am a Fugitive from a Chain Gang* (1932), and Charlie Chaplin's immortal *Modern Times* (1936), the desperation of the masses and the perceived "soullessness" of the political, economic, and social leadership that would manipulate them from war to unrewarding work to want are all too painfully apparent. It cannot be too strongly observed that this is a generation in which danger, desolation, and deprivation permeate the atmosphere, and it is small wonder that this Value Population, in its adulthood, so unashamedly embraces a peaceful life of tract housing, Sunday dinners, and all the glories of a consumer economy.

Group Hug (Families and Other Personal Belongings)

Once in the gang, you know the rest.
—Joe, *Little Caesar* (1930)

Alone bad. Friend good.
—The Monster, *The Bride of Frankenstein* (1934)

A message that is not always in the forefront of this era's movies, but that obviously represents a value so ingrained to this value-formation period that it is almost incessantly in the background, is the importance of belonging to a group in which everyone holds similar, if not identical, values. Not to put too fine a point on it, but a generation racked by war and poverty obviously feels that survival is vested in loyalty to a clan that will help support them in the bad times and watch their backs in the good. Generally, one's "allegiance to clan" consists of family, close friends, and/or culturally similar neighbors, rather than a dogmatic following of political, social, or economic philosophy or institutions.

Interestingly, the first "talking" picture ever made, Al Jolson's *The Jazz Singer* (1927), deals with a son who betrays his father's expectations (he's supposed to become a cantor in the synagogue like his father, but he wants to sing jazz instead). The movie's uplifting ending is an affirmation of traditional values. The son sings in the synagogue, and there is reconciliation.

Although Patriots are generally characterized as strongly devoted to their children, movies of the late 1920s and 1930s rarely feature children. It can be argued that this stems from the group's view of children as fertile perpetuations of the clan, rather than strong and highly individualized members of society. In the immensely popular "escapist" Shirley Temple films of the mid- and late 1930s (Temple is America's most popular box-office attraction between 1935 and 1938) it is interesting, and perhaps a bit ironic, to note how often this oddly precocious thousand-watt singing and dancing phenomenon is portrayed as an orphan. In other words, who could possibly be her parents?

Arguably, the cinematic phenomenon that best captures the visceral sense of the clan is the ubiquitous gangster movie. Although they most often approach matters from the criminal side, there's no denying that films such as *Little Caesar* (1930), *The Public Enemy* (1931), *Scarface* (1932), *Manhattan Melodrama* (1934), and *Angels with Dirty Faces* (1938) are testaments to the principles of allegiance to a code, respect for a hierarchy founded upon a meritocracy (the meanest and shrewdest gets to be the boss), physical and mental toughness, and life-and-death loyalty in service to the brotherhood. Not only are such principles attractive to movie audiences of the time, they are also more than a little useful as "instructional guides" when the generation is conscripted to fight a war.

Misogynists, Misanthropes, and Money (Love for Sale)

We're fighting for this woman's honor, which is more than she ever did.
—**Groucho Marx as Rufus T. Firefly in** *Duck Soup* **(1933)**

"Haven't you ever met a man who could make you happy?"
"Sure, lots of times."
—**Cary Grant and Mae West,** *She Done Him Wrong* **(1933)**

Angel, ha! She's a female! And all females is poison! They're full of wicked wiles!
—**Grumpy,** *Snow White and the Seven Dwarfs* **(1937)**

It was beauty killed the beast.
—**Reporter,** *King Kong* **(1933)**

Perhaps men and women have always mistrusted and/or misunderstood each other's motives, but in an era of unguarded speech, occurring decades before the days of political correctness, there's no mistaking the rift. Some of the boy/girl tension in the films of the Patriot value-formation era is doubtlessly an expression of sexual frustration in a less sexually free time. Yet, in this era, women are also for the first time becoming real participants in the worlds of commerce, politics, sports, science, and exploration—and men react by creating a popular culture full of sexual objectification.

In reviewing literally dozens of popular movies of the era, such as the ones quoted above, one gets the reasonable, if artistically exaggerated, impression that to the Patriot man, the contemporary woman is basically irrational, insincere, and headstrong (not to mention quite often a trollop). To the Patriot woman, the contemporary man is basically dumb, duplicitous, and disposable—not to mention extremely sex starved.

A lot of this is, of course, intensified by a crippled economy in which the practice of gold-digging is presented as an understandable, even if also hurtful and morally wanting, survival strategy. It is joked about in movies, such as 1933's *Duck Soup* (Margaret Dumont: "I don't think you'd love me if I were poor." Groucho Marx: "I might, but I'd keep my mouth shut."); *Dinner at Eight* (Jean Harlow: "If there's one thing I know it's men. I ought to. It's been my life's work."); and *She Done Him Wrong* (Mae West: "I wasn't always rich. No, there was a time when I didn't know where my next husband was coming from."); but the humor doesn't entirely mask the visceral knowledge that there is real want in the world. In all, relationships entered into for the sake of material security are hardly ill advised or unfortunate.

In the context of all of this, it is particularly interesting to consider Frank Capra's *It Happened One Night* (1934), an immensely popular movie that is the first ever to win all five major Oscars. In this good-natured story, a love match develops between a working class reporter (Clark Gable) and a willful little rich girl (Claudette Colbert). It is generationally significant in that there is so much appeal to a story in which simple shared events, and a little animal magnetism, lead to love and to triumph over class differences. Still, it is hard to ignore the long-term value implications for Patriots when the reporter scores a major coup with his future father-in-law by observing (about the man's daughter): "What she needs is a guy that takes a sock at her once a day whether it's coming to her or not."

The Patriot Ideal

If you lose this war, don't blame me.
—**Buster Keaton in The General (1927)**

I'll do it. We'll get a home even if I have to work for it!
—**Charlie Chaplin as The Little Tramp, Modern Times (1936)**

I'll wash and sew and sweep and cook!
—**Snow White, Snow White and the Seven Dwarfs (1937)**

He's got goodness, Mabel. Do you know what that is? No, of course you don't.
We've forgotten. We're too busy being smart alecks. Too busy in a
crazy competition for nothing.
—**Jean Arthur as Babe, Mr. Deeds Goes to Town (1936)**

The idealized Patriot is a combination of Buster Keaton, Charlie Chaplin, Snow White, and Gary Cooper. This is not necessarily who a Patriot is, but it is who he'd figuratively like to be.

In *The General* (1927), Buster Keaton is informed that he is of no use to the confederacy as a soldier in the civil war, and subsequently his girlfriend rejects him. He instead becomes a train engineer and, of course, saves the girl and almost single-handedly wins the war for the South. Courage and humor are part of the package, but the real Patriot virtue manifest here is accepting the unsought role and turning it into a benefit for oneself and the greater society.

In the remarkable *Modern Times* (1936), Charlie Chaplin's Little Tramp character comes up against every imaginable dehumanizing attribute of industrialization, job-hunting, and deprivation in an era of economic depression. Through a combination of simplicity, goodness, resilience, and indomitability, he never suffers a loss of what can only be described as happiness (many critics have pointed out the similarity between the Little Tramp and Mickey Mouse). In the movie's famous final scene, the Little Tramp walks down the road with his sweetheart—there's only trouble behind them, but there is an amazing feeling of hope regarding the future.

The feminists of later Value Populations might take exception to Snow White's "some day my prince will come" take on life in *Snow White and the Seven Drawfs* (1937), but that doesn't change how Patriots look at it. Keeping up spirits and managing the domestic life of the clan (Snow White first assumes she has stumbled upon an orphanage, not a den of dwarves) is just another example of accepting a role that works for the good of the many. It is not just the courage it takes to escape the wicked queen, charm the knife-wielding woodsman, or survive a life with Dopey and Grumpy in an enchanted forest—it is the lack of complaint.

Ultimately, one finds the total Patriot wish-package in Gary Cooper's portrayal of Longfellow Deeds, the title character in Frank Capra's Academy Award–winning *Mr. Deeds Goes to Town* (1936). A tuba-playing greeting card poet in a relentlessly folksy New England village, Deeds becomes heir to a $20 million fortune (a truly astounding sum in 1936) left by a distant uncle. Though targeted for exploitation by attorneys, by a female reporter who eventually falls in love with him, by "opera lovers," and by a host of other shrewd operators, Deeds foils everyone's plans by simply being democracy's model common man—kind, courageous, funny, subtly sagacious, and very aware of whose hand is in his wallet.

Because Deeds first has the audacity to state that he doesn't need the money (there must have been an audible movie audience gasp) and then decides to use the entire amount to underwrite a fund for poor family farmers, he is of course made to stand trial for his sanity. This concern with "sanity" is a meaningful echo of the themes introduced throughout the Patriot value formation period—when monsters and madmen roamed the movie screens, hacking through the audience's sense of self-worth. It must have felt more than comforting when the Deeds' trial judge announces his finding that this quintessentially good everyman is simply "the sanest man I've ever met."

7

THE PERFORMERS
An Overview

POPULATION OVERVIEW

Age: Born 1938–1957
Size: 23% of the U.S. Population
Spending: $1.32 Trillion Annually
Themes: The Atomic Age/Personality
Values: Freedom/Drama/Adventure

Summary

If Performers sometimes seem unduly self-absorbed and self-indulgent, one must first consider the conditions of their value-formation period before passing too blithe a judgment. Born during and just after global war, and heirs to the advent of "we will bury you" communism and its consistent threat of nuclear annihilation, offspring of the Patriot Value Population—most notably characterized by caution and an obsessive allegiance to the prevailing practices of the clan—the Performer generation might well have emerged as a tribe of crushed gray spirits quivering in the darkest corners of their own repressive nightmares. But be it a matter of fate, fortune, or their own sheer numbers, the Performers take the exact opposite generational tack—that of lighting their own inner flames rather than cursing the darkness.

There are always exceptions to these broad generalities, but no other Value Population quite compares with Performers for their lust after life's sheer drama—for the belongings, feelings, and events that make an individual feel unique and very much alive.

PERFORMER HISTORICAL EVENT MATRIX

Hope/War/Prosperity

Hope

Although the New Deal legislation of the FDR administration is eventually disqualified by the courts, the economy appears healed from the Great Depression and headed in the right direction, as is evidenced by steeply growing employment, national minimum wage legislation (1938), and a broadly recovering stock market.

A comprehensive and coherent vision of a materially-flush consumerist future takes shape at the New York World's Fair of 1938. Simultaneously, there is a great opening up of the possibilities of the human creative spirit via the birth of television and the proliferation of Technicolor movie epics (e.g., *Wizard of Oz* and *Gone with the Wind*).

Despite ominous political and military developments in Europe, there is still ample faith that policies of isolation, appeasement, and neutrality will prevent direct U.S. involvement in a broad military conflict.

War

World War II (1941–1945), with global military and civilian fatalities numbering upwards of 45 million people, brings death and destruction to humanity on a scale that can barely be contemplated.

Essential historical icons for the era are the genocidal German concentration camps and the Japanese cities of Hiroshima and Nagasaki, whose populations are instantly devastated by atomic bombs.

The threats of military dictatorship and nuclear weaponry, and the fragility of human life in their shadows, linger long after WW II and throughout the Korean (1950–1953) and "Cold" Wars.

Prosperity

The end of WW II ushers in a period of unprecedented economic growth, particularly reflected in the rise of automobiles, suburbia, disposable consumer goods, and the overall growth of the middle class.

The United States becomes the world's foremost nation, and New York City becomes the center of economic, political, and cultural civilization—the cornerstone for the United Nations building is laid in New York City in 1949.

Children are born to returning soldiers and their wives in the greatest historical numbers ever (i.e., the Baby Boom); and these children soon become the focus of American culture.

PERFORMER POPULATION VALUES

Personal Freedom

- *Historical drivers.* Survival of WW II and the Cold War; the cultural pendulum swings away from restrictive "collective" doctrines of the Patriot period; parental indulgence; automobile culture.
- *Value manifestation.* Vastly educated and incredibly affluent by historical standards, this entitled Value Population appropriates the right to freedom of belief, expression, affiliation, location, and life change. Wealth and power are desirable facilitators, but these are means not ends.

A Place in the Sun

- *Historical drivers.* Popular culture (soap operas, movies, kid-centric television, Disneyland) and historical events (war and nuclear annihilation) conspire to present life dramatically, urgently, and in fairly strict terms of heroes and villains.
- *Value manifestation.* The quest is not necessarily for a center-stage spotlight or real glory (although that might occasionally be nice), but for a place where one is recognized, respected, and ultimately rewarded for one's unique attributes and contributions—and if it is fun, all the better.

Courage and Adventure

- *Historical drivers.* The true war hero and the cowboy myth; the national highway system; the psychological survival imperative of an A-bomb burdened age.
- *Value manifestation.* Life is too short to let fear be the boss. A happy heart is a racing heart. Experience is life's greatest treasure.

Creativity

- *Historical drivers.* An enormous influx of variety in goods, services, and diversions; a pendulum swing away from the closed-off and self-protective insularity of the Patriots.
- *Value manifestation.* The urge to produce, express, or accomplish something unique—artistically, intellectually, athletically, socially, politically, financially, and so forth—is powerful. Child bearing and raising is definitely included here.

Youthfulness

- *Historical drivers.* From *The Wizard of Oz* to Disneyland to *Leave It to Beaver* to *The Catcher in the Rye* to Dr. Benjamin Spock, the child becomes, for the first time in American history, the consistent center of cultural preoccupation and commentary.
- *Value manifestation.* The hope, self-infatuation, energy, and resilience of Performers are best suited to the young and young-at-heart. Unsurprisingly, this Value Population puts a premium on parental encouragement of, and identification with, their own young.

Romance

- *Historical drivers.* The intensification of relationships against the backdrop of war—the agony of loss, the joy of discovery and return; the *Casablanca* myth.
- *Value manifestation.* Flirtatious, sexual, and/or everlasting romance is the perfect blend of reward, excitement, and essential validation of one's worth. In all endeavors, the ultimate adventure is the adventure of the heart.

Glamour and Style

- *Historical drivers.* The vivid colorization of life, ranging from movies to food to cars to clothes to household appliances; Hollywood is brought into the home via television.
- *Value manifestation.* There is a deep affection for all things that help to transcend the ordinariness of life—from fashion to fine dining to luxury automobiles to exotic vacations to the work of a good plastic surgeon.

Headlines, Summaries, and Generalizations

- *Historical drivers.* Global historical events of extreme urgency meet the dawn of the television age; proliferation of dramatic formats yields expectation of sudden changes; President Eisenhower introduces one-page summary to government reports.
- *Value manifestation.* Details are deemed too sticky. There is a preference for broad generalizations that can be summarily rallied behind or easily dismissed. Performers hate not being able to have or change a personal opinion.

Friendship

- *Historical drivers.* Empowerment at early age leads to unique youth affiliations; increased suburban population and "playing" become important social trends.
- *Value manifestation.* Here friendship is uniquely fashioned as a relationship between kindred spirits associating on the basis of freely chosen beliefs, empathies, and experiences, rather than on the basis of heritage or hierarchy.

PERFORMER MACRO INTERESTS

(Life-phase considerations projected through 2010)

Business Problems

In terms of the old ant/grasshopper fable, Performers have had their share of being ants, but they have really been much more disposed toward being grasshoppers. Brought into the world in a time of economic optimism and growing material affluence, they were counseled about rainy-day savings, but inevitably they seemed to get a shiny new toy before the lecture was over. Now in their middle age, they are confronting the reality that economies do grow soft from time to time, that markets change, that new hard-to-learn technologies and other required job skills emerge, and that good jobs and entire industries sometimes go away forever. The insecurity such changes breed often seems to become a terrible fly in the ointment of their self-satisfaction. This group really never expected to run out of resources or the ability to recover—but now?

Children

With the youngest of Performers now nearing 50, Performers are generally confronting that time in their children's development cycle when high school, college, careers, and their children's own families are looming large on the horizon. Issues of resources are of great importance in all these endeavors but so is the matter of their offspring's success and creative fulfillment—which, most Performers strongly feel, reflects on their own life's accomplishments.

Credit Problems

Taken as a whole, the Performers' credit "abuse" is not as striking as those of younger Value Populations, but their situation is certainly serious enough; stock-market fickleness, an unkind job market, and a general propensity to be less savings-conscious than their parents are catching up with Performers—an enormous problem for a group that is not into self-denial.

Education

Performers need no prompting to understand the link between a child's education and his or her success. However, this concern with education is also true of their own development, as the Performer generation prepares to live, work, and "grow" longer than any preceding generation in history.

Heart Disease and Other Ailments

Although medical science continues to make remarkable strides, the deck still seems stacked against middle-aged men (and many women) when it comes to serious health issues, including heart disease, the leading cause of death in the United States. Even beyond genetic risk, many of the stress-causing and health-impairing conditions of modern life are minimized by a generation whose tickers have been tocking for a good long while now.

Pleasure and Fun

Although they are aging, Performers seem little inclined to dispense with activities that are performed for pure pleasure. This group is not likely to retreat gracefully to the front-porch rocker, although they may have to take up the issue of endurance with their hearts and backs. Look for this group to seek active fun, including travel, for as long as they can stand it—and social stimulation when they can no longer even stand.

Personal Passions

Even more than pleasure and fun, Performers are indelibly imprinted with a desire to feel and express their essential life urges—this may mean a passion for writing poetry, collecting stamps, cooking, performing charity work, or flying stunt airplanes. It is also likely to manifest in a substantial increase in the tens-of-millions of prescriptions that have already been written for Viagra. Performers need to do more than live—they need to feel alive.

Property Appreciation

They might not care to admit it to their own parents, but the Performers have been convinced by the vagaries of market investment that there is no asset like a real one and no real asset like a home. Indications are already strong of a spate of second-home buying by this Value Population, which is looking to turn retirement into both a pleasure and a sound financial plan.

Public Morality

Morality is a very interesting area with regard to Performers who, frequently during their maturation process, have dismissed as "square" many of the socially "uptight" customs and concerns of their elders. Now, though, the mantle of gray is on the heads of Performers, and one can only wonder if their tolerance will be tested as they now become the collective voice of experience.

Risk-Taking

Whether it is a trump card or a trouble spot, Performers have historically been adventurous and risk-tolerant. How this may manifest physically, socially, and economically in an aging population is a matter of uncharted territory—but it pays to flatter Performer courage.

Relaxation for Performers

Performers enjoy just about any public spectacle or display (participatory or spectator), including concerts, theatrical presentations, sporting events, glamorous parties and social occasions, escapist vacations, romantic outings and getaways, club and organization social events, as well as elective classes and workshops.

8

THE PERFORMERS
History Creating Values

ost modern demographers consider the World War II era almost exclusively as a phenomenon of the Patriot Value Population that actually fought the war and then celebrated victory. We certainly agree that the war era itself was a manifestation of the values of the adult population of the time. However, in a key departure from standard analysis, our primary emphasis regarding these events is on the youthful segment of the population whose values were formed during and in the close aftermath of this worldwide test and reorganization of political, economic, and social realities.

When one gets beyond birth-rate demography and the reasoning that events have validity only for the adults who are acting them out, an alignment of history according to something other than the "common wisdom" occurs. With this in mind, one of the most fascinating insights into Performers is that much of this group's value-formation story is thematically foreshadowed in the brief period between 1938 and 1940, just prior to the U.S. entrance into war. The war itself does, of course, become a key part of the story, but the earlier period gives a valuable look into the value-formation themes of the period as a whole.

VULNERABILITY TO DANGEROUS GLOBAL FORCES

At the beginning of the Performer period, there is still hope that isolation and appeasement can be successful strategies to halt the spread of tyrannical global imperialism. In 1938, France and England sanction Nazi Germany's annexation of Austria and dismemberment of Czechoslovakia, and in 1939, the United States formally declares neutrality with regard to "the war in Europe." In 1939, however, Germany's armed invasion of Poland forces France and England to declare war. In Asia, an expansionist Japan occupies Indochina in 1940, and the bombing of Pearl Harbor and the U.S. entrance into world war take place the following year. The mood of this period is characterized by a growing and desperately oppressive awareness that the world is a fiercely dangerous place where every man, woman, and child is at risk and where burying one's head in the sand is no longer a viable option—and never will be again.

UPWARDLY MOBILE ECONOMY

It may sound almost inconsequential in light of the above, but at the New York World's Fair of 1938–1939, an economically recovering global civilization gets its first look at the future as conceived by capitalist forces confronting the desperate "want" experienced during the global depression. The fair's central exhibit is General Motors' Futurama, a prescient vision of the United States "in 1960" as a society dominated by automobiles, urban skyscrapers, suburbs, and kitchen appliances. Although the World's Fair is temporarily disrupted by hostile global developments and ends badly (mostly sold as scrap materials for the war effort), postwar society would largely fulfill this vision of a consumer-centered, highway criss-crossed, civilization into which the generation of Performers would be born.

INDIVIDUALS VERSUS SOCIETY

It is an issue that is soon swallowed up by the collective practical necessity of building an army, but John Steinbeck's *The Grapes of Wrath*, published in 1939, and Richard Wright's *Native Son*, published in 1940, eloquently argue that America does not just practice discrimination against its poor and its racial minorities, but that the rights and opportunities of all "common" individuals in the American "system" are tenuous at best, when opposed to the interests of the rich and powerful. The issue is to grow much more significant and divisive after the war, particularly when war "heroes" return to lives at the lower end of the social spectrum. This coming to terms with the injustices of the "system" stamps itself upon the very soul of Performer value formation.

TRANSITION TO THE TUBE AND TECHNICOLOR

In 1939, President Franklin Delano Roosevelt becomes the first U.S. President to appear on commercial broadcast television when he gives a short speech at the reopening of the New York World's Fair. The very next day, RCA introduces its first television sets to the buying public and announces a broadcast schedule on its NBC subsidiary. The new technology is adapted slowly (only 9 percent of U.S. households own sets as late as 1950) and does not reach sophistication or saturation until the end of the Performer period—but, the early eager development of this world-changing new entertainment-oriented medium and the youthful population born in its wake go hand-in-hand.

Along with this milestone in television development, movies in 1939, according to many film historians, had their single greatest year ever. Among the now-classic movies released in that one year are *The Wizard of Oz, Gone with the Wind, Mr. Smith Goes to Washington, Stagecoach, Destry Rides Again, Wuthering Heights,* and *The Hunchback of Notre Dame.* While the specific thematic relevancies of many of these movies will be explored in the next chapter, it is well worth noting that this veritable all-at-once explosion of intense and artfully crafted movies reflects an essential shift of perception that is to dominate this value-formation period. With the Performers comes the evolutionary moment in which media itself become transcendent—first through movies and then along with television—via the creation of stories and technologies that not so much capture reality, but in all ways dramatize and enhance it.

WORLD WAR II (1939–1945)

A nuanced discussion of the effects of war in general, and of World War II specifically, might rightfully run to encyclopedic length. But, as has already been indicated, the issue in this discussion is the effect such an event has on the value formation of a population just coming into being at the time of the event. What, in other words, is the impact of such an all-consuming and deathly dangerous conflict on the children being born in its shadow?

In the manner of nursery stories, one encounters a classic mythology (albeit populated by real people performing real acts) of heroes and villains. Especially as filtered through the adults acting out the story, one gets the most compelling and clear-cut sense of a war between good and evil. Drama is everywhere in such a tale, and it is this drama as well as an innate expression of knowing what is right (even when this is entirely subjective) that becomes a keynote of the Performers as they mature.

Ultimately, from the perspective of American Performer value formation, the most important fact of the war may be that it concludes in victory for the American side. One must assume that such an outcome engenders many desirable virtues in an emerging population, from courage to optimism to a prevailing sense that time and fate, and perhaps even God, are on one's side.

Even allowing for the sweet psychological fruits of victory, there's little denying that World War II opens up a Pandora's box of evil that permeates the climate of global affairs and generational consciousness during the entire Performer value-formation period. The cost of victory, if one counts the world's total military and civilian casualties during the WW II era, is an incredibly demoralizing 45 to 50 million lives. In the United States alone, more than a million soldiers are listed as killed, injured, captured, or missing in action.

Assuredly, the post-war discovery that six million people have died in concentration camps because of their religious and ethnic affiliations may have left some sort of scar on the collective psyche of Performers. But perhaps even more devastating is the image of the mushroom cloud over Hiroshima that carries away 200,000 lives during a few moments in August of 1945. Forever afterward, and quite manifestly in the politics and culture of the Performer value-formation period, the possibility of the annihilation of the human race in a brief exchange of button pressing is to hang over humankind.

Quotes from Leaders of the Performer Era

As long as I live I shall think only of the victory of my people. I shall shrink
from nothing and shall annihilate everyone who is opposed to me . . .
I want to annihilate the enemy!

—Adolph Hitler, German Chancellor (1938–1945)

A single death is a tragedy, a million deaths is a statistic.
—Joseph Stalin, Russian Premier (1941–1953)

Bombs do not choose. They will hit everything.
—Nikita Khrushchev, Russian Premier, *Time* Magazine's Man of the Year (1957)

The object of war is not to die for your country, but to make the other bastard
die for his.

—George S. Patton, U.S. General (1941–1945)

COLD WAR (1945+)

New Enemies for Old

Had WW II resulted in a clear and absolute victory for the forces of democratic capitalism, it would be possible to put a less guardedly upbeat spin on the implications of the event. Quickly, though, it becomes apparent that there is a powerful new brand of despotism abroad in the world. The Soviet Union, a former ally possessed of its own fearsome nuclear capabilities, reveals that the challenge to Western dominance has simply changed its color (to communist red), not its stripes. The everything-at-risk tension between superpowers is to grind away at global society for the next half-century.

New Enemies at Home

Names such as Alger Hiss, Ethel Rosenberg, and Joe McCarthy, grab a fair share of the domestic headlines between 1949 and 1953. The issue here is the sometimes real, more-often imagined, threat of communist infiltration into the domestic, political, and cultural affairs of the nation. As a vocal and powerful faction of the Patriot generation uses "witch-hunt" tactics to insulate itself against perceived enemies of the state, the Performers begin to grow up in a world where there is fuzzy delineation between the just operations of democratic law and the belligerent designs of a lynch mob.

KOREAN WAR (1950–1953)

More War

In a world clearly grown weary of war, the American-led United Nations police action fails to capture the patriotic spirit of the era's previous conflict and is essentially fought to a draw. Still more communists, this time Chinese, become dangerous enemies of the United States. During the same period, Jews and Arabs engage in armed hostilities in Palestine, and the division of India and Pakistan also leads to thousands of refugee deaths. In short, world war has ended, but dangerous and deadly world turmoil has not.

AMERICAN PROSPERITY (1940S AND 1950S)

Consumer Goods Heyday

The silver lining that nearly blots out the mushroom cloud is the remarkable affluence of America's postwar economy. At the end of WW II, America goes on a celebratory production and spending spree that involves, according to one commentator, "an awesome and bewildering array of stuff." Coupled with continuing mammoth expenditures on defense, the American gross domestic product (GDP) grows 51 percent in the decade after the war. See Figure 8.1. More Americans join the middle class than at any time in history—a threefold increase from 1940 to 1960. The United States, with 6 percent of the world's population, becomes the producer and consumer of one-third of the world's goods.

It is worth noting that the emergent American passion for material goods, and the culture that champions them, attract mostly ardent support. But the same culture also quickly engenders a "movement" of influential, articulate, and passionate critics of the bland uniformity that a consumer society engenders. In addition to the prodigious outpouring of the antimaterialistic and antiestablishment "beat generation," key commentaries of the period include John Kenneth Galbraith's *The Affluent*

FIGURE 8.1

U.S. Gross Domestic Product (GDP)

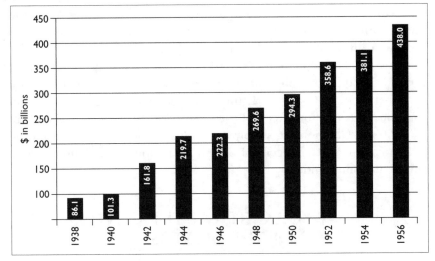

Source: U.S. Department of Commerce—Bureau of Economic Analysis

Society, William H. Whyte's *The Organization Man,* Sloan Wilson's *The Man in the Gray Flannel Suit,* and Ayn Rand's *Atlas Shrugged.*

Although adult Performers are often criticized for their materialism, it is essential to acknowledge that the conspicuous consumption frenzy and the middle-class homogenization of the postwar period are essentially Patriot (Performer parents) phenomena. Performers grow up in an environment where material comfort is bestowed upon them as the most loving act of a generation brought up in an economic depression (and to this day, it is fair to say that Performers often respond to material goods as a return to mother's milk). But they also grow up in a culture that probingly questions the value of all this "stuff" and cultural sameness, and whether the acquisition of goods is a rewarding and interesting enough premise upon which to build a worthwhile life. Performers, who tend to embrace the clash of opposites, the very soul of drama, have always derived a lot of their value character from the "war" of this material ambiguity in their natures.

Automobiles and Suburbia

Central to the postwar economy is the automobile. By the mid-1950s, automobile sales in the United States average around 9 million new units per year. Government money pours into highway construction during the Eisenhower administrations, reaching its apex with the passage of the Federal Highway Act of 1956 that essentially creates and funds the nation's interstate highway grid. The Performer generation is the first to grow up with the car trip as its birthright.

The rapid development of suburbia reinforces and justifies the need for additional automobiles, highways, and domestic consumer goodies. Built between 1946 and 1951, the tract homes of Long Island's Levittown become a national icon of the future of U.S. domestic civilization. By 1960 the U.S. housing supply has increased by 25 percent from the 1950 total, and 30.5 percent of the entire national population lives in suburban communities.

NEW YORK CITY AT THE CENTER OF THE UNIVERSE

After WW II, America is at the summit of global civilization, and New York City is, from that indelible moment of victory celebration in Times Square, at the summit of America. The great symbolic crowning as world capital comes with the opening of the United Nations in 1952. As previously ethnic residential neighborhoods are bulldozed, New York City commits itself to commerce and the skyscraper. In the last eight years of the 1950s, more new office space is created in New York City than exists in the entire city of Chicago. During the Performer period, "the city that never sleeps" becomes the world's foremost center for trade, culture, style, and information. Its "bright lights and Broadway" and its advertising mecca, Madison Avenue, become for the Performer generation symbols of what "making it" is all about.

THE SOCIAL COST OF URBAN RENEWAL

With the postwar federal government developing highways, sponsoring highrise real estate development (Title 1), and giving attractive tax breaks to suburban mortgage holders (Title 2), major cities become less demarcated by the vibrant ethnic neighborhoods and street life that has defined them in the past. Groups who can afford it flee to the new suburbs, taking a good portion of the tax base along with them. Less-upwardly-mobile populations—particularly blacks and Puerto Ricans—find themselves, while already reeling from the disruptions of war, increasingly uprooted, "ghettoized," distanced from familiar support networks, denied civic services, and forced into menial jobs. This metropolitan-based cauldron of poverty and disenfranchisement is to come to a full boil in the era of the Techticians, but the heat starts here.

CHILDREN—SEEN AND HEARD

What deserves a bit of special emphasis here is the unique historical nature of the Performer perspective itself: Performers are the first modern Value Population that imposes a strong and unique point of view on its society from the time of its early youth. Although many reasons for this influence on society can be debated, such as the sheer number of young Performers, a doting adult generation, the need for atomic escapism, or something like fate, it is nonetheless a powerful influence.

Assuredly, general affluence, a strong educational system, and the advent of television enable Performers to form what may be called "generational consciousness" faster than preceding Value Populations. There are countless icons of this phenomenon, but surely nothing like the vision of Disneyland—a child-centered vision of the U.S. "dream culture" opened in July of 1955 (with an astounding 90 million people watching on television)—could or would have been rendered into reality at any preceding moment in history.

Although, the exact dates of value-population demarcation are arguable, the mid-to-late 1950s are a profound turning point in history, because by then, young people begin to fully emerge with an independent and often predominant cultural perspective and voice. A voice that will exist in conflict with the Patriot value culture and from which, the next Value Population, the Techticians, will largely be formed. Indicative of this timing are three landmark 1957 television events: the first national telecast of *American Bandstand,* the famous "waist up" appearance of Elvis Presley on *Ed Sullivan,* and the airing of the first episode of *Leave It to Beaver,* the first television series to tell its story from the point of view of a child protagonist.

It is interesting to note that while most demographers consider the Baby Boom to have lasted through 1964, the absolute peak year in U.S. births is 1957, with just over 4.3 million live births that year. See Figure 8.2. After 1957, the number of live births steadily declines while the cultural acting out of a fully formed Performer Value Population moves to center stage and begins influencing the formation of Techtician values.

FIGURE 8.2

U.S. Total Birth Rates

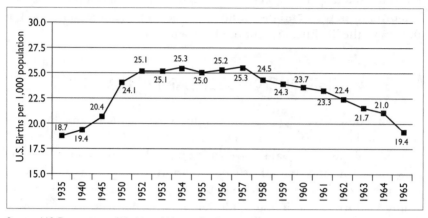

Source: U.S. Department of Health and Human Services

9

THE PERFORMERS
Cultural Expressions of an Era

Your choice is simple. Join us and live in peace or pursue your present course and face obliteration. We shall be waiting for your answer. The decision rests with you.

—**Klaatu, The Day the Earth Stood Still (1951)**

WORLD WAR AND ITS COMPLICATED AFTERMATH

For an unprecedented number of Americans, victory in WW II ushers in an era of economic and social upward mobility. In fact, most superficial sociology and trends analysis derives its understanding of Performers as a product of Chevrolets on the road, Donna Reed in the kitchen, and good times at the malt shop. It is argued here, however, that while the material blessings of the postwar period are coveted and enjoyed by the Patriot generation acting out its own values, to Performers, there is a much darker tone to the times in the midst of their value formation.

An important basic truth of the Performer era is, "Just because a war ends, does not mean its influence goes away." The angst, anxiety, sadness, and loss that linger after WW II are hugely magnified by the Cold War and the revelation of the destructive capacity of atomic weapons. Movies, more than any other media of the era, give a frightening vision of what is forming in the collective psyche of the Performer generation.

If there is a cinematic "establishing shot" for Performers, it is the panoramic display of human carnage—the destruction of the Confederacy—in *Gone with the Wind* (1939). For the next 20 years, thoughts and visions of meaningless and terrifying destruction hang over movie-house fare like an invading army from hell. War images, massacres, crowd violence, personal violence, and murders by the bushel become the staple of the silver screen. Eventually these enemies of mankind's survival are joined by legions of monsters, such as the giant mutant ants in *Them* (1954) and the intergalactic bad boy *Godzilla* (1956)—products of atomic radiation and a future almost too terrifying to contemplate.

In addition to the images of violence and doom, the psychological somberness of the period is reflected in at least the following four major recurring themes: disaffection; mistrust of vested and powerful interests; the western way; and death, an interesting neighbor.

DISAFFECTION

I'm not an officer and a gentleman anymore. I'm just another soda jerk out of a job.

—Fred Perry, The Best Years of Our Lives (1946)

Many movie buffs might have a hard time identifying the most commercially and critically successful American movie made between *Gone with the Wind* (1939) and *Ben Hur* (1959). That movie is *The Best Years of Our Lives* (1946), which tells a torturous tale of back-to-normal adjustment for returning heroes—American soldiers who are attempting to fit back into the families, the jobs, and the social order they left behind when they headed off to war. It is a "sobering" saga of battered relationships and crushed economic expectations punctuated with binge drinking.

In many of the great iconographic films and books of the Performer era—*Catcher in the Rye* (1951), *Shane* (1953), *On the Waterfront* (1954), and *Rebel without a Cause* (1955)—it is the disaffected antihero, the person who simply can no longer pretend to fit into the prescribed order of things, regardless of the personal consequences, who captures our attention and, most frequently, our sympathies.

MISTRUST OF VESTED AND POWERFUL INTERESTS

"Why should I?"

"Patriotism."

"That word gives me a pain. No thank you. I don't go for patriotism, nor patriots."

"I could dispute that with you."

"Waving the flag with one hand and picking pockets with the other. That's your patriotism. Well, you can have it."

—Ingrid Bergman and Cary Grant, as Alicia and Devlin, *Notorious* (1946)

Considering how real and painful the blacklisting of actors, writers, and directors was to become during the so-called "communist witch hunts" of the McCarthy era, it is particularly impressive to note the number of popular films of the era that take at least some jabs at the nation's most cherished social, political, and economic ideals and institutions. The particular target in many films is the stereotyped fat-cat businessman who prospers in good times and bad, and who seems little inclined toward gratitude, generosity, or the rules he endorses for the rest of society. The greatest of these antientitlement statements is made in *Citizen Kane* (1941), but the sentiment is echoed throughout the era, particularly in its many great Westerns.

THE WESTERN WAY

A man has to be what he is, Joey. You can't break the mold. I tried and it didn't work for me.

—Alan Ladd as the title character, *Shane* (1953)

It is useful to think of the great Westerns of the Performer era—including *Stagecoach* (1939), *Destry Rides Again* (1939), *My Darling Clementine* (1954), *Shane* (1953), *The Searchers* (1956), and countless others—as compelling hybrids of a private psychological dreamscape (famed Western director John Ford's great visionary insight was that the actual Monument Valley was no less a fantastical setting than Oz) and an eminently public meeting on the town square. Here is the artistic genre that, via its examination of the conflict between a human being, as a heroically free individual, and the land as a communally exploitable resource, truly does provide the mythological context for an examination of postwar America.

In the Western, one gets a bare-knuckled examination of what sort of person—the cowboy or the capitalist—should hold the purse and the political power. See Figure 9.1. The genre consistently presents compelling drama and dialogue regarding the appropriate shape of the national future, accomplishing this in part by always putting death on the line. It is the Western that asks (and dramatizes the answer as a life-and-

FIGURE 9.1

Top Ten Western Films of the Performer Era

 1. *High Noon* (1952)
 2. *The Searchers* (1956)
 3. *Red River* (1948)
 4. *The Ox-Bow Incident* (1943)
 5. *Stagecoach* (1939)
 6. *My Darling Clementine* (1946)
 7. *Shane* (1953)
 8. *Destry Rides Again* (1939)
 9. *Winchester '73* (1950)
10. *She Wore a Yellow Ribbon* (1949)

Source: As voted on by the members of Internet Movie Database, Inc.

death matter) whether a society is best served by courageous individual-ism or whether safety, stability, and prosperity are obtained through allegiance to a more politically orthodox and socially responsible col-lectivism, a profoundly relevant postwar discussion.

As in a good fight, heavy blows are given and taken in all aspects of this complex ideological exploration. Remarkably, and with sincere ap-preciation of the difficulty of what is being examined, there really is no clear-cut answer. Yet it is hard not to notice that John Wayne, Henry Fonda, Jimmy Stewart, and Alan Ladd (and then TV's Hopalong Cassidy, The Lone Ranger, Gene Autry, Roy Rogers, etc.), rather than the settlers or capitalists, always seem to be among the courageous individualists—even when they wear badges. This is a glamorous fact certainly not lost on the young toy-gun-toting Performers.

DEATH, AN INTERESTING NEIGHBOR

In Italy for 30 years under the Borgias, they had warfare, terror, murder, and bloodshed, but they produced Michelangelo, Leonardo da Vinci, and the Renaissance. In Switzerland they had brotherly love; they had 500 years of democracy and peace; and what did they produce? The cuckoo clock.

—Orson Welles as Harry Lime, *The Third Man* (1949)

Is there no exemption for actors?

—Erik Strandmark as Jonas Skat, in response to Death coming for him, *The Seventh Seal* (1957)

The prevailing war sentiment of movies during the Performer value-formation era (especially after the war) is that war and death are rarely good for society or the individual and should be avoided if at all possible. However, because some argue that, at times, wars are morally justifiable, then it becomes necessary to produce soldiers who are willing to die for a cause. Thus, a fair number of Performer movies talk up the nobility of death for a worthy objective. Assuredly, John Wayne's bravery in the fight against Indian "savages" provides spiritual fuel for some Performers who will later fight in Vietnam.

Beyond the "worthy cause" point of view, it is useful to note the memorable Performer-era movies that further address war and death as some sort of complex, not-always-unsatisfactory answer to an extremely difficult question. One thinks of Hamlet's "To be or not to be" soliloquy, which is actually delivered by Doc Holiday in *My Darling Clementine* (1946)—perhaps the strangest scene ever filmed in an American Western. There is also the compelling *From Here to Eternity* (1953) which, although a postwar movie, presents the start of the war, even with its certainty of death and crippling injury for some, as a somehow satisfactory resolution to many of the difficult relationships and situations in which the movie's main characters are embroiled.

Perhaps one should not make too much of these philosophical meanderings. But, to the emergent generation of Performers, war and potential personal annihilation occupy much the same role as poverty does to the Patriots. To a large portion of the Performer population, the threat of death is not some abstract condition of life, but an enormously present and persistent influence on value formation. How could anyone be surprised when, in their late adolescence and early adulthood, a significant portion of the newly minted middle-class Performer population turns its backs on materialism in a symbolic gesture of life affirmation and their hearts towards a peace movement?

LIFE AS SOAP OPERA

By gad, sir, you are a character. There's never any telling what you'll say or do next, except that it's bound to be something astonishing.

—Kaspar Gutman describing Sam Spade (Humphrey Bogart), *The Maltese Falcon* (1941)

A person doesn't always get what she deserves. Remember it. If there's anything in life you want, go and get it. Don't wait for anybody to give it to you.

—Mrs. Thornton, *Peyton Place* (1957)

Perhaps the most noteworthy and remarkable observation about Performers is that they do not immediately, collectively, and permanently retreat right back into the womb. Traditional interpretation attributes this not to some amazing generational survivalist response, but to the fact that this event era has parents who indulge them in all the ways it is possible to indulge children, with the result that these children become insufferably cocksure and egomaniacal. But that, besides being arguable, is almost a comical slight when one considers the ferocity with which this generation has tried to work out its relationship with the world.

Leaving the ultimate "why" to the sociologists and psychologists, there is just no avoiding the truth that the "typical" Performer life manifests, from the perspective of the individual Performer, as a soap opera wherein he or she is the star. According to the Museum of Television and Radio, soap operas (a radio phenomenon of the 1930s brought to television in 1952 with *The Guiding Light* and established as an essential television form in 1956 with *As The World Turns*) are characterized by an intense and dramatic preoccupation with birth, death, marriage, romance, current social issues, and villainy. At their very core, soap operas are relentless multiyear, sometimes multidecade, character studies that explore the helpful and harmful nuances of every emotion, thought, value, relationship, and capacity for transformation that can occur within an individual's lifetime.

The reason it is so hard to describe, sell to, or manage the Performer generation is that one is dealing with people who see themselves not only as individualists, but also as individualists who zealously reserve the right to grow, change, change back, make things more interesting, and, as suits them, perform as brilliantly as master artists or as self-destructively as drunken sailors. This is a generation that apparently operates on the principle that an ego must be both strong and flexible to survive. Ultimately, the only description that really comes close to capturing the Performer personality is one that recognizes their capacity for willfulness and self-styled complexity.

Cinematic examples of this character complexity in Performer movies are many: Rhett Butler does not join the Confederate army until its cause is obviously and totally hopeless *(Gone with the Wind);* Jimmy Stewart intends to "clean up" the west's most degenerate town as a pacifist sheriff *(Destry Rides Again);* Humphrey Bogart's motives and machinations are so convoluted that even the screenplay's author admits that he doesn't know who actually commits one of the film's murders *(The Big Sleep);* and too numerous to mention are the films where the reformed prostitute and the town drunk are the characters of true ethical superiority. Particularly interesting, considering the stereotypical notion of his dramatic persona, is the character complexity that is written into so many of John Wayne's best "heroic" roles (stretching from *Stagecoach* in 1939 to *The Searchers* in 1956), in which he is variously an outlaw, a racist, a tragic loner, and a very morally ambiguous soul.

For all of the above, though, there are some themes and preoccupations that do consistently cycle around in the films of the Performer era. Taken collectively, they seem to address characteristics that are important in a philosophy made of equal parts intensity, individualism, and survival.

LOVE BETWEEN SOUL MATES

Maybe if I told you a story, you'd change your mind about the dead coming back. Maybe you'd know, as I do, that there is a force that brings them back, if their hearts were wild enough in life.

—Ellen, *Wuthering Heights* (1939)

The stories of Heathcliff and Catherine, Rhett and Scarlett, and Rick and Ilsa are so well known that often neither their last names nor the movies wherein they appear need be identified. But even in less-famous romances of the period, there is frequently something powerful and larger than life in the apparently fated pairing of these couples. These matches rarely end happily but, thanks to the intensity of the match, there is always the hope of the next life—or a next meeting in Paris. One should never underestimate the Performer preoccupation with love and romance as some sort of key to eternity.

DRAMATIZATION AND STYLE

I don't want realism. I want magic!

—Vivien Leigh as Blanche DuBois, *A Streetcar Named Desire* (1951)

If one wants to identify the exact instant when the Performers come into being, it is at the moment in *The Wizard of Oz* (1939) when Dorothy's house drops on the wicked witch and everything goes from black and white to Technicolor. To understand Performers is to appreciate their desire to have things vivid. This can and often does refer to character and plot points, but it just as frequently refers to style. The shadows of film noir, the warbled story lines and crazed costuming of musicals, the wide-screen panoramas in Westerns, and the drama of war stories are compelling not because they capture reality, but because they enhance mood. Such dramatic overdoing and aggressive preoccupations with style have generally continued to appeal to Performers, as they help to make life a little more vibrant and perhaps also constitute a little laugh at death.

CHEMICAL MOOD ENHANCEMENT

It shrinks my liver, doesn't it Nat? It pickles my kidneys, yeah. But what it does to the mind. It tosses the sandbags overboard so the balloon can soar.
—Ray Milland as Don Birnum, *The Lost Weekend* (1945)

Judging solely from the breadth of its appearance in the popular movies of the era, it would be virtually impossible to overestimate the adult Patriot population's preoccupation with boozing. And despite the strong antidrinking message of the Academy Award winning film, *The Lost Weekend,* quoted above (which the American liquor industry is reported to have tried to suppress by offering to buy the negatives), one can only come to the conclusion that drinking is something generally done by the good guys. In film after film of the Performer value-formation era, alcohol not only helps to deaden the pain of a bad situation, it makes people absolutely pleasant, funny, cool, spontaneous, and, not infrequently, wise.

In *Casablanca,* the impossibly urbane Rick Blaine (Humphrey Bogart) observes that he doesn't trust people who say "when" if they are being poured a drink because that means they're dishonest and don't trust themselves being drunk. In *Harvey* (1950), drinking clearly helps the pleasantly addled James Stewart to be both imaginative and kind. This tolerance for alcohol (perhaps "endorsement" is actually the right word), is even extended to the early television era in "charming" skits such as Lucy's bout with Vitameatavegamin (an alcohol-laden vitamin drink) and Brett Maverick's quotes from "my old pappy," such as, "Never cry over spilt milk—it could've been whiskey."

Perhaps the most interesting observation regarding alcohol's influence in the Performer's formative years is that of Margot Fontaine (Bette Davis) in *All about Eve* (1950), when she comments that infants would "get drunk if they knew how." This prescient comment simply fails to take into consideration that Performers were being formed to have their mood alteration and mind expansion take place on the more stimulant rather than depressant end of the spectrum. How could Patriots ever have been shocked when their kids got into pot and LSD? And why would we be surprised that this generation looks for new miracle pills and additives (the Vitameatavegamin without the alcohol) to enhance their lives today?

FATALISM AND A SENSE OF HUMOR

I'm not only a philosopher sir, I'm a fatalist. Somewhere, sometime, there may be the right bullet or the wrong bottle waiting for Josiah Boone. Why worry where or when?
—Doc Boone, Stagecoach (1939)

There's a tone to the movies of the Performer era that can only be called philosophical. Unlike the preceding Patriot generation which pretty much collectively knew what it wanted from life (work, security, somewhere to belong), the Performers' intense preoccupation with the individual twists and turns of life against a backdrop of potentially broad and personally inevitable annihilation lends little in the way of common generational goals. It doesn't make a marketer's life any easier, but to understand Performers is to acknowledge the insight that one's personal outlook is everything—and the selection of that outlook is a birthright.

This message comes through in various expressions and appreciations of life's ephemeral nature made throughout the movies of the era. But it is even more apparent in the era's comedy—which at its best is a wry appreciation of how fate and chance can so easily and suddenly turn situations for the better or worse.

Consider the scene in which Butch the bartender counsels a young soldier who has returned from the war with prosthetic hands (a role played by an actual war hero who received a special Academy Award for his work in the movie) in *The Best Years of Our Lives:* "Give 'em time kid. They'll catch on. You know, your folks will get used to you, and you'll get used to them. Then everything will settle down nicely, unless we have another war. Then none of us have to worry because we will all be blown to bits in the first day. So cheer up, huh?"

A KID'S LIFE

If you really want to hear about it, the first thing you'll probably want to know is where
I was born and what my lousy childhood was like and all that David Copperfield
kind of crap, but I don't feel like getting into it, if you want to know the truth.
—Opening lines, J.D. Salinger's *Catcher in the Rye* (1951)

So much is made of the Performer childhood, of the life of material
goods, and of the behavioral permissiveness furnished by a generation
of doting parents—Patriots—who had just gone through a depression
and a war. But even though there is little denying the self-involvement of
Performers, the "spoiled brat" analysis is a story told by the Patriot generation, not by Performers themselves. What the Patriots believe to be
parental purpose—"produce 'em, feed 'em, school 'em, church 'em, give
'em a nice bike on Christmas, and then they'll hang around to plant the
crops, procreate the tribe, and protect the traditions when they're grown
up"—is eventually challenged by Performers, not without some reason,
as a form of manipulation by a generation with its own shortcomings.

One could call it ingratitude but, unlike Patriots, young Performers
are not that interested in the past (especially the recent past with its gas
chambers, global war, and nuclear detonations). It is sometimes leveled
as a criticism of Performers that they live too much in the moment (and
indeed they have not prepared well for retirement, if the truth be told)
but from their perspective, neither the past nor future holds anywhere
near as much promise, allure, and credibility as an interesting, fulfilling,
and, pun intended, manifested present.

When Performers start having the story told from their point of view
in books such as *Catcher in the Rye* (1951) and movies such as *Rebel without a Cause* (1955) and *Blackboard Jungle* (1955), not only is there a lot of
poignancy in the protagonists' alienation from the values of the society
into which they have been born, but there is also a relentless observation
that no adult really listens to them. Rock and roll soon comes along to
get the Performers "heard," of course, but the parental response to this
"noise" is generally even more outrage and denial. But if one wishes to
truly appreciate the more solemn side of growing up as a Performer,
they might do well to fully attend to the following bit of dialogue from
Rebel without a Cause:

> *Planetarium narrator:* "In all the immensity of our universe
> and the galaxies beyond, the earth will not be missed. Through

the infinite reaches of space, the problems of man seem trivial and naïve indeed, and man existing alone seems himself an episode of little consequence." (There is a reddish burst of fire, and the show ends.)

Jim (James Dean to Sal Mineo, who is hiding under a seat): "It's all over, the world ended."

Plato (Sal Mineo, whose busy parents are rarely around except to dole out money): "What does he know about man alone?"

THE PERFORMER IDEAL

With enough courage, you can do without a reputation.
—Clark Gable as Rhett Butler, *Gone with the Wind* (1939)

Kiss me. Kiss me as if it were the last time.
—Ingrid Bergman as Ilsa Lund, *Casablanca* (1942)

I'm impatient with stupidity. My people have learned to live without it.
—Klaatu, *The Day the Earth Stood Still* (1951)

My pa did it the old way and I'm gonna do it the new way.
—Jimmy Stewart as the pacifist sheriff Tom Destry, *Destry Rides Again* (1939)

Once more, it is not necessary to go much further than Oz to understand the ideals that are most precious to Performers. (Interestingly, when *The Wizard of Oz* was released in 1939, it was critically acclaimed but *not* commercially successful. Ahead of its time, it did not reach "phenomenon" status until young Performers could watch it on television). The key elements that *Oz* introduces, and which are to hold sway over Performer value definition in movies ranging from *Casablanca* to *Alice in Wonderland* for the next 20 years, include the following:

- *Leaving Home.* There is the familiarity and safety of all the things associated with home. Opposed to these is the call to adventure. Adventure invariably entails danger and sometimes ends badly but, given a sense that life is fleeting and there is much evil to be defeated in the world, the call to adventure wins.
- *Adventure Survival.* Life is an adventure, and the three qualities an individual needs to survive an adventure are: courage, a heart, and a brain. Personal qualities are essential—pedigree is not.

- *Vivid Stimulation.* The land of adventure is invariably more stimulating than one's familiar turf. It is likely to be in Technicolor, and it may very likely include singing munchkins, flying monkeys, mad hatters, or the Gestapo. Stimulation by the vivid and the exotic is a sure sign that you are alive.
- *Fellowship before Authority.* The world is full of scarecrows who deserve closer attention and snake-oil salesmen who pretend to be wizards. Fellowship is always to be valued. Authority is always suspect. Some way, somehow, everyone is interestingly and uniquely acting out a part.

Certainly, Dorothy does come to the tacked-on Patriot-induced conclusion that there's "no place like home." Yet the greater Performer truth is revealed in her look of wonder and the excitement of her impending adventure when she realizes that she's finally made it "somewhere over the rainbow." To a Performer, Kansas will always be a little disappointingly black and white.

10

THE TECHTICIANS
An Overview

POPULATION OVERVIEW

Age: Born 1958–1971
Size: 22% of the U.S. Population
Spending: $1.45 Trillion Annually
Themes: Science/Speed/Service
Values: Self-Reliance/Pragmatism

Summary

Techtician (technician + tactician) values derive from a complex mix of social idealism and world-weary cynicism. Born into a world flush with scientific, social, economic, and personal potential, some of which did manifest in very positive ways during their value-formation period, the Techticians were ultimately subjected to a degradation of events. President John F. Kennedy invoked outer space as a metaphor for man's unlimited potential for advancement. Unfortunately, advancement did not occur, and the times instead declined in the forms of political assassinations, violent generational confrontations over moral attitudes, and the ethical calamities of the Vietnam War and the Watergate scandal.

While simultaneously disposed toward altruistic acts of service and a cautious, if not cynical, approach toward swallowing too much of anyone's pitch, Techticians now seem to be marked by nothing so much as their pragmatism. They accept few absolutes—relying mainly on "the facts" and a rational process for stringing them together for the benefit of some greater, albeit conditional, good.

> *We choose to go to the moon. We choose to go to the moon in this decade and do the other things, not because they are easy, but because they are hard, because that goal will serve to organize and measure the best of our energies and skills . . .*
> —John F. Kennedy

TECHTICIAN EVENT MATRIX

Hope/Hyperdrive/Chaos and Exhaustion

Hope

The specter of global war fades from cultural prominence as WW II and the Korean War recede into history. Society comes to accept that "peaceful" nuclear standoff between the United States and the Union of Soviet Socialist Republics (USSR) is a far more desirable scenario than no-win mutual destruction.

The energy, enthusiasm, and idealism of youth become the keynotes of U.S. culture, as the post-war babies surge into their adolescence, teen years, and early adulthood. Peace and love have their cultural heyday—in concept anyway.

Idealistic future-oriented political leadership surfaces, particularly during the "Camelot" period of the Kennedy administration (1960–1963). Even after Kennedy's assassination, the Johnson administration continues the "Great Society" drive toward a humanitarian social agenda and a space agenda that lands a person on the moon in 1969.

Hyperdrive

The scientific research advances of military and space technology begin to flood into the private sector. Satellite communications, integrated circuit technology, and commercial jet travel are just some of the developments that alter the speed and orientation of the world. In an historical eye blink, the "Age of Information" is rooted.

Progressive social agendas flood the cultural landscape. The Techtician period witnesses the true birth of the civil rights, antipoverty, feminist, environmentalist, consumer, and peace movements.

Running huge deficits to fund the war in Vietnam, the government spurs the gross national product (GNP) to its greatest period of historical growth ever (a 50 percent increase between 1961–1969). A 15 percent real rise in wages and the advent of revolving credit also aid the rapid economic expansion.

Chaos and Exhaustion

The assassinations of the idealistic and inspirational leaders—John and Robert Kennedy and Martin Luther King, Jr., lead to a feeling of chaos and unrest.

The Vietnam War becomes an enormous political, social, and ethical morass that deeply divides the nation, largely along generational lines (Patriots versus Performers).

The Richard Nixon administration is burdened by a deteriorating postwar economy, and its own sorry ethical stance in the Watergate break-in scandal, ending in Nixon's "I am not a crook" speech.

TECHTICIAN POPULATION VALUES

Self-Reliance

- *Historical drivers.* Self-involved emotional confrontations between Patriots and Performers during Vietnam era; assassination of capable and charismatic leaders such as John F. Kennedy, Robert Kennedy, and Martin Luther King, Jr.
- *Value manifestation.* It is unwise to count on anyone else to make *your* well-being his or her priority. Even the best leaders may let you down.

Service

- *Historical drivers.* The JFK "what you can do for your country" legacy; an era of broad social activism regarding civil rights, environment, consumer protection, etc.; the beginning of the service economy.
- *Value manifestation.* The world is a difficult place in need of improvement. Active commitment to a cause, or just sheer helpfulness, trumps lip service.

Pragmatism

- *Historical drivers.* Inevitable response to the Vietnam War and the cultural excesses of the 1960s; the appeal of the real science underlying the dreams of the space age.
- *Value manifestation.* Results are far more impressive than motivations. One should make the best practical use of people, places, and things, avoiding unnecessary excess if it is not useful.

Data and Logic

- *Historical drivers.* For the first and only time in contemporary history, science is esteemed as a servant of mankind and not just some extension of military affairs; an era of engineering begins to produce marvels throughout society.
- *Value manifestation.* The single most desirable apparatus at one's disposal is a sound piece of information processed by an orderly mind.

Time

- *Historical drivers.* The advent of the Age of Information, commercial jet travel, and the space age.
- *Value manifestation.* What is worth doing probably needs to be done now . . . and quickly.

Skill

- *Historical drivers.* The doctrinal certainty of the Patriots and the dramatic self-valuation of the Performers seem too lightly won; contrast to the first landing on the moon—a miracle of preparation and precision.
- *Value manifestation.* Words are cheap. Life is not a dream—practice and heavy lifting are usually required.

Technology

- *Historical drivers.* Satellites, commercial jets, interplanetary probes, moon landings, heart transplants, miracle drugs, microprocessors, etc.

- *Value manifestation.* Techticians were born to be the creators and stewards of the technology boom of the 1990s. "Personal computer" is an apt description of the individual Techtician, reflective of much that is valued here.

Alienation

- *Historical drivers.* Inner cities in turmoil; growing extremes in wealth and poverty; assassination; lack of victory and perceived meaning in Vietnam; technology.
- *Value manifestation.* Beyond the survivalist's awareness of the need for self-reliance is the debate over the existence of God versus the absence of God. Techticians reserve the right to move between the extremes of belief and nonbelief while questing for a sort of objective personal perfection..

Nature

- *Historical drivers.* An enormous upsurge in ecological activity as reflected in phenomena like Earth Day and Rachel Carson's classic book, *Silent Spring*, the cultural balance to technology.
- *Value manifestation.* In many ways, nature becomes the essence of Techtician spirituality, and stewardship of the biosphere the most spiritual of all acts. Natural law is ultimately accepted as a reflection of God's perfection.

TECHTICIAN MACRO INTERESTS

(Life-phase considerations projected through 2010)

Base-Building

Because techticians understand that a strong building begins with a strong foundation, they are likely to be literal base-builders in terms of employment, income, and property ownership—working hard to create long-term foundations for mature life.

Domesticity

Often ambiguous about traditional family relationships, especially parenting, which frequently strikes them as an irrational "roll of the dice." When considering their roles associated with home life, Techticians tend to think in terms of improvement of people, places, and things.

Issues with Authority

One of the sobering aspects of maturity is learning that you rarely get to be in charge. Ironically, Techticians are mostly disposed to being okay with this because their orientation toward service makes them excellent functionaries in the execution of someone else's larger vision. Nevertheless, Techticians tend to be frank in their estimation of an authority figure's shortcomings, and the outcomes of this social dynamic will be most interesting to see, as will the sort of leadership this Value Population produces.

Living Conditions

In their homes, Techticians appreciate pragmatic conveniences such as electronic compatibility of appliances, office and workshop areas, and good insulation—natural settings are also usually a plus.

Parents

Rarely disposed toward sentimentality about the plight of the aged, Techticians confronted with the needs of their own aging parents tend nonetheless to be pragmatic and loyal.

Private Life

With maturity often comes an inner-directedness that makes the stresses of dealing with the public world tolerable. Gravitating toward self-improvement activities—from bodybuilding to book clubs, from tap dancing to transcendental meditation—helps Techticians maintain their sanity and stay grounded.

Property

Techticians tend to value the tangible and are likely to want to own "real" property in their maturity. Their adulthood could easily coincide with an upsurge in hard assets, rather than financial instruments.

Public Enemies

The fact that an adult generation must confront its common antagonists is often a struggle for Techticians, as they tend to have "value trouble" with moral and ethical absolutes and may tend to see villainy in shades of gray. By the same token, they have little sympathy for self-promoters and self-righteous perpetrators of pain, who are absolutely certain in their cause.

Security—Physical and Spiritual

While broadly reflected in some of the preceding issues, the Techtician propensity for finding reassurance in the rational, the tactile, and the factual, bears repeating. One of the emerging macrotrends in today's world is the bridge building that is going on between science and religion, with scholars on both sides attempting to prove that the hand of God is obvious in the precise mechanics of the natural world. This is a comforting proposition to most Techticians and is useful in understanding what makes the average Techtician feel safe and secure.

Accountability and Accommodation

Another principle of maturity is that one becomes fully accountable for one's decisions and actions. Hoping for the best and expecting the worst may have the ring of truth for the Techticians, who may thus be blessed with an appreciation of, and an accommodation for life's up and down cycles.

Relaxation for Techticians

High tech gadgetry, self-improvement projects, reading, physical exercise, activities in nature, domestic projects, walking the dog, games of skill, intelligent conversation, etc.

11

THE TECHTICIANS
History Creating Values

A NEW DEMOGRAPHY

Born between 1958 and 1971, the Value Population we named the Techticians is unique in the field of modern demography. Although major works on generational analysis most often acknowledge that the children of the 1960s arrived during a period that was unparalleled in its social eccentricity, these works rarely ascribe to this group a value matrix that is uniquely their own. Due in part to the common sociological ideology that a generation is reproductively decreed to last for 20 years, the Techticians are seen either as a second wave of Baby Boomers or as a first wave of Gen Xers.

This unique group, while in some ways an odd hybrid of the self-actualizing Performers and the disenfranchised Believers, is really not best characterized by an understanding of their predecessors or their successors. The largest of all of the Value Populations (hardly a generational afterthought!), the Techticians share among themselves so much more than the vivid self-absorption of the Performers or the hope of rescue that describes the Believers. Ironically, it is the very fact of a society sped up by emergent mass communications, technology, and radical social change that begins to define the Techticians and call into question the appropriateness of double-decade value formation analysis.

SCIENCE, SPEED, AND INFORMATION

One fails to properly understand the Techticians if one fails to emphasize the importance that science and technology play in the era of Techticians' value formation. See Figure 11.1. This Value Population began with an unprecedented bright hope of scientific and social potential. While admittedly the Techtician value formation story does not have a particularly happy ending, the rush to combine the Techticians' failures and frustrations with that of the following generation as their prevailing keynote, completely and inappropriately diminishes an understanding of the Techticians' real virtues—their pragmatic devotion to accomplishments via rational, detailed, fair-minded, efficient, and roll-up-your-sleeve endeavors that ultimately seek to facilitate and serve some greater good.

FIGURE 11.1
Scientific and Technological Breakthroughs of the Techtician Era

1958—First transatlantic jet passenger service begins.

1959—Navy launches Vanguard satellite; first integrated circuit developed by Texas Instruments.

1960—First working laser is built; Digital Equipment Corporation builds the first minicomputer.

1961—First American man goes in space; contraceptive intrauterine device is developed.

1962—First interplanetary probe reaches Venus; first industrial robot is introduced.

1963—Quasars are discovered; first liver transplant is performed; sedative Valium is developed.

1964—U.S. Surgeon General affirms cigarette smoking causes cancer.

1965—First commercial communication satellite is launched; first American walks in space.

1966—FDA approves "the Pill" safe for human use; DNA code is fully deciphered.

1967—World's first successful human heart is transplanted; Pulsars are discovered.

1968—Largest American petroleum reservoir is discovered in Alaska.

1969—Scanning electron microscope is developed; first humans walk on the moon.

1970—Floppy disk is introduced; bar codes are developed for retail and industrial use.

1971—Microprocessor is introduced; Mars is orbited and photos reveal its surface.

Source: Family Education Network, Inc.

THE SPACE RACE

With Russia's launch of Sputnik in 1957 and the U.S. launch of Explorer in 1958, the space race was on in earnest. What began as another expression of Cold War competition quickly morphed into something more hopeful . . . a sense that humanity was living in infinite space and possessed the genius to unlock the productive secrets of technology and push its domain toward the stars. The Mercury and Apollo space programs were important driving forces of the Techtician era, and confidence culminated with the first human landing on the Moon in 1969. This sense of expanding domain also had a political correlative in the granting of statehood to Alaska and Hawaii in 1959.

CIVILIAN JET TRAVEL

At virtually the same historical moment that those early satellites were being launched, airlines introduced international and domestic jet service, and the demolishing of New York City's Penn Station, in 1963, was the symbolic end of the long-distance passenger rail age. Besides helping to foster the sense that science and technology were capable of lifting people above their earthly limitations, widespread jet travel also stamped this emergent event era with one of its most salient defining characteristics—the need for speed.

Similarly, popular culture began to change its own primary soundtrack from country and pop ballads to the jet-fueled beat of rock and roll. The landmark jet-fighter-inspired tail fins of the 1957 Chevrolet Bel Air are legendary to this day.

INFORMATION TECHNOLOGY
AND THE SERVICE AGE

In 1959, Texas Instruments introduced the first integrated-circuit technology. In 1960, Digital Equipment Corporation built the first minicomputer, and the U.S. Department of Defense literally invented the earliest version of the Internet. In 1962, the first communications satellite was sent into orbit.

These events, and other early iconic rumblings of the electronic Age of Information, went largely unnoticed by the general population of the time. However, it is important to note that, by as early as 1957, the num-

FIGURE 11.2

U.S. Service-based Employees Versus Production-based Employees

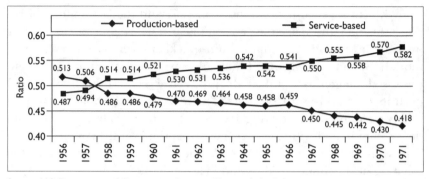

Source: U.S. Department of Commerce—Bureau of Economic Analysis

ber of managerial, clerical, and service jobs in the United States had sur-
passed production-based blue-collar jobs. See Figure 11.2. This marked
the Techtician era as truly the dawn of the information and service ages.

What did not go unnoticed by the general public was a mass communications device called television. Whereas in 1950, only 9 percent of
American households had televisions, by 1960, the household penetration had reached an astounding 87 percent, with the average household
set turned on more than five hours per day. See Figure 11.3.

Virtually unavailable at the end of the 1950s, by the end of the Techtician era in 1972 color televisions were in more than half of American

FIGURE 11.3

*Average Time Per Day Television Is Turned On and Percentage of Households
with a Television Set*

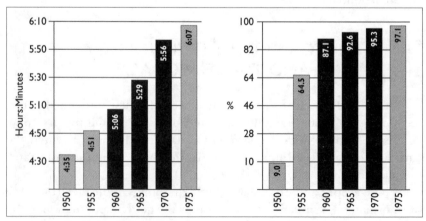

Source: Television Bureau of Advertising, Inc., and Nielsen Media Research

households. What began as an entertainment novelty quickly became a social force, with the often-cited turning point being the televised 1960 Kennedy/Nixon presidential election campaign debates. Inarguably, among all its other impacts, this new mass medium forever changed the world by speeding up the time frame and vastly broadening the scope of information and experience delivered to the human race.

SOCIAL TURMOIL

Symbolized by the inspired and inspiring leadership of individuals such as John F. Kennedy and Martin Luther King, Jr., the Techtician era began with a profoundly idealistic sense of human potential. It soon became apparent that society's growing infatuation with speed, coupled with the broad access of conflicting interest groups to a mass-media pulpit, was going to severely challenge comprehension and change in U.S. contemporary culture. Ideas, expectations, and agendas were suddenly flying around much faster than people could respond or adapt to—with the result being a severe fracturing of the social mass exemplified by a sad inclination toward acts of confrontation and violence. See Figure 11.4. Although it was a difficult time, it is also important to acknowledge that much vitally important social legislation was enacted during this era.

FIGURE 11.4
U.S. Crime Index Rate

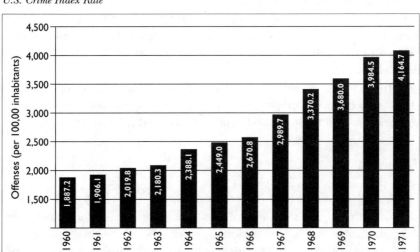

Source: U.S. Department of Justice—Bureau of Justice Statistics

CITIES IN TURMOIL

The broad political and economic policies of the 1950s, which developed highways, encouraged the growth of middle class suburbs, and directly funded the development of office-tower urban centers and high-rise apartment projects, had a devastating effect on the nation's cities. With the destruction of traditional neighborhoods, the decline of the tax base, and the diminishment of municipal services, the poorer classes found themselves deeply disenfranchised drones in the "American Dream." This story has other important aspects, but the bare facts are incontrovertible: riots in Los Angeles' Watts neighborhood caused 34 deaths and $200 million in damages (1965); riots in Newark led to 26 deaths, 1,500 injuries, and 1,000 arrests (1966); riots in Detroit killed 40, injured 2,000, and left 5,000 homeless (1967). And every other major city in the United States was a proverbial powder keg—barely short a match.

Civil Rights

Beyond the poverty and the overcrowding, there was the gut-level issue of racism itself. In the period between the court-ordered integration of schools in Little Rock, Arkansas, at the end of 1957, and the 1963 March on Washington, where Martin Luther King delivered his famous "I Have a Dream" speech, hundreds of thousands of primarily young blacks and whites participated in peaceful protests for racial tolerance and equality. Despite the passage of the Omnibus Civil Rights Bill, and significant War on Poverty legislation in 1964, it was not much of a "time-step" from peaceful protest to the radical Black Panther movement, race riots, and the ultimate iconic in-your-face megalomania of "The Greatest," Muhammad Ali.

To society's less liberal members, it seemed as if more than a hundred years of social order was to be eliminated—violently—in the space of a season, and this was more than many could tolerate or accept.

Feminism

In the same year as the March on Washington (1963), the publication of Betty Friedan's *Feminine Mystique* launched the feminist movement. A contentious and confrontational exploration of perceived sexual inequities and gender-based entitlements, this early feminist activism eventually led to the 1972 passage by the Senate of a constitutional amendment barring gender-based discrimination; however, it was never ratified by the full Congress. While the real feminist moment would peak during the next Value Population era, that of the Believers, here is where the seeds of the movement that would forever change sexual roles and relationships, perhaps not entirely to anyone's satisfaction, were sown.

Environmentalism

In the same way that Betty Friedan's book launched feminism, Rachel Carson's *Silent Spring,* a polemic against the environmental harm of pesticides, inaugurated the environmentalist movement in 1962. The Techtician era is when humanity realized that population growth and industrial practices were manifestly at odds with ecological survival. A reflection of how important this issue was becoming (some commentators contend that it has always been the single most historically important social issue of the 1960s) was the celebration of Earth Day on April 22, 1970, by 20 million Americans and the subsequent creation of an aggressive Environmental Protection Agency later that same year. It is worth noting that consumerism also got its start in the 1960s, with the publication of Ralph Nader's *Unsafe at Any Speed,* an indictment of the automobile industry, published in 1965. Many of the issues of the consumerists proved to be environmental issues, and the two causes became politically allied.

Vietnam

In terms of Value Population analysis, the Vietnam War was the focal point for a desperate collision between the most fundamentally incompatible values of the Patriots (sacrificial allegiance) and the Performers (sanctity of individual life). Although there is no way that the importance of this conflict (both the real war abroad and the ideological conflict at home) can be over-expressed in the history of the era, the point here is to understand the influence that this remote (albeit televised) and confusing war, and the related student protest movement, might have had on the value formation of the Techticians.

Techticians were born into a world where "hawks" (bombastic, cold, manipulative, and clearly materialistic group, arguing an unconvincing "love of country" ideology in the face of enormous American casualties) were opposed by "hippies" (stoned-out, smug, self-indulgent, and anarchical, arguing that "feeling groovy" is the divine law of life). In its negative extreme, the war was not an issue likely to produce any heroes or meaning to an emergent generation, who perhaps best appreciated that the United States did not win this war, honor its participants, or even celebrate its end.

Leadership and Moral Ambiguity

I do not believe that any of us would exchange places with any other people or any other generation. The energy, the faith, the devotion which we bring to this endeavor will light our country and all who serve it . . . and the glow from that fire can truly light the world.
—John F. Kennedy, 1963

Without making it sound like too much of a polemic, the fact is that the Techtician era begins with the emergence of John F. Kennedy and the immense hope for the future of mankind and concludes with Richard Nixon's humiliating resignation over Watergate, a botched political burglary. Historical perspective has smoothed out the evaluations of these two presidents (Kennedy down some in stature, Nixon up some), but the experience, as lived and as reported on contemporary television, was hardly an uplifting story of human progress.

It is well worth noting that, because of the proliferation of television and the intense image scrutiny it allowed, the mass population had never before in history been so close to its leaders or current events. Partisans of the true social dreamers of the era, most notably John F. Kennedy, Martin Luther King, Jr., and Robert F. Kennedy, lost far more than agenda advocates when these leaders were assassinated; they lost very real presences that stood for hope in their daily lives. In addition, the traits of leaders who were less "telegenic," or less well-spoken, or who simply endorsed less-populist agendas, were magnified into something bordering upon evil.

Having established this, an important part of the story of the Techticians is how the events and dealings surrounding the leaders of their developmental period seem so consistently dishonest and/or tragic. The Warren Commission Report (1964), which found the assassination of John F. Kennedy to be the work of a solitary gunman, was highly suspect even at that time—with even less-convincing stories emerging after the murders of Robert Kennedy and Martin Luther King, Jr., both in 1968.

Almost all government-released information related to the war in Vietnam seemed a bit too neatly fabricated, a suspicion that was justly proved in many respects by subsequent historical studies. A recent book on the Lyndon B. Johnson White House reports that, during a discussion of the Gulf of Tonkin incident, a deadly naval confrontation that was the prime justification for the escalation of American troops from "advisor" to "combatant" status in Vietnam in 1964, Johnson is captured on tape as remarking, "for all I know, our Navy was shooting at whales out there."

Ultimately, when it comes to the people in charge of selling or defending their take on events, Techticians tend to find it all a little suspect. In their value-formation period, good leaders came to bad ends, bad leaders came to bad ends, and the assumption of authority, moral or otherwise, is never to be entirely trusted. On their bad days, Patriots may be described as fearful of authority, and Performers can be characterized as contrary for the fun of it, but Techticians really seem to have little choice about authority but to doubt it.

Economic Ambiguity

In terms of gross domestic product, the period between 1961 and 1969 was, on a percentage basis, the strongest growth period in the history of the modern U.S. economy. See Figure 11.5. Not only did real, adjusted-for-inflation, economic output grow by more than 50 percent during these years, but real wages increased by 15 percent. Vietnam may have been an ethical morass, but the huge debts the federal government

FIGURE 11.5
U.S. Gross Domestic Product and Percent Annual Change

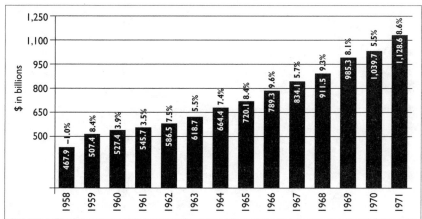

Source: U.S. Department of Commerce—Bureau of Economic Analysis

ran to fund the war effort, while simultaneously holding the line on new taxes, not to mention the extra stimulative kick given by the advent of the revolving-payment credit card in 1966, proved to be very good for the broad economy.

Nevertheless, by the end of the Techtician period, it was apparent that inflation was likely to become an enormous problem. Initially resistant to devaluation of the dollar and to wage and price controls, in 1971, the Nixon administration finally acquiesced to the issue, but by most accounts, it was too late. What went up in the 1960s was going to come down hard in the 1970s. Although most of the decline is part of the story of the Believer era, Techticians are defined in part by great prosperity turning into gloomy economic writing on the wall.

Perhaps it is fair to surmise that the Techticians primarily have a pragmatic sense that wealth is a facilitator of independence, a tool of personal growth, and an aid to causes, rather than as a guarantor of security, a tool of indulgence, or an emblem of social status (although there is likely some appeal to wealth as a measure of one's "smarts"). To a Techtician, ultimately, financial stability may not be "easy," but it is certainly something to work on.

12

THE TECHTICIANS
Cultural Expressions of an Era

This world is so full of crap, a man's gonna get into it sooner or later, whether he's careful or not.

—Paul Newman as Hud Bannon, *Hud* (1963)

SOCIETY AND THE INDIVIDUAL: BEYOND ALIENATION

The single most important difference between the art of the Techtician period and that of their predecessors, the Performers, is that the Techticians' heroes and heroines are represented as much more uncertain about the role of individual passion and personal preference in the affairs of the real world. It is not that Performers are always successful or well integrated into their circumstances, but the solution to social disenfranchisement in Performer terms is generally an acting out of a stronger or different facet of one's personality. What is essentially accepted as self-actualizing drama in the Performer world view, though, veers very close to social pathology in the faster, exponentially more complex, and morally ambiguous universe of the Techtician.

Perhaps the most common protagonist of the Techtician cinema is the social pariah, the individual whose consciousness, characteristics, and/or circumstances make participation in the affairs of "normal" society an unimaginable impossibility. A short list of these indelible Techtician-period characters include the following:

- Norman Bates, *Psycho* (1960), a momma's boy as a homicidal maniac.

- T.E. Lawrence, *Lawrence of Arabia* (1962), a successful warrior but also a dangerous desert madman who sees himself as a latter-day Moses.
- Raymond Shaw, *The Manchurian Candidate* (1962), a brainwashed war hero who is set up by his politically powerful mother to assassinate a presidential candidate. (As an interesting aside, this movie so eerily foreshadowed the Kennedy assassination and its surrounding sense of political subterfuge that the movie's release was suspended and the movie's star, Frank Sinatra, bought all the rights to insure that the movie would not see general release for decades.)
- The Man with No Name, *A Fistful of Dollars* (1967), the ultimate morally ambiguous gunfighter.
- Rosemary Woodhouse, *Rosemary's Baby* (1968), Satan's unwitting concubine and mother of the Antichrist (another ominous foreshadowing, as the film's details of a pregnant woman tortured by a cult came horrifically true for the film's director, Roman Polanski, whose pregnant wife, Sharon Tate, was tortured and murdered by the Charles Manson "family" the following year).
- Captain America, *Easy Rider* (1969), whose decision to drug-deal his way to easy money and drug-take his way to easy enlightenment ends in personal and social tragedy.
- Yossarian, *Catch-22* (1970), a bombardier of questionable mental competence who attempts to flee the insanity of WW II in a rubber raft.
- Alex DeLarge, *A Clockwork Orange* (1971), a murderous sociopath delinquent who is psychologically conditioned (ultimately unsuccessfully) to avoid violence.

For the most part, these characters are not merely romantic loners or alienated outsiders, but individuals who are cast out by the established social framework in the same way that a healthy body rejects a foreign pathogen—violently, and frequently with deadly effect. Even when society appears not to have driven the characters to mental incapacity, there is so often an irredeemable incongruity between the values and/or circumstances of the central figures and the societies in which they must perform. Consider Dustin Hoffman as both Ben in *The Graduate* (1967) and as Ratso Rizzo in *Midnight Cowboy* (1969), the doomed lovers Tony and Maria in *West Side Story* (1961), the archetypal bug-squashed "Organization Man" C.C. Baxter in *The Apartment* (1960), or even the wrongly convicted Dr. Richard Kimble of television's *The Fugitive* (1963).

Techticians seem to be not so much interested in the creative power of the ego as they are in its vulnerability to complex social conditions. They are not essentially hopeful and do not believe everyone escapes in the final reel. Ultimately to Techticians, society may have its positive moments, but, given tendency and enough time, it has an alarming tendency to drive even the strong individual toward insanity, corruption, violence, or despair.

LEADERSHIP AND DOCTRINE: MAY THE FARCE BE WITH YOU

World domination. The same old dream. Our asylums are full of people who think they're Napoleon. Or God.
—Sean Connery as James Bond, Dr. No (1962)

We have to shoot and kill and destroy. We represent everything that's wholesome and good in the world.
—Don Adams as Maxwell Smart, Get Smart (1965)

Ample mention of the Techticians' mistrust of political leaders and their self-serving, socially menacing tactics and agendas has been made earlier in this book, so the point will not be overly elaborated upon here. It is worth mentioning, however, that certainly one of the richest thrusts of the popular art of the Techtician period is the excoriation of political leaders, their methods, and their doctrinal beliefs. This is sometimes handled with thoughtful sensitivity in such great historical dramas as *Inherit the Wind* (1960), *A Man for All Seasons* (1966), and *The Lion in Winter* (1968), but the typical tone of the period is satire and farce.

Indicative are movies such as *One, Two, Three* (1961), *A Funny Thing Happened on the Way to the Forum* (1966), and *The Producers* (1968), the latter two starring Zero Mostel in the originals and both enjoying successful Broadway revivals with the Techtician audiences of today. Much popular television fare employed satire and farce, including *F Troop* (1965), *Get Smart* (1965), *Hogan's Heroes* (1965), *The Monkees* (1965), and particularly, the BBC's *Monty Python* (1969). Perhaps the greatest work ever in this thematic vein, however, is Stanley Kubrick's *Dr. Strangelove* (1964), a dark comic treasure trove of over-the-top leaders and knuckle-headed statesmen whose actions resulted in the destruction of the world via a largely mechanical nuclear-retaliatory disaster.

In summary, Techticians have reservations about society at large—reservations that naturally extend to the individuals who seek to govern that society. For those whose interests run toward organizational dynamics and/or mass marketing, it is worth keeping in mind that the Techticians may not be the first to embrace the wisdom emanating from the executive suite or the first to raise their hand in a salute to the flag—any flag.

THE DOMAIN(S) OF DHARMA

There's nothing wrong with you Ray; your only trouble is you never learned
to get out of spots like this; you've let the world drown you in its horseshit
and you've been vexed . . .

—Jack Kerouac, *The Dharma Bums* (1958)

Just because Techticians often feel they are denied meaningful personal integration into a "crazy" world created by their predecessors, in no way automatically implies that they have abandoned the search for personal peace and enlightenment. On the contrary, although the search often comes at a cost in social terms, many Techticians are concerned (consciously and unconsciously) with finding their *dharma*—roughly translated as one's appropriate place and sustaining characteristics within the totality of the universe.

It is remarkable that Jack Kerouac, the same author who so forcefully captures the spiritual essence of the Performers in his book, *On the Road* (written in the early 1950s, published in 1957), is so elegantly attuned to the different spiritual vibration of the Techticians in his 1958 work, *The Dharma Bums*. The former work is an exuberant tribute to the intoxicating glory of the unfettered ego let loose in an immense physical and spiritual realm of personal creative freedom. The far more devotional and precise second work suggests that the least among us, even if we are literally bums, may fulfill a spiritual duty greater than ours by surrendering their "vexed" egos to appropriate places of peace and performance within the immensity of consciousness.

As abstract and esoteric as this may sound, it is very helpful in appreciating the quest of Techticians to find some places of peace—and actually, there turn out to be a few.

NATURE

The human beings believe everything is alive. But the white man believes
everything is dead.
—Old Lodge Skins, Little Big Man (1970)

The hippie "flower people" sometimes made an appreciation of nature seem saccharin and dopey as heck, and the budding environmentalist movement sometimes made nature seem like just another battlefield. However, there is also an important spiritual aspect to this awareness of nature's primacy that serves Techticians to this day. In a value system, so heavily influenced by technology and the urge to speed things up, and amidst general cultural commotion, it is not surprising that many Techticians would grow up to find a restorative sense of peace, righteousness, and order in nature. In the seminal movie *Easy Rider* (1969), a very downbeat vision of an American youth/drug culture that had cashiered its idealism, the only genuine admiration expressed is for the people who are working the land. And it is in a small cabin on Desolation Peak that the protagonist of *The Dharma Bums* eventually finds ecstasy through immersion in the nature all around him.

THE LOGICAL MIND

In a child's ability to master the multiplication table, there is more holiness than in
all your shouted hosannas and holy holies.
—Spencer Tracy as Henry Drummond, Inherit the Wind (1960)

"Thank heavens!"
"Mr. Scott, there was no deity involved. It was my cross-circuiting to B
that recovered them."
—Exchange between Scotty and Mr. Spock, Star Trek (1966).

They're awful hard to buy for. Besides it was something they could use.
—Don Knotts as Barney Fife (explaining why he bought his parents a septic tank as an anniversary gift),
The Andy Griffith Show (1960)

From the most mundane daily activities to the most abstruse technological challenges, pragmatism and rational thought provide the average Techtician great comfort and strength. Brought up in an era that seemed to be spinning off its axis in so many literal and figurative ways, the Techticians have generationally embraced functionality and its help-mates, efficiency and precision. Even while people, events, abstractions, and causes were failing and perplexing them, the Techticians discovered that physical principles remained comfortingly constant and good old "two plus two" could reliably be counted on to equal four.

In general, the popular art of the Techtician value-formation period exhibits great admiration for science and technology. This ranges from lighthearted amusement with gizmos and inventions in movies, such as *The Absent-Minded Professor* (1961) and *The Nutty Professor* (1963), to a fond appreciation for stirring science adventure in movies like *Journey to the Center of the Earth* (1961) and *Fantastic Voyage* (1966), to deep fascination with the complex technical gadgetry and plots of the James Bond movies (which premiered with *Dr. No* in 1963), to absolute devotion to the amazingly thoughtful, ambitious, and influential *Star Trek* (first released on television in 1966 and still running strong today). Other technological "fascinations" of the period range from Scientology, a highly structured mind-based religious system that had its first great burst of prominence during the Techtician value-formation period, to the so-called "Marvel Age of Comics," in which comic book genius Stan Lee explored (via characters such as Spider-Man and The Hulk) both the awesomeness and the angst of technology-based superhuman transformations in "normal" people.

While hardly an unmitigated endorsement of a technological and rational value system, the movie *2001: A Space Odyssey* (1968) deserves a brief mention here. When it first came out, the contemporary (Performer) audience largely rejected it as aloof and cerebral, complaining that the only fully developed character was Hal, the supposedly "infallible" computer that adapts human self-preservation traits and murders most of the crew on its space mission. What is interesting is that the movie eventually achieved its enormous popularity in a series of re-releases between 1975 and 1982, when the Techticians were movie-going teenagers.

SERVICE

Ask not what your country can do for you, ask what you can do for your country.

—John F. Kennedy (1961)

Ah chrysanthemums. Such serviceable flowers.

—Maggie Smith as Jean Brodie, *The Prime of Miss Jean Brodie* (1969)

Of all the overlooked virtues of this overlooked generation, likely the most significant to the world's well-being is the Techticians' willingness to perform service. In many demographic analyses, Generation X either receives sympathy or catches mild disdain for being drafted into the worker-bee positions of the service economy. However, it is the Techticians' value conditioning that makes them well suited to the acknowledgment that self-sacrificing service is an unimpeachable good.

Unlike Patriots (who may give blindly loyal service to the causes of their clan), or Performers (who may render service for the glory), Techticians possess a sense of service that is more situational and coolly efficient. Their innate sense of empathy for personal dilemma allows them a special gift for recognizing the need for unconditional help. Pragmatic by nature, they give service as, and in the amount, it is needed.

If this sounds overly abstract, remember that the popular art of the Techtician value-formation period rewards those who give remarkable service with special powers and protections. Such is the case with the "practically perfect" *Mary Poppins* (1964), the odds-beating town-saving *Magnificent Seven* (1960), the always-surviving galactic "good scouts" of the Starship Enterprise, and the world's ultimate world-saving Secret Service agent, James Bond.

Perhaps the most memorable example of the true heart of spiritual and selfless service appears in the documentary *A Night to Remember* (1958), when the officers of the Titanic, facing certain personal doom, do their best to load the lifeboats, while equally dedicated chamber musicians play to their deaths in a gesture of peace amidst panic and despair.

RELIGION

Almost at the moment he died, he said, "Father forgive them, for they know not what they do." Even then, and I felt his words take the sword from my hand!
—Charlton Heston as Judah Ben-Hur, Ben Hur (1959)

This is madness, my Lord. Don't do it. I could not serve both God and you.
—Richard Burton, as Thomas Becket (advising the king not to make him archbishop), Becket (1964)

I'm not a beatnik. I'm a Catholic.
—Jack Kerouac, in a New York Times article—Joseph Lelyveld, October 22, 1969.

There is evidence of a meaningful religious urge in the Techticians. They exhibit not so much an involvement with the mysteries of faith or divine love but rather a profound intellectual appreciation of God's manifest perfection. In a world so full of compromised leadership, moral equivocation, false doctrine, selfish materialism, and general tribulation, God remains for many Techticians the only conceivable source of truth, authority, and enlightenment.

Needless to say, this does not always bode well for society, as the human corruption that manifests itself in the name of God is often the most pernicious of evils. This is amply demonstrated in the brilliant 1960 movie *Inherit the Wind*, in which religious fundamentalism faces off against science in a confrontation that still fascinates Techticians to this day. Nevertheless, one shouldn't overlook the Techticians' urge to understand and serve some greater good. Compelling movies of the Techtician value-formation period, including *Ben-Hur* (1959), *Spartacus* (1960), *Barabbas* (1962), *Becket* (1964), *Godspell* (1971—Broadway, 1973—movie), and *Jesus Christ Superstar* (1971—Broadway; 1973—movie), demonstrate that there is no greater good to serve than God.

WHAT'S LOVE GOT TO DO WITH IT?

I find the moment that a woman makes friends with me, she becomes jealous, exacting, suspicious, and a damned nuisance. And I find the moment that I make friends with a woman, I become selfish and tyrannical. So here I am, a confirmed old bachelor, and likely to remain so.
—Rex Harrison as Professor Henry Higgins, My Fair Lady (1964)

Women! I could have conquered all of Europe, but I had women in my life!
—Peter O'Toole as Henry II, The Lion in Winter (1968)

You're NOT a girl! You're a GUY! Why would a guy wanna marry a guy?
Security.
—Tony Curtis and Jack Lemmon as Joe and Jerry, Some Like It Hot (1959)

Traditional romantic love comes in for fairly shoddy treatment in the value system of the Techticians, Doris Day notwithstanding. This was exemplified by the rise of feminism, the contemporary overthrow of many social traditions and cultural taboos, the conflicting demands and options of modern life, and the commercial need for cinema to differentiate itself from family-oriented television.

Further examination of social issues, among them the simple truths regarding love, sex, and relationships, reveals the Techticians' view that just because something is biological, doesn't necessarily make it logical. See Figure 12.1.

Notwithstanding romantic love, some of the breakthrough "romantic" preoccupations of the Techtician-era cinema include the following:

- *Homosexuality: Some Like It Hot* (1959), *Spartacus* (1960), *The Boys in the Band* (1970)
- *Incest: Lolita* (1962)
- *Impotence: Bonnie and Clyde* (1967)
- *Mixed marriages: Guess Who's Coming to Dinner* (1967), *Harold and Maude* (1971)
- *Prostitution: Midnight Cowboy* (1969) (the only X-rated film to ever win the Best Picture Oscar)
- *Confirmed bachelorhood/spinsterhood: My Fair Lady* (1964), *The Odd Couple* (1968), *The Prime of Miss Jean Brodie* (1969)
- *Adultery: The Graduate* (1967), *Bob & Carol & Ted & Alice* (1969), *Carnal Knowledge* (1971)

In addition, several mother-son relationships of the era seem to have been taken from a term paper on Freud, and written by Satan (or vice versa). *Psycho* (1960), *The Manchurian Candidate* (1962), *The Birds* (1963), *Bye Bye Birdie* (1963), *My Fair Lady* (1964), *Who's Afraid of Virginia Woolf?* (1966), an imaginary son, but no less powerful for that, and *Harold and*

FIGURE 12.1
U.S. Divorce Rates

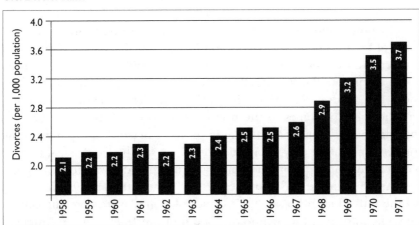

Source: U.S. Department of Health and Human Services

Maude (1971), among others, are all films that feature mothers who intend to keep a stranglehold on their son's lives, most particularly their romantic interests. Although explaining this should truly be the work for a psychiatrist, not social-trends historians, it is hard to ignore the cinematic proliferation of would-be emasculating mothers in the Techtician value-formation era.

Finally, it is hard to resist mentioning the television introduction of *The Newlywed Game* (1966). The show's major draw was the tension that developed between competing and frequently belligerent newlyweds who discovered all the comical (to the audience) ways in which they were emotionally incompatible and clueless about one another. This popular, long-running show demonstrates clearly the Techticians' largely dispassionate perception of Cupid.

COMMERCE: THE NECESSARY EVIL

It's real hard to be free when you are bought and sold in the marketplace.
—Jack Nicholson as George Hanson, *Easy Rider* (1969)

He's got 92 credit cards in his wallet. The minute anything happens to him, America lights up.
—Walter Matthau as Oscar Madison, *The Odd Couple* (1968)

There was a time when I used to get lots of ideas. I thought up the Seven Deadly Sins in one afternoon. The only thing I've come up with recently is advertising.
—Peter Cook as The Devil, *Bedazzled* (1967)

By now it should be clear that Techticians are both pragmatic and wary of the prevailing socioeconomic system. Furthermore, as discussed earlier, their values formed in an era of remarkable debt-financed affluence, albeit one that eventually spiraled into painful inflationary recession. See Figure 12.2. Many Techticians, therefore, experience inner conflict when it comes to the notion of amassing wealth. The obvious benefits of good material fortune in terms of personal autonomy in the present and future play off against the broad spiritual and social costs of collectively worshipping a demonstrably mean and fickle golden idol.

As a brief aside, it is extremely useful to note that many, if not most, of the individuals who saw their options-laden/day-trading ships about to come in during the technology boom of the 1990s were Techticians.

FIGURE 12.2

U.S. Real Weekly Wages and Percent Annual Change

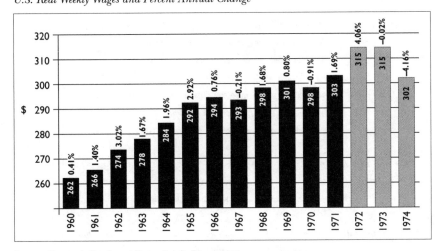

Source: Economic Trends and Data—Labor Research.org

Then this same group watched these vessels sink as the tech bust suddenly hit with the fury of a typhoon. A useful defining characteristic of the realist Techticians is their "what goes up must come down" attitude toward this turn of events. This same storm manifested as panic in the Patriots and heroic poise in the Performers.

Although judgments regarding matters of commerce are not all negative in the popular art of the Techtician-formation period, the most singularly consistent and arresting trend of this period is a pronounced and growing sympathy for the criminal adversaries of capitalism, i.e., thieves. They may reach bad ends, but everyone in the theatre roots for, or at least admires, the crooks in movies such as *Bonnie and Clyde* (1967), *The Producers* (1968), and *Butch Cassidy and The Sundance Kid* (1969). In other movies, including *How to Steal a Million* (1966) and *The Thomas Crown Affair* (1968), not only are the thieves cool; they also get away with their crimes!

That this trend toward rooting for the bad guys is an antisocial attitude is not lost on the Techticians. Nevertheless, the notion of "antisocial" is as much a dark comic thought as a cause for concern to the Techticians. Surely, a group as assaulted by moral ambiguity, social chaos, and failed leadership in their value-formation period is not entirely above the belief that ends justify means—a notion worth keeping in mind, if one's own commerce involves them.

THE TECHTICIAN IDEAL

Anything can be great. I don't care, brick laying can be great if a guy knows what
he's doing and why, and if he can make it come off.
—Paul Newman as Fast Eddie Felson, The Hustler (1961)

There are some men in this world who are born to do our unpleasant jobs for us.
Your father's one of them.
—Maudie Atkinson, To Kill a Mockingbird (1962)

Let me help. A hundred years or so from now, I believe, a famous novelist will write
a classic using that theme. He'll recommend those three words over 'I love you'.
—Capt. James T. Kirk, Star Trek (1966)

I am putting myself to the fullest possible use, which is all I think that any
conscious entity can ever hope to do.
—Hal the Computer, 2001: A Space Odyssey (1968)

To be blunt, there probably is no such thing as a Techtician ideal. An ideal is an abstraction that implies absolute principles, and there is something about a belief-based system that repels Techticians more than any other Value Population. Rendered virtually incapable of reconciling a smooth fit between the fulfillment of the individual and the conditions of society, the Techticians are most likely to accept that the system is flawed and that they don't comfortably "fit in."

Having established this conditionality, however, there is no denying the Techticians' high regard for individuals who do their personal best under whatever circumstances they happen to find themselves in. Many of the "outsider" roles of Paul Newman come to mind, including that of the pool hustler in *The Hustler* (1961), the convict in *Cool Hand Luke* (1967), and the train robber in *Butch Cassidy and the Sundance Kid* (1969). In all of these characters, no diminishment of will and skill occurs in the face of harsh personal conditions and an unjust authoritarian society. To the Techtician, that's exactly what makes a good guy.

Although there is often a hint of vivid Performer egoism about them, the fictional heroes of the Techtician value-formation period most often derive their essential essences from performing their actions, often at mortal risk, for the benefit of someone or something other than themselves. James Bond gets the cool toys and the babes; Capt. Kirk and Mary Poppins both get to fly; Spider-Man gets web throwers, a neat looking suit, and superpowers. The key to their heroic drives is that they are all in service to human needs greater than their own personal happiness or survival. The fact is rendered even more poignantly in Gregory Peck's Atticus Finch in *To Kill a Mockingbird* (1962). Here, the defense of an unjustly accused black man puts a white Southern lawyer's own family at mortal risk. Of course, those brave doomed officers and musicians on the Titanic in *A Night to Remember* (1958) will always come to mind.

Although films such as *Dr. Strangelove* (1964), *2001: A Space Odyssey* (1968), and *A Clockwork Orange* (1971) demonstrate that science is not the cure-all for the world's problems, Techticians firmly hold the belief that reasoned analysis abetted by technology have to be ultimately more helpful to mankind than the crazed ambiguities of life on the planet as it now stands.

In many ways, the Techtician ideal is best summed up by Charlton Heston, as George Taylor, in *Planet of the Apes* (1968): "I'm a seeker too. But my dreams aren't like yours. I can't help thinking that somewhere in the universe there has to be something better than man. Has to be."

13

THE BELIEVERS
An Overview

POPULATION OVERVIEW

Age:	Born 1972–1983
Size:	17% of the U.S. Population
Spending:	$861 Billion Annually
Themes:	Withdrawal/Watergate/Women
Values:	Relationship/Diplomacy

Summary

It is tempting to dismiss Believers as victims of a bad patch of history and to simply offer generational condolences. Certainly Believer value formation takes place in an era of broad political, economic, and social dissolution, and there is hardly a more representative phrase than "power outage" to describe the general tone of the times. But to be frank, the term "power outage" is a common aspect of the characteristic Believer personality. What makes the Believers such a fascinating group, however, is an appreciation of the skills they develop to cope with and survive the issues posed by such a low-wattage value formation period. Along these lines, some of the defining qualities of Believers include empathy, patience, and, perhaps most importantly, the faith that rescue may be near at hand. To some observers, the idea that things are simply going to get better of their own accord may seem rather naïve and escapist, but the overriding "truth" of the Believer value-formation period is that at its darkest hour the Ronald Reagan administration comes along and things suddenly do get better. Grace, Believers seem to inherently know, can only arrive if one makes room in the spirit for its possibility.

BELIEVER EVENT MATRIX

Exhaustion/Downturn/Rescue

Exhaustion

America's effort to extricate itself from the Vietnam War finally succeeds with withdrawal of ground troops in 1972, but the result of retreat is fatigue, anxiety, and cultural malaise, rather than relief and celebration.

The OPEC oil embargo of 1973 highlights a historically unprecedented year of energy shortage problems punctuated by brownouts, restrictive fuel allocations, service-station gas-pump lines, and rapidly escalating oil prices—this coupled with "defeat" in Vietnam reveals extraordinary U.S. vulnerability to external powers.

A decade-long political leadership vacuum is initiated by the Watergate scandal in 1972 and Nixon's resignation in 1974.

Downturn

After the boom of the 1950s and 1960s, the Believer period is marked by a weak economy, including recessionary gross domestic product (GDP) periods, a flat stock market, historically high loan defaults, and "stagflation" (high inflation with little job growth).

Social dysfunction becomes systemic with huge rises in abortions, unwed mothers, divorces, latchkey kids, and school dropouts. Concurrently, the so-called "Me Generation" is symbolized by a debauched club-and-cocaine culture and a pervasive attitude of self-righteous self-gratification.

Adding to this downturn is "America Held Hostage, " CNN's relentless coverage of the Iranian hostage crisis, where 63 U.S. citizens are held for 444 days (11/1979–1/1981) at the U.S. embassy in Tehran, and all negotiations and rescues fail.

Rescue

Ronald Reagan's persona, perhaps more than his policies, symbolizes the return of the absent father to a society in need of a strong hand on the social rudder.

Although the economy weakens during Reagan's first years in office, inflation finally abates, unemployment peaks in 1982, and a turnaround begins in 1983. Deficit spending, lower interest rates, and a tax increase to preserve social security are an odd mix of "fix," but they work.

The Iranian hostages are released and the country takes heart from feel-good news, such as the first launch of the space shuttle (1981), the first woman U.S. Supreme Court Justice (1981), and the first woman in space (1983)—and on a symbolic level, a military victory in Grenada (1983).

BELIEVER POPULATION VALUES

Friendship and Love

- *Historical drivers.* Crushing social trends related to the family include rising divorce rates, abandonment by fathers, unwed mothers; drug usage; difficult economic times for many; children given short shrift in public policy.
- *Value manifestation.* The best way to emotionally navigate dark times is with empathic friends in the same boat. Love between kindred spirits is life's ultimate reward.

Suspicion of Leaders

- *Historical drivers.* The Nixon, Ford, and Carter administrations cast doubts on motives and effectiveness of traditional leadership; negative father-image trends.
- *Value manifestation.* You may have to accept the bosses, but you don't have to believe they know what they are doing.

Feminism

- *Historical drivers.* The 1970s represent the move of feminist principles from theory to practice; politics, business, the arts, and many

traditionally male-dominated fields experience an influx of female talent and leadership; *Ms. Magazine; Roe v. Wade;* Charlie's Angels.
- *Value manifestation.* Never send a man to do a woman's job.

Peace and Diplomacy

- *Historical drivers.* The post-Vietnam era ushers in a period of conflict avoidance; Anti-Ballistic Missile Treaty with Russia; trade relations with China; Carter-led Israel-Egypt peace talks.
- *Value manifestation.* The world periodically wearies of war—it causes great pain and doesn't promise much of a future. Peace seems so much easier and talking less messy.

Comfort and Ease

- *Historical drivers.* Resource deprivation is a reality throughout society; inflation and job growth stagnation dominate the downbeat economic feeling of the times; crime-riddled New York City—the great symbol of capitalism—declares bankruptcy.
- *Value manifestation.* It is not the same as the abject material want of the Great Depression, but the deprived state of the Believer value formation era fosters a healthy respect for having enough . . . and for locating a nice place to enjoy it.

Justice

- *Historical drivers.* The resignation of Richard Nixon over the Watergate scandal; landmark Supreme Court women's rights cases and the appointment of the first woman Supreme Court justice; peace and arms control treaties instead of armed conflict.
- *Value manifestation.* Peoples' rights are important. Tyranny is the use of force when fairness is not even considered as an available option.

Patience

- *Historical drivers.* Energy shortages and gas lines; 55 mph national speed limit; 444-day "America Held Hostage" crisis in Iran.

- *Value manifestation.* Sometimes problems are resolved overnight, but probably not this night.

Grace

- *Historical drivers.* Eventual release of the Iranian hostages; uptick in emotional milieu and economic fortunes during the Reagan administration; presidential pardons of Nixon and Vietnam draft dodgers.
- *Value manifestation.* One must never lose hope and faith, for rescue may be near at hand, and it would be a shame not to have left a light on.

Art

- *Historical drivers.* Tough times breed a strong strain of hopeful Star Wars/Superman/Raiders of the Lost Ark escapism; design trends move away from modernism towards humanism; love as redemption becomes central theme in literature; dancing and the romantic ballad make a return.
- *Value manifestation.* Creativity can be a type of hopeful transcendence. It gives mankind the ability to write happy endings, even if they just occur in the imagination.

BELIEVER MACRO INTERESTS

(Life-phase considerations projected through 2010)

Children

Believers have a complicated generational outlook regarding kids. Having had their values formed in an era of broad parental and social dysfunction, many Believers will decide that life has far more satisfying and less stressful purposes than parenthood. By the same token, many Believers could decide that their greatest personal achievement might be an enlightened and enthusiastic attitude toward offspring (their own and others). Stay tuned!

Communication

Believers' emergence into adulthood has ramifications for both the form and content of communications in our society. On a very obvious level, this is a population that has been exposed to interactive computer-driven electronic media from a very early age and seems to prefer participation to passive reception (e.g., chat rooms to newspapers). The key is communication that breeds active community, even if narrowly defined as pertaining only to Believers themselves.

Local Gathering Places

Believers, who prize community, are entering the gathering places of the adult world with a fair amount of enthusiasm. They appear to like the courtship places (restaurants, clubs), the cultural places (museums, theaters), the consumer places (malls, contemporary metro centers), and anywhere they can collectively kick back and be comfortable. While style definitely does matter, environments that appeal tend to emphasize ease over edginess.

Ideas and Learning

To hear some college professors tell it, Believers are a uniquely uninspired and uninspiring group of scholars. But one must consider: 1) Believers formed their values in an era of political, social, cultural, and economic enervation that has led to a generational indifference toward the potency of institutional wisdom; and 2) Believers have a fondness for the sort of learning that allows things to seem better than they are. Call it "art," but the real key is that too much reality, rationalism, and regulation tend to poison the potential of a good rescue fantasy. In all, Believers are far less likely than Techticians to worship at the altar of scientific empiricism.

Neighbors

As Believers move into their first apartments and starter homes, it is interesting to observe how inherently wary many of them are of neighbors. Capable of being quite sociable and respectful of community, Believers are nevertheless very protective of their own need for recuperative privacy and dislike being vulnerable to the implicit aggression of neighbors whose music is too loud, whose cooking smells too pungent, or whose demands for scout cookie sales is too incessant. Whatever their personal behavioral tastes, Believers, more than any other Value Population (except maybe Patriots), need to be among like-minded and like-valued neighbors.

News

Value Populations entering adulthood suddenly come to realize that news is something that involves them on a participatory and reactive basis, rather than just being something that pertains to their parents and other adult populations. Yet, despite the difficult situation of the world today, Believers may be very value-inclined to not pay too much attention to "hard" news, preferring to keep an illusion of equanimity through a devotion to the features aspects (celebrities, fashions, entertainment, etc.) of the news. This could be their Achilles' heel, but Believers have faith that it won't be.

Offices and Office Workers

Believers tend to bring a very particular set of personal requirements to the workplace, particularly regarding a preference for order, peace, and harmony in the environment. Ironically, this is sometimes frustrating to managers of other Value Populations who view business as a battlefield and are far more willing to prize urgency and competitiveness over tranquility. But such managers should be wary of jamming their Believer colleagues' very sensitive radars.

Restlessness

For a Value Population that had the enormous economic promise of the late 1990s as a background to its school years, the less generous reality of the early twenty-first century is quite the disappointment. Given their smaller numbers and the boom in the economy, Believers were brought up believing that their hardest choice would be which great job offer to take. Now they are confronted with a national malaise similar to that of their birth years, and the specter of dissipation looms again.

Independent Contractors Not Company People

Entering the workforce, Believers offer their employers an odd mix of artistic entrepreneurism and an ability to fit comfortably into an orderly environment. Even though they bring a lot of potential grace to impersonal institutions, polls of Believer college students indicate they are not interested in joining those large organizations, which are, after all, too impersonal.

Vehicles

Just as media started to become less "mass" and more individually interactive with the advent of Believers, the reign of the American automobile industry was challenged by a slew of foreign imports selling individual feature benefits rather than vested brand loyalty. While Believers can sometimes follow a fashion with the best of them, it is with this generation that the notion of loyalty to a particular automobile brand is likely dead as an Edsel.

Relaxation for Believers

Believers enjoy activities of courtship and socialization—both in person and electronically. All work and no play make Jack a dull boy—or at least not part of the in crowd. The desire to maintain personal peace and equilibrium often manifests in the desire to go off by oneself to pursue some reflective personal pleasure or to just tune out.

14

THE BELIEVERS
History Creating Values

Traditional Generation X analysis
tends to lump the value-formation events of the 1960s and 1970s together. Certainly, issues of failed leadership and broad social disruption
are common to both eras. However, there are key and crucial differences
to these periods that are not easily glossed over by traditional reliance
on a 20-year generational cycle that begins at the end of a birth rate
boom and bust cycle.

POWER OUTAGE (1972–1982)

First and foremost, it is not simply an abstraction to point to the
widely dissimilar, actually *opposite* is not too strong a term, energy levels
of the two periods. Whereas the dynamic Techtician era is characterized
by an enormous amount of intellectual, political, and societal engagement with breakthrough technological advances and economic robust-
ness, the far less vigorous Believer period is a time of limited energy
(both actual and political), flagging economic hope, and a pervasive
sense of social ennui and isolation. It is as if a switch is turned off at the
beginning of the Believer period (symbolically, in 1973, the White
House decides not to light the national Christmas tree as an energy saving measure), and the nation embarks on a restless national nap, in

which the cultural emphasis switches from "save the world" to "save anything you can."

The two events that most dramatically demarcate entrance into the Believer period are Watergate (1972–1974) and the withdrawal of all combat troops from Vietnam (1972). While the impact of both events as challenges to political and ethical consciousness have been discussed as part of the Techticians value-formation time frame, the significance of these events is different for Believers. In the case of Watergate, the federal government's immersion in the political scandal, which culminates with the resignation of President Nixon (1974), precipitates an era in which the United States is beset with extremely ineffectual leadership (including the Ford and Carter administrations which *seem* somehow absent in office). In regard to military withdrawal, the country discovers that the costs, both financial and psychological, of involvement in Vietnam are largely to be felt as debt, apathy, and alienation in the war's aftermath.

The sense of the times as "running on empty" is not at all abstract or far-fetched in light of the very real resource shortages related to an OPEC oil embargo (1973), an OPEC price manipulation that doubles the price of a barrel of oil (1979), the perceived failure of nuclear energy (most dramatically evidenced by the partial meltdown of a reactor at Three Mile Island in 1979), and a worldwide food-production crisis (lasting most of the 1970s).

ECONOMIC WOES: THE LIMITS OF GROWTH AND STAGFLATION (1972–1983)

In the landmark book, *The Limits of Growth* (1972), an influential team of economic, environmental, and population scholars argue that there is no way the world economy can sustain a boundless rate of development. The "prophecy" seems to come true almost immediately, as energy shortages and recession curb growth around much of the globe. In the United States, the period, further exacerbated by the debt of the Vietnam war and a reduction in military spending, is punctuated by recessionary decreases in the real GDP (1974, 1975, 1980, 1982), a virtually flat stock market (1965–1982), the loan default of America's capitol of capitalism, New York City (1975), and, quite important symbolically, the establishment of a national 55 mph speed limit (1974).

While economic historians are still arguing over who deserves the blame for the darkened economy (as well as who deserves the credit for the eventual recovery), the key economic reality of the Believer period becomes stagflation, a confusing and pernicious period of rising prices unexpectedly coupled with little or no job growth. The Misery Index (a sum of the inflation rate and the unemployment rate) breaks 11 for the first time in post-World War II history in 1973, rises rapidly to a peak of 20.7 in 1980, and does not return to under 12 until the first year of the Transformers' value-formation period in 1984. At their worst, interest rates hit 20 percent in 1980 and the unemployment rate jumps to 10.8 percent at one point during 1982. In 1979, the consumer price index jumps 13.3 percent, the largest one-year rise in more than three decades. See Figure 14.1.

The economy, like the public mood, is simply overwhelmed and exhausted.

THE IRONY OF PEACE

The Believer Value Population is the first modern generation to live through a value-formation period in which the United States does not have a significant number of troops involved in a military conflict abroad. In fact, it can be persuasively argued that the most outstanding accomplishments of the Believer era, certainly as far as the United States is concerned, are its contributions to conflict containment and world

FIGURE 14.1

The Misery Index (Inflation Rate + Unemployment Rate)

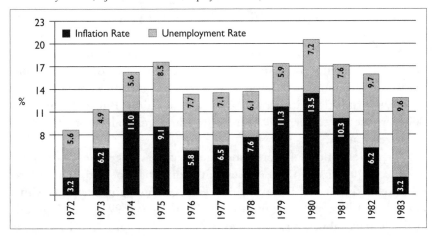

Source: U.S. Bureau of Labor Statistics

peace. During the Nixon administration, the war in Vietnam ends (in 1972 troops are withdrawn, and in 1973 bombing stops), relations are "normalized" with China (1972), a strategic arms limitation treaty is signed with Russia (1972), and the military draft is eliminated (1973). Jimmy Carter's landmark Middle East diplomacy leads to the Camp David accords and a Nobel Peace Prize for Anwar al-Sadat, the President of Egypt and Menachem Begin, the Prime Minister of Israel (1978).

Despite these considerable accomplishments, the national feeling seems to be one of anxiety and vulnerability, rather than calm control. In addition to the emotional aftermath of Vietnam, America's first lost war, the nation learns how vulnerable its economy is to foreign interests as the Arab-Israeli conflict leads to the Arab Oil Embargo in 1973. The feeling of powerlessness crests with the taking of 63 hostages at the American Embassy in Tehran by militant Iranian students, an event made especially dispiriting by a failed military rescue attempt and the incessant media coverage ("America Held Hostage" is ABC's label for a relentless dose of depression dished up throughout the 444-day ordeal that lasts from November of 1979 through Ronald Reagan's inauguration day in January of 1981).

National confidence does not seem to reemerge until Ronald Reagan sends a small force of U.S. marines to liberate the island nation of Grenada from a Marxist regime apparently buttressed by a few hundred Cuban "construction workers" in 1983, renovating the notion of a Communist "menace."

SOCIAL DYSFUNCTION AND WOMEN'S RIGHTS

Much of the research on Generation X focuses on the social dissolution that becomes most apparent in the 1970s. Indeed, there is more than enough aberrant behavior to cluck over and no shortage of demoralizing statistics with which to tar a generation. But in all honesty, Believers are no easier to capture with grand generalizations than any other generation.

To understand Believers, one must acknowledge the undeniably harsh social truths of the Believer value-formation period, particularly those related to family life and child-rearing. This rightfully starts with a nod to the Supreme Court findings in *Roe v. Wade* (1973), which greatly facilitate legal abortions. Arguments of ethics, religion, and social responsibility will be left to other forums, but there is little denying that the *timing* of this event in the context of broad social disruption appears significant.

BELIEVER-ERA SOCIAL TRENDS

- *Birth rate decline.* Some commentators select the year 1972 as the opening demarcation of "Generation Y" (which they extend, we believe mistakenly, all the way to 1995), because it is the year that the U.S. birth rate slips below the population replacement rate. Interestingly, in this same year, the Rockefeller Commission, a joint presidential-congressional effort, tacitly approves this trend, when it issues a report that concludes, "we have not found any convincing argument for continued population growth."
- *Rise in abortions.* In 1972, the number of legal abortions represents 13 percent of all known pregnancies. By 1976, that figure has grown to 21 percent and by 1980 it has reached 25 percent.
- *Rise in births to unmarried mothers.* In 1969, 10 percent of all live births in the United States are to unmarried mothers; by 1985, that figure has more than doubled to 22 percent. See Figure 14.2. The last year that a majority of black children are born into married two-parent households is 1975.
- *Rise in divorces.* Divorce rates climb steadily throughout the 1970s, peaking from 1979 to 1981 when 22.8 of every 1,000 married women over the age of 15 got divorced each year—double the rate of the mid-1960s.

Additional troubling statistics, particularly related to education, religious practice, and child welfare, paint a generally glum picture of

FIGURE 14.2

U.S. Birth Rates to Unmarried Mothers

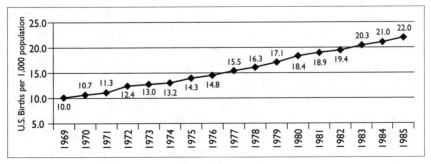

society's regard for children and family. When the 1970s are referred to as the "Me Decade," it is adults turning away from a child-first doctrine that is most damning in the eyes of traditional family-value supporters. The facile abandonments by fathers, the well-chronicled nightlife scene, the drugs, the glib profaning of conservative institutions, and the libertine sexual experimentation make it hard to grant a sympathetic spin to this story, even as historical artifacts.

Yet, one should not entirely mistake the caricature for the reality. First, amidst all the hue and cry over *Roe v. Wade,* it is sometimes conveniently forgotten that this seven-to-two majority decision of the Supreme Court is a profound acknowledgment of women's rights. It may be seriously argued that if the number-one overlooked achievement of the Believer era is its relative military peace, then the creation of a climate allowing the empowerment and individuation of women is the second. More than just a time of abstract feminist philosophy, the 1970s usher in a mainstream change in the perception of women's roles and their influence on society. The first year of the Believer period, 1972, is noteworthy for such developments as the launch of *Ms. Magazine;* the total domination of popular culture—especially music charts and awards—by women artists such as Helen Reddy, Carole King, Carly Simon, and Aretha Franklin; and the passage of Title IX legislation that puts women's educational activities, especially intercollegiate sports, on an equal government-funding footing with men's activities.

Arguably, most of the era's women remain in traditional roles or choose not to push the envelope much farther than the fictional career women on the *Mary Tyler Moore Show* (1970–1977). But suddenly there is at least the implied "right" to fantasize about becoming a crime-fighting Charlie's Angel (1976–1981)—or to actually become a revolutionary, like Patty "Tania" Hearst (apprehended in 1975), or a Supreme Court Justice like Sandra Day O'Connor (1981), or the first woman in space, like Sally Ride (1983). And if failure more often becomes reality, as is so sadly illustrated by the abortion and divorce statistics quoted above, well at least there was now a right to fail. Intriguingly, the Believer era ends on a rising tide of "family values," with the U.S. Congress voting against the Equal Rights Amendment in 1982.

Ultimately, it should simply be acknowledged that there is often a conservative bias in much of the social analysis done on the Believer period. The aim here is not to judge the analysts or to approve of socially deviant behavior, but simply to suggest that there is more to this "Me Decade" stuff than cocaine and contraception. For just as individuals from other event eras form unique value attributes to deal with economic challenge, war, or even mass prosperity, Believers have grown to develop values that work in the context of social dysfunction and economic malaise.

Ultimately, and maybe a little ironically, one cannot help but notice that many of the values that "work" for both men and women in this period are values that are associated with traditional feminine virtues. Among these are nonviolence, creativity, personal empathy, patience, faith, and an orientation toward accepting assistance. Maybe the truth is best expressed by Cyndi Lauper by the title of her sassy 1983 hit, "Girls Just Want to Have Fun."

RESCUE

A terrible year by most anyone's standards, 1980 is plagued by a horrible economy; a hostage crisis; a deterioration of the relationship with the Soviet Union (because they invade Afghanistan), which results in a suspension of the SALT agreement; a U.S. boycott of the Moscow-based Olympics; the reinstitution of draft registration; the murder of John Lennon; and the legend-ending destruction of Muhammad Ali at the hands of Larry Holmes. America is badly in need of an economic and emotional boost.

That lift arrives in the person of Ronald Reagan who, preaching the gospel of lower taxes, business-friendly deregulation, American military might, and, especially conservative family values, becomes the strong American father-figure who has been absent for the better part of a traditional generation. There is little arguing that Ronald Reagan's election as U.S. President, in late 1980, has a profound impact on the mood of the country.

The reason the early years of the Reagan administration are included in the Believer analysis is two-fold. First, although many books, articles, and doctoral theses have been written about the economic maneuverings of this period, the truth is that the economy actually worsens during the early years of the Reagan presidency (as mentioned earlier, unemployment soars to 10.8 percent at the end of 1982). Second, both in terms of its revivification of spirit and in the advocacy of an economic policy that is willing to incur huge debt, the early Reagan administration is directly addressing solutions to specific Believer circumstances.

While it will be fully explored as a cultural trend in the next chapter of this book, it is worth noting the importance of acts-of-rescue and forgiveness in the events of the Believer era. President Ford's unconditional pardon of ex-President Nixon (1974), the marine rescue of the merchant ship *Mayaguez* from Cambodia (1975), the admission of 140,000 Vietnamese refugees into the United States (1975), the Israeli commando raid to free hijacked passengers at the Entebbe airport (1976), the unconditional pardon of Vietnam-era draft evaders by President Carter (1977), the failed hostage rescue attempt in Iran (1980—surely the final nail in the Carter popularity coffin), the freeing of the hostages on Reagan's inauguration day (1981), and the rescue of American medical students during the Grenada "war" (1983) all illustrate this point. Although the taking of the hostages in Iran brushes the story from the nation's headlines three days later, perhaps the most illustrative example of this phenomenon takes place on November 4, 1979, when the federal government announces an unprecedented $1.5 billion loan guarantee to Chrysler, which has just reported a $460 million loss for the third quarter of the year.

Along these lines, the most relevant act with regard to Believer value formation of the early Reagan years, despite the president's reputation as a tax cutter, may well be his grudging willingness to raise taxes in order to save the Social Security system from bankruptcy (1983).

In the end, Believers seem to have an unnatural expectation, no matter how dire their personal situation may be, of being provided for and protected by forces outside their own direct command. And really, why shouldn't they?

Chapter

15

THE BELIEVERS

Cultural Expressions of an Era

I used to think that if I died in an evil place, then my soul wouldn't make it to heaven. Well, fuck. I don't care where it goes as long as it ain't here.

—Frederic Forrest as Chef, *Apocalypse Now* (1979)

Performers were value-formed to appreciate that a strong personality might surmount a challenge from society. Techticians learned that it is not often that society's challenges can be surmounted, but that there is still virtue in making oneself useful. Believers are casualties.

Lest this sound too harsh an evaluation, please remember that this is not the Believers' fault, as we are merely exploring the cultural conditions of their value-formation period. As already indicated, Believers do develop appropriate and compelling survival traits—arguably the most charming and worthwhile set of such traits at the disposal of any Value Population. But to see how they get there, one must first consider a value-formation period predicated upon all the ways a human organism and a human society can run out of gas.

MATERIAL RESOURCES

I'm just here for the gasoline.

—Mel Gibson as Mad Max, *The Road Warrior* (1981)

Movies of the Believer value-formation period are saturated with a heavy preoccupation over resource, depletion (whether it is oil, money, or food), and pervasive want. Taken to the violent extremes of fantasy (an important concept for good and evil in the Believer era), one encounters plots about resource-related gang warfare in movies such as *Mad Max* (1979), *The Road Warrior* (1981), and *Blade Runner* (1982); desperate acts of personal and political poverty in *Mean Streets* (1973), *The Taking of Pelham One, Two, Three* (1974), and *Dog Day Afternoon* (1975); and even cannibalism in *Soylent Green* (1973) and *The Texas Chain Saw Massacre* (1974). Beyond their thematic linkage, and despite being fantasies, many movies of this era have an almost documentary-style quality that comes across as grainy, dreary, dark, bleak, and anxious—and that certainly augments their fearfulness. Their heroes and survivors, when there are any, are at the very best conditionally victorious and will almost invariably have to fight the same fight another day.

In all, it is a compelling set of fantasies for people in the real world who have just left a grocery store where beef prices have doubled and who are now sitting in line for an hour to get their car filled with gasoline.

PERSONAL POWER

At this moment I don't feel shame or fear, but just kind of blah, like when you're sitting there and all the water's run out of the bathtub.
—**Sissy Spacek as Holly Sargis, *Badlands* (1973)**

While the fantasies mentioned above are generally violent in nature, the films that concentrate on character study tend to portray fairly ordinary individuals who are without the willpower to effect positive change. In *Badlands,* the 15-year-old Holly Sargis simply accompanies her 30-year-old boyfriend on a killing spree until ennui overtakes them both. In the era's *noir* movies, such as *Chinatown* (1974) and *Body Heat* (1981), the male protagonists progressively discover they haven't a clue as to what's actually been going on around them, and that almost all of their actions have been performed blindly and ineffectively. It is a vast creative leap downward, but the popular teenage sitcom *Welcome Back Kotter* (1975–1979) captures this miasma of inertia, cluelessness, and slow pace of discovery to perfection.

Some of the more compelling movies of the Believer period, such as *One Flew over the Cuckoo's Nest* (1975), *The Deer Hunter* (1978), and *Apocalypse Now* (1979), do feature brave protagonists who try to take effective action. But at the end of these movies, respectively, Jack Nicholson's Murphy is rendered a lobotomized zombie, Robert DeNiro's Michael

Vronsky is surrounded by death and mutilation, and Charlie Sheen's Capt. Willard, having looked into the heart of darkness, becomes a burned out messenger for a dead madman. In short, it is not exactly a Stephen Covey *(The 7 Habits of Highly Effective People)* era.

THE ABSENCE OF GOD

If it turns out there is a God, I don't think he's evil. I think the worst you can say about him is that basically he's an underachiever.

—Woody Allen as Boris, Love And Death (1975)

It is not surprising that the era as described to this point is challenged when it comes to the issue of God's concern for his flock. Many of the "realistic" films of the era such as *Mean Streets* (1973) and *Midnight Express* (1978), as well as landmark horror films such as *The Exorcist* (1973) and *The Omen* (1976), take great pains to point out that evil is strong, life is often a wicked beating, and neither church nor God exists to provide personal protection. This outlook is even alluded to in the era's comedies, including *Oh, God!* (1977) *and Monty Python's Life of Brian* (1979), where it is made clear that although God may care for humanity, he's really not inclined to get bogged down in the details of personal salvation or flock tending.

Ironically, in the cinematic fare of the Believer value-formation period, it is God himself who is portrayed as the agnostic!

What is especially interesting about this portrayal is that Believers today show a very high statistical involvement in organized worship and a general propensity toward faith in a benign providence (the issue of providence is discussed a little later in this chapter—and we are talking about a group named the Believers, after all!). So many qualities essential to the Believer experience—community support, the need to repair relationships with fathers, the need to find some sustaining order in the world, the need to be rescued, and the need to participate in love and grace—are encountered in the realm of devotion that it is not all that surprising that Believers would become a Value Population engaged in the search for a meaningful relationship with the Divine. But it is also fairly characterized as a "search"—as in looking for something that's not necessarily or obviously here right now, and that was certainly portrayed as remote in their value-formation era.

BANKRUPT INSTITUTIONS

*Screw the goddam passengers! What the hell did they expect for their lousy 35 cents
. . . to live forever?*

—Dick O'Neill as Frank Correll, The Taking of Pelham One, Two, Three (1974)

All of the value-population eras take their swipes at vested institutions, but in the Believer era one encounters a panicky and near-total sense of ethical and financial collapse. While pictures such as *Magnum Force* (1973), *Three Days of the Condor* (1975), *All the President's Men* (1976), and *And Justice for All* (1979) attempt to realistically capture the nuances and dirty dealings of political and legal power brokers, the heart of the Believer-era matter is laid out in films such as *The Taking of Pelham One, Two, Three* (1974), in which an advisor to the mayor of New York argues that the city simply does not have enough money to ransom a trainload of citizen hostages. This theme is repeated throughout the era, most notably in *Jaws* (1975), in which the Amity city fathers disastrously refuse to close a shark-infested beach because it might depress tourist revenue, and *Capricorn One* (1978), in which government scientists fake a Mars surface landing and then attempt to kill off the reluctant astronauts because of a funding crisis.

What is interesting in the midst of all this is a suddenly very ambiguous consideration of business institutions. On the one hand, greed, manipulation, and the oppression of workers are still portrayed as bad during the Believer value-formation period. But there is also an implicit admiration of financial success—of the people and institutions that can create wealth and control it, even if rules are bent in the process. Movies such as *Network* (1976) and *Arthur* (1981) look at this issue ironically and fondly, respectively, but the real thought provokers in this regard are *The Godfather* (1972) and *The Godfather Part II* (1974), in which the inestimable value of an orderly and successful hierarchy makes even murder seem a reasonable expense of doing good business.

MEDIA POLLUTION

You're television incarnate, Diana . . . indifferent to suffering, insensitive to joy.

—William Holden as Max Schumacher, Network (1976)

By the Believer era, mass media has become both omnipresent and vested. In movies, which must be understood as a competitive medium and therefore suspect in its motivations, there is endless sniping at television. While newspaper people are both heroes and villains in the film work of the Believer era, television personnel are almost invariably portrayed as crass, conformist, insensitive, intrusive, manipulative, and inane. In *Annie Hall* (1977), Woody Allen remarks that Los Angeles is clean because "they don't throw their garbage away, they turn it into television shows." In *Taxi Driver* (1976), Robert DeNiro, as the crazed would-be political assassin Travis Bickle, is turned into a media hero for inadvertently saving an unrepentant young prostitute during a deadly confrontation with her pimp.

Believers are the most self-doubting of the contemporary Value Populations and the first Value Population to be born into a mature television culture. These are best illustrated in the brilliant film *Network* (1976), written by Paddy Chayefsky and acted by a flawless cast. It is difficult to render all the film's insight into a single observation, but the following speech by Academy Award winner Peter Finch, as network news anchor Howard Beele, is well worth keeping in mind:

> You're beginning to believe the illusions we are spinning here, you're beginning to believe that the tube is reality and your own lives are unreal! You do! Why, whatever the tube tells you: you dress like the tube, you raise your children like the tube, you even think like the tube! This is mass madness, you maniacs. In God's name, you people are the real thing. WE are the illusion.

NEW YORK, NEW YORK

I think someone should just take this city and just . . . just flush it down the fuckin' toilet.
—Robert DeNiro as Travis Bickle, *Taxi Driver* (1976)

One of the great insights into Believer values may be derived from the era's various cinematic representations of the city of New York. In the real world, NYC reaches the lowest point of its municipal history during the 1970s with soaring personal and property crime rates and a vast array of municipal service problems. In 1975, the city announces it will likely have to declare bankruptcy, and President Ford's initial reaction to a request for aid is basically, as is recorded in a now-famous *New York Daily News* headline, "Drop Dead!" (As a relevant aside, Ford's initial cold decision to forsake a fiscal rescue ranks right up there with Carter's failed Iranian hostage recovery and is probably the event that quashes Ford's bid for a second term).

What is symbolically devastating in movies such as *Mean Streets* (1973), *The Taking of Pelham One, Two, Three* (1974), *Dog Day Afternoon* (1975), *Taxi Driver* (1976), *The Warriors* (1979), *Escape from New York* (1980), and *Fort Apache the Bronx* (1981), is the abject failure and total renunciation of New York city, America's most important symbol of capitalism, culture, and diversity. A few films, most notably Woody Allen's *Manhattan* (1979) and Dudley Moore's *Arthur* (1981), try to paint a prettier picture, but for most people the Big Apple, and what it stands for, has become rotten to the core.

ROLE ADJUSTMENTS

I Am Woman, Hear Me Roar . . .
—Helen Reddy (1972)

It should come as little surprise that the Believer period is further characterized by a radical rebalancing of traditional gender roles in the family, in the work place, and in society at large. Although it is a vast oversimplification of a complex matter, one needs to recognize that the energy and authority traditionally associated with males in our society is at low ebb during the Believer value-formation period. Be this an issue of enlightened personal choice or desperate cultural circumstance (and it is probably both), the world simply moves away from an idealized, some would argue "fantasized," notion of virile male father/soldier/hunter/provider/protector and toward a more inclusive stance regarding the potencies and potentialities of women.

THE LIBERATION OF WOMEN

"Hi, Diana Christensen. A racist lackey of the imperial ruling circles."
"Laureen Hobbs. Badass commie nigger."
—Faye Dunaway and Marlene Warfield, Network (1976)

There is no simple observation that encapsulates all the roles that women suddenly start to play in art or in real life during the Believer value-formation period. This is, of course, a large part of the point. To illustrate, consider even a modest list of memorable Believer-era actresses and their Oscar-winning characters, who help define this cultural trend toward women's emancipation:

- Louise Fletcher as Nurse Ratched, *One Flew Over the Cuckoo's Nest* (1975)—an unrepentant emasculator of a ward full of dysfunctional male patients—takes some lumps but ends up lobotomizing her chief tormentor.
- Faye Dunaway as Diana Christensen, *Network* (1976)—a driven media executive, gleefully exploiting anyone and anything that can improve her TV shows' ratings—openly discusses her sexuality as similar to a male's (quick to arouse, quick to consummate, and immediately ready to get back to work).
- Diane Keaton as Annie Hall, *Annie Hall* (1977)—a talented but unsophisticated Midwestern girl eventually outgrows her male mentor and moves on to stardom. (The "masculine" Annie-Hall look starts a major fashion trend of the late 1970s.)
- Sissy Spacek as Loretta Lynn, *Coal Miner's Daughter* (1980)—a talented but unsophisticated country girl eventually outgrows her male mentor and moves on to stardom.
- Sally Field as Norma Rae, *Norma Rae* (1979)—far braver than any of the males she works with in a textile mill, this young single mother risks everything as she agrees to become a union organizer.

This brief list barely touches the dozens of memorable characterizations in which women are variously shown as sexual aggressors, strategy instigators, social experimenters, and staunch defenders of their own self-worth. Even in *10,* a movie that celebrates nothing so much as the female form's effect on the male libido, there is a wonderful moment when Julie Andrews, Mary Poppins herself, gives a finger to the man who's done her wrong. And thanks to Katherine Ross in *The Stepford Wives* (1975), the persona of a traditional suburban housewife takes a memorable knife through the heart.

Some male backlash to all of this does inevitably take place, of course. It is hard to erase an image of a totally buff, virtually naked Arnold Schwarzenegger in *Conan the Barbarian* (1982), commenting that what is "best" in life is "to crush your enemies, see them driven before you, and to hear the lamentation of the women." But it may be safe to assume that more men are acknowledgers, however begrudgingly, of the essential indomitability of the newly liberated woman. As George Wendt playing Norm Peterson observes on an early episode of the classic television sitcom *Cheers* (1982–1983): "Women. You can't live with'm. Pass the beer nuts."

GENTLE MEN

"If a man said that to me I'd break his neck."

"I am a man."

"Well, I mean a much shorter man."

—Woody Allen as Boris Grushenko and Harold Gould as Anton Inbedkov, Love and Death (1975)

Traditional male action heroes do exist in the Believer era, particularly and therefore significantly, in "fantasy" films. Harrison Ford certainly comes on strong as Han Solo in *Star Wars* (1977) and *The Empire Strikes Back* (1980), as Indiana Jones in *Raiders of the Lost Ark* (1981), and as Rick Deckard in *Blade Runner* (1982)—although he is deathly afraid of snakes in *Raiders of the Lost Ark* and turns out not to be human in *Blade Runner*. The Believer era also yields the "comic book" triumphs of Sylvester Stallone as Rocky (1976), Christopher Reeve as Superman (1978), and, as previously mentioned, Arnold Schwarzenegger as Conan the Barbarian (1982).

For the most part, though, the films of the Believer era that play it a little more closely to everyday reality are noteworthy for the reflective, rather than the active, qualities of its male protagonists. The Believer era is the heyday of films and television programs that star the likes of Woody Allen, Alan Alda, Richard Dreyfuss, Dudley Moore, John Denver, Peter Sellers, and Peter Falk. All of these actors, and most of the characters they play, have virtues aplenty, ranging from empathy to charm to intelligence to sincere artistic temperament to ethical conviction to great wit. But it is hard to ignore a lack of "true grit" or "right stuff" in these figures, who are somehow "safe" and "passive" in ways that more macho heroes are not.

Admittedly, one can point to the characterizations of actors like Jack Nicholson in *One Flew over the Cuckoo's Nest* (1975) and *The Shining* (1980) and Robert DeNiro in *Taxi Driver* (1976) and *Raging Bull* (1980) as being virile enough. But if there is a defining characteristic to these portrayals, it is simply that all of these characters are certifiably crazy or, at the very least, just plain mean—so much for Believer testosterone.

FATHERS AND FAMILIES

"It just seems that you and me have been mad at each other for so long."

"I didn't think we were mad. I just thought we didn't like each other."

—Real-life daughter and father Jane and Henry Fonda as fictional daughter and father Chelsea and Norman Thayer, On Golden Pond (1981)

As has already been noted here, 1980 is an enormously trying year for the United States—filled with downcast conditions and disturbing events. But if one wants to capture the single defining sociological moment that summons up the zeitgeist of the era, it is when, in *The Empire Strikes Back* (1980), Darth Vader, the chief operations officer of universal evil, turns to Luke Skywalker and announces "I am your father."

Darth Vader represents an extreme in paternal shortcomings, but his character lurks in the nightmares of an inordinate number of children whose values are formed in the Believer era. As may quickly be surmised from a glance at the statistics earlier in this report, there is an historical level of family disruption and disappointment during the Believer value-formation era. Dads become delinquents, dropouts, or at best grumpy old men in a society that challenges vested roles and spurns moral authority, and in which an anxious peace and a weak economy frustrate traditional male strengths.

The artistic representations are sometimes terrifying. In *Badlands* (1973), a father who disapproves of his daughter's date murders her dog; in *Chinatown* (1974), there is paternal rape, incest, and kidnap; in *The Deer Hunter* (1978), there are unprovoked beatings of a devoted daughter; in *The Shining* (1980), a dad, who is having a bad career patch, tries to axe-murder his wife and son. Far too many to list are the movies that somehow involve a father's emotional detachment, divorce, and/or abandonment.

However, not all representations are unsympathetic. In movies such as *Close Encounters of the Third Kind* (1977), *Oh, God!* (1977), and *Altered States* (1980), one gets the message that dads are sometimes summoned on truly urgent missions that are really, really important, no matter how wacked-out those missions may seem to an abandoned family. One wonderful treatment along these lines is William Katt's character Ralph Hinkley in *The Greatest American Hero* (1981–1983), a television show about a divorced father who is enlisted into the aid of the Secret Service when he discovers a costume that provides superpowers (over which, like everything else in his life, he has the most tenuous and intermittent control, as he promptly loses the costume's instruction manual).

Surrogate fathers sometimes do the trick. In *Arthur* (1981), much of the title character's and the film's redemptions are to be found in John Gielgud's Oscar-winning portrayal of Hobson, the avuncular yet firm butler who works to keep Arthur on a moral and responsible path (there is a great moment when Gielgud, unexpected to viewers, is sitting on the bed and wearing a cowboy hat—perhaps a prescient cultural nod to Ronald Reagan). Father figures Ben Obi-Wan-Kenobi and Yoda are there to make sure that Luke Skywalker uses "the force" responsibly in *Star Wars* (1977) and *The Empire Strikes Back* (1980). Henry Fonda's Norman Thayer, having botched his relationship with his own daughter, discovers he might do yeoman service as a grandfather to her stepchild in *On Golden Pond* (1981).

Ultimately, though, it will be particularly interesting to observe how Believers respond to male authority figures, as well as how male Believers may perform in authority roles themselves, as they fully enter their social maturity. Meanwhile it is definitely a case of *caveat employer*—let the employer beware!

THE KIDS ARE TO BLAME

Then one day I hear "Reach for it mister!" I spun around, and there I was
facing a six-year-old kid. Well, I just laid down my guns and walked away.
Little bastard shot me in the ass!

—Gene Wilder as The Waco Kid, *Blazing Saddles* (1974)

Given all that has been observed about the Believer era to this point, it comes as little surprise that the status and welfare of children leave a lot to be desired during this time. Whether one cares to blame parents, society, economic problems, or just a bad crop of eggs (at times all are blamed), kids are sort of beaten off their pedestal during the Believer value-formation period. In a "Me Generation" society virtually flooding with divorce and abortion, children stop becoming the hope of the future and are reclassified as problems, inconveniences, expenses, issues, and, as in The Waco Kid's case, all-around pains-in-the-ass.

This bleak assessment is not universal, (thank God!), but it is a powerful and inescapable aspect of the times. It is one hell of a leap from Shirley Temple dancing on the Good Ship Lollipop or Timmy hugging Lassie to the vomit-spewing 13-year-old Linda Blair in *The Exorcist* (1973) or the incarnation of the Antichrist as 8-year-old Harvey Stevens in *The Omen* (1976). A few movies of the period, most notably *Kramer vs. Kramer* (1979) and *Ordinary People* (1980), go so far as to acknowledge that the problems involving children are rarely their fault, but this is by far more exoneration than embrace.

Perhaps the Believer-era scene that resonates most in this regard occurs in *The Godfather Part II* (1974), when Diane Keaton's Kay Corleone tells Al Pacino's Michael Corleone that she had their "evil" fetus aborted. This moment has particular impact, as *The Godfather* sagas, despite their embrace of criminal culture, embrace even more passionately the sanctity of family. In all, it is going to be extremely interesting to observe what percentage of the Believer Value Population simply chooses to opt out of the child-bearing experience and what percent commits themselves to doing a better job of it than they were exposed to in their own childhoods.

REDEMPTION THROUGH RELATIONSHIPS

I wanna be in love with something. Anything. Just the idea. A dog, a cat. Anything. Just something.
—Jack Lemmon as Harry Stoner, *Save the Tiger* (1973)

Believers sometimes manifest behavior that seems emotionally shell-shocked or bruised, but it is an enormous mistake to therefore consider them as heartless. On the contrary, the heart is pretty much where they seem to make their home. Value-formed during a dismal economic and social era that often depreciated their very existence, Believers find themselves validated by the esteem of others—in other words, through friendship and love.

On one level, this valuing of alliances almost harkens back to the clannish Patriots, but what the Believers are expressing is anything but a blind loyalty to the belief system into which one is born. That families can cause a lot of pain is not an insight lost on the Believers. When it comes to whom they believe will actually watch their back, Believers are more inclined to follow their hearts than their heritage.

EMPATHY

Well, boys, it would be hard to call what we've been through fun, but I'm sure glad we went through it together.
—Harry Morgan as Col. Sherman Potter, bidding farewell to Hawkeye and B.J., *MASH* (1972–1983)

If a single creative work captures the essence the Believer era, it is the television show *MASH*, which extends precisely the length of the Believer period (1972–1983). Nothing comes quite as close as this show to representing how the most hellacious of environments can be endured, and occasionally even vicariously escaped, through the qualities of empathy, humor, and friendship (sometimes with a little boost from fantasy, liquor, and lust). While so much more can be written about *MASH* as a Believer archetype than will be attempted here (for example, in its main and recurring characters almost all of the chief types of Believer value-influencers are present), it is particularly compelling to note that problems in the world of *MASH* are most often personal, but solutions are almost invariably the result of heartfelt ministrations by others.

Throughout the Believer value-formation era, one encounters stories of "misfits" thrown together by circumstance who somehow manage, by emotionally banding together, to achieve if not outright victory at least conditional survival with a little grace. Movies such as *The Bad News Bears* (1976), *The Boys in Company C* (1978), *Convoy* (1978), and *The Warriors* (1979) illustrate this point. So does the television show *Soap* (1977–1981), which brilliantly demonstrates that the only thing that will keep a "modern" family at all functional is a tolerant and flexible empathy, not a reliance on tradition.

LOVE

Every age is the same. It is only love that makes any of them bearable.
—Malcom McDowell as H.G. Wells, *Time After Time* (1979)

The height of empathy is love, and therefore love is the great prize in the Believer value system. While love of course exists long before the Believers, it is really they who give it a pure definition. In the Believer value system, absolutely nothing else matters if, and while, the connection is there.

Although one encounters a bevy of more-or-less "classic" love stories in the Believer era, *The Way We Were* (1973), *Rocky* (1976), *The Electric Horseman* (1979), *Time after Time* (1979), *The Jerk* (1979), *The Main Event* (1979), *Arthur* (1981), *On Golden Pond* (1981), what really linger are the nontraditional love stories—loves that are only occasionally between traditional couples. Among these are *Harold and Maude* (1972), a 20-year-old male depressive and an 80-year-old female free spirit; *Badlands* (1973), a small-town, 15-year-old high-school girl and a 30-year-old mass murderer; *Manhattan* (1979), a 15-year-old WASP high-school girl and a 30-year-old Jewish intellectual; and *Dog Day Afternoon* (1975), where two 30-year-old male bank robbers are romantic partners attempting to finance a sex-change operation for one of them.

The Believer value-formation era is also characterized by stories of friendships that are virtually love stories—in that a life-and-death context drives relationship development and empathy beyond what anyone might reasonably construe as mere friendship. *Bang the Drum Slowly* (1973), *Blazing Saddles* (1974), *48 Hours* (1982), and *E.T.* (1982) are examples. There is even Art Carney's Oscar-winning-performance in *Harry and Tonto* (1974), essentially a love story between an old man and his cat.

Ultimately, in the Believer universe, external differences are rarely impediments to love. Love makes the world go round. Nobody mentioned anything about making it go straight.

THE ART OF TRANSCENDENCE

Boy, if life were only like this.
—Woody Allen as Alvy Singer, *Annie Hall* (1977)

Commentators throughout the ages have observed that great art is created out of suffering. The explanation offered for this is that art has the power to at least temporarily reshape and provide some measure of control over reality. The more difficult the reality, the more art is necessary.

Woven into the fabric of the Believer value-formation period is this awareness about the power of art to help make difficult times more endurable. Major Believer-era films such as *American Graffiti* (1973), *The Godfather, Parts I and II* (1972 and 1974), *Close Encounters of the Third Kind* (1977), *Grease* (1978), *Apocalypse Now* (1979), *E.T.* (1982), and *Blade Runner* (1982) are every bit as important for their amazing breakthroughs in music, set design, costuming, lighting, cinematography, and production values as they are for their plots. The hugely influential movie *Star Wars* (1977) is ultimately just a good guys versus bad guys movie set in space— but man, those special effects! All three Star Wars' Oscars came in "technical" categories.

A great example of what "art" means in the Believer value system is found in the John Travolta's star-making film *Saturday Night Fever* (1977). As famed film critic Roger Ebert observes, "Travolta's Tony Manero character inhabits a bleak, sad, and painful world with next to zero prospects for his personal advancement." But all anyone really remembers about the movie is Tony's primping, dancing, and strutting to a BeeGees soundtrack, which is an experience, for the character and for the audience, of no small transcendence.

GIVING PEACE A CHANCE

An eye for an eye only ends up making the whole world blind.
—Ben Kingsley as Mahatma Gandhi, *Gandhi* (1982)

As has already been discussed, the historical peace of the Believer era is a complex blessing. It is not just mitigated by the onerous reality that a reduction in military spending badly hurts the general economy. It is also that a time of peace, at least in the Believer case, seems to correspond with a lack of energy regarding other worthy interests of mankind, like a concern for society's posterity.

Yet for better or worse, whether as a matter of conditioning or conviction, Believers are generally inclined to choose negotiation over a knife fight. It is not that they lack convictions worth fighting for; they just seem to feel that direct aggression is hardly the best way to reduce the world's or their own already generous allotment of pain and chaos.

Powerful antiviolence/antiwar movies of the Believer era like *Deliverance* (1972), *The Deer Hunter* (1978), and *Apocalypse Now* (1979) are pretty adamant about the poison fruits of hostility. But perhaps shows like David Carradine's *Kung Fu* (1972–1973) and Bruce Lee's *Enter the Dragon* (1973) are more balanced in dealing with what is basically a passive-aggressive predicament. If you have any idea what Bruce Lee means when he says, "My style you can call the art of fighting without fighting," then you are well on your way toward understanding Believers.

PROVIDENCE

Use the Force, Luke!
—Alec Guiness as Ben Obi-Wan Kenobi, *Star Wars* (1977)

Many downtrodden Believers are secure in the belief that there is some small miracle out there with their name on it. This miracle can manifest as a person, a place, a professional breakthrough, or as some universal energy ray that can beam away the baddies in a heartbeat. This may seem naïve to some, but luck has a tendency to change, even if it takes a very long time to do so, and Believers can be quite patient about waiting for a good thing.

The payoffs of belief are both profound and strangely subtle. It is Charlie in *Charlie's Angels* (1976–1981) who foots the lifestyle bills for three beautiful women and doesn't even expect a back rub.

It is the hedonistic future of *Logan's Run* (1976), where everything feel-good is free for the asking, and, apparently, nobody has to grow the food or clean the toilets. It is Rocky Balboa, in *Rocky* (1976), being selected randomly out of the boxing phone book to have a chance in the ring with the champ. It is the heavenly angels in *Heaven Can Wait* (1978), who, when you are accidentally killed, give you a second chance to be a millionaire football star. Also, with the deadly light saber at your very throat, it is Obi-Wan Kenobi in *Star Wars* (1976) with a very timely reminder about the availability of the Force.

The trump card in the Believer value system is an intuitive awareness that to enter a state of grace one has to be open to grace as a possibility (a fact that ironically screens out many of the world's deep thinkers). This premise is explored brilliantly in *Being There* (1979), in which Peter Sellers plays Chance, a simple, passive gardener, whose innocent banalities regarding gardening and liking to watch television are misconstrued as deep profundities by a distressed society, including its president, hungry for anyone who might deliver a message of hope. As the audience, we are in on the joke until the very end—until Chance actually does walk across water.

THE BELIEVER IDEAL

"That's quite a lovely Jackson Pollack, isn't it?"

"Yes it is."

"What does it say to you?"

"It restates the negativeness of the universe. The hideous lonely emptiness of existence. Nothingness. The predicament of Man forced to live in a barren Godless eternity like a tiny flame flickering in an immense void with nothing but waste, horror, and degradation forming a useless bleak straitjacket in a black absurd cosmos."

"What are you doing Saturday night?"

"Committing suicide."

"What about Friday night?"

—Woody Allen as Allan Felix and Diana Davila as "Museum Girl," in *Play It Again, Sam* (1972)

To be truthful, the above-quoted conversation does not fully capture the Believer ideal. What makes it fall a little short is that the come-on is without a happy ending. In the movie, museum girl gives Woody a chilly once-over and walks away.

So much of the rest of this exchange, though, is right on the mark: the museum setting; the empathic appreciation of art; taking a chance on love; the situational domination by the woman; the nerdy but not un-inspired wit of the man. Then of course, there is the astoundingly dis-heartening description of the universe in which all this is taking place.

The great thing about Believers is not simply that they dare to hope, but that they dare to hope for so much against their own previous ex-perience and life's horribly stacked odds—all of this while simultane-ously not taking themselves too seriously.

The Believers' true gift is believing that if an essential talent is miss-ing from one's life, a solution will inevitably show up to provide all the necessary instructions, as does Humphrey Bogart's ghost in *Play It Again, Sam.*

In the end there may just be two less lonely people come Friday night.

16

THE TRANSFORMERS
An Overview

POPULATION OVERVIEW

Age: Born 1984–1995
Size: 16% of the U.S. Population
Spending: $200 Billion Annually (est.)
Themes: The Long Boom/Constant Chaos
Values: Personal Power/Clarity

Summary

While Transformers are still in their childhood and adolescence as this is being written, one may safely assume that this Value Population is likely to take a back seat to none when it comes to claiming a share of the world's wealth and power. Whereas Believers, who preceded them, appear to have accepted peace as a path through turmoil, Transformers have received their value conditioning in an era that endorses a far more energetic and assertive approach toward personal survival and self-satisfaction. Created in a complex time of personal power resurgence amidst chaos, built by the speed and perception-bending qualities of the computer age, and fraught with streetwise intelligence about what separates winners and losers, Transformers, already exquisitely adept and savvy, are likely to survive on their own terms.

The poet called Miss Liberty's torch "the lamp beside the golden door." Well,
that was the entrance to America, and it still is. And now you really know
why we're here tonight. The glistening hope of that lamp is still ours. Every
promise, every opportunity is still golden in this land. And through that golden
door our children can walk into tomorrow with the knowledge that no one
can be denied the promise that is America.

—Ronald Reagan, Republican National Committee speech (1984)

TRANSFORMER EVENT MATRIX

Revitalization/Chaos and Contention/Redefinition

Revitalization

After more than a decade of economic difficulty, America's finances take a dramatic turn for the better—by 1984 the United States begins a 15-year period of dynamic economic growth—"The Long Boom."

The United States again becomes the world's premier political power through "symbolic" military victories in Grenada (1983) and Iraq (1991). Even more significant is the victorious conclusion of the 40-year Cold War with the breakup and democratization of the Union of Soviet Socialist Republics (USSR) (1989–1991).

Economic and political stability breed social optimism, and the period sees a sharp rise in U.S. births and a rededication of society to youth and family interests.

Chaos and Contention

Good financial fortune rules the period, but an ugly and pervasive counterpoint of insider stock trading, banking scandals, and financial hucksterism makes the road to riches a tricky one for average citizens.

Sudden geopolitical changes (Japan's economic dominance, the USSR's breakup, Iraq's attempt to annex Kuwait), geological disasters (droughts, earthquakes, floods), and humanmade messes (oil and chemical spills, wayward missiles, a space shuttle explosion) corroborate the validity that reality is essentially chaos.

Although many black Americans benefit from the improving economy, a rising tide of dissatisfied poor black youth culturally embrace drugs and gangs as their only route to the status and riches of society.

Redefinition

The 1994–1995 transition period is marked by a time of attempted cultural reorganization that ultimately fails as it expands beyond its "intended" delineations.

The North American Free Trade Agreement (NAFTA) and the European Monetary Institute (1994) redefine national economic borders forever—globalization, for good or bad, is given financial wings.

The Republicans sweep Congress in 1994, and the GOP advocates conservative social values, reduced federal spending, and a free-market economy.

The 1995 bombing of the Oklahoma City federal building, the acquittal of O.J. Simpson, and the arrival of Monica Lewinsky at the White House, all hint at a new world without any (ethical) borders.

TRANSFORMER POPULATION VALUES

Power

- *Historical drivers.* From politics to economics to international diplomacy to popular art, the virtue of being more energetic, more resilient, more clever, stronger, and bolder than one's opponent comes back into cultural vogue; the new name of the game is "winners and losers."
- *Value manifestation.* In all fields of endeavor the quest is to be the victor rather than the vanquished, the leader rather than the follower.

Edge

- *Historical drivers.* Inside information is widely presented as the Holy Grail of political and economic success; meanwhile, in popular culture, preparation merged with "street smarts" is praised as central to victory.
- *Value manifestation.* An advantage is an advantage, and the other person is looking for one too.

Control

- *Historical drivers.* The unexpected reigns in geopolitical (Japan, Soviet Union, NAFTA), geological (droughts, earthquakes, floods),

and macro-industrial (oil spills, chemical leaks, space shuttle crash) affairs; "chaos theory" becomes a central concept in the scientific explanation of reality.
- *Value manifestation.* To achieve stability in a world, whose only constant is the unanticipated, is an achievement of heroic proportions.

Challenge and Competition

- *Historical drivers.* America's brilliant showing in the 1984 Los Angeles-based Summer Olympics; the beginning of the Michael Jordan era in the NBA; activities ranging from chess to baseball enjoy huge surges in popularity among youth.
- *Value manifestation.* Tests of will and skill, particularly in contests that directly involve opponents, are far more than tolerated—they are enjoyed.

Loyalty

- *Historical drivers.* Grenada military victory invokes power of allegiance to one's comrades in arms; popular art becomes fixated on bands of strange outcasts and on marginalized contributors banding together to protect the weak and overthrow evil (*Ghostbusters, Revenge of the Nerds, Power Rangers, Beverly Hills Cop,* etc.)
- *Value manifestation.* Alliances are sometimes risky propositions, but the right alliances can increase power beyond all reasonable expectations and their value kept in high regard.

Tradition

- *Historical drivers.* "Family values" orientation of the Reagan administration; "Echo Boom" and the return of children to a place of prominence in social consciousness; recovery of American political and economic institutions.
- *Value manifestation.* Rules, rituals, customs, and associations that endure must have power to do so—and are therefore greatly respected.

Enhanced Perception

- *Historical drivers.* Computer involvement from birth yields a historically unique interactive filter on reality; new paradigms of learning and response are driven by technological capabilities.
- *Value manifestation.* The ability to adapt the speed, accuracy, and versatility of technology to *subjective* purposes will always be perceived as an ace in the hole.

Money

- *Historical drivers.* The economic Long Boom; the broad ascension of Wall Street in the cultural consciousness; the age of the Yuppie.
- *Value manifestation.* Materialism has both good and bad aspects, but in the "power game" there is no better means than money to enhance leverage or to keep score.

Transcendence

- *Historical drivers.* The movement from an era of passive resistance to one in which effort and enterprise are essential to success; in particular, the fall of the USSR lends an "anything can be achieved" aura to the period; popular culture deals extensively with death defiance and immortality.
- *Value manifestation.* The word "can't" is not easily accepted here.

TRANSFORMER MACRO INTERESTS

(Life-phase considerations projected through 2010)

Allowances

Transformers have a particularly astute grasp of money from an early age. Interestingly, however, surveys indicate that rather than receiving allowances, many young Transformers have become more like junior partners in the family economy, receiving money on an as-needed basis for specific goods and services, and contributing an important voice to major purchase decisions such as electronic equipment, cars, and vacations.

Family Friends

The importance of protective alliances is not a notion wasted on young Transformers. But this notion is hardly confined to the relationships they may have with other children. Transformers also seem to have more meaningful interaction with the friends and colleagues of their parents, with adult neighbors, and with their own friends' parents than did children of preceding Value Populations. Adults simply have the power in society, and Transformers want the security of approaching people for their insights or, if need be, their protection.

Freedom

Inherently wary of the world's dangers, Transformers are still generally eager to try out their skill and mettle in the realms beyond the family "rec room." The real road to success, they quickly intuit, is not a passive path through safety-seeking and closed-off experience. The phenomenon of competitive interactivity on the Web is significantly appealing to this group of youths, as it provides both an outlet for testing aggression and the dual safety of masked identity and an on/off switch.

Income

The anecdotal evidence is mounting regarding not only the Transformers' willingness to pursue paid employment but their absolute eagerness to do so. Quick to the point, the astute Transformers clearly understand that it is one's work that in large part makes or breaks an adult life. Starting early, they realize, has to yield some sort of advantage in ultimately getting the good jobs, and it is the sort of learning experience that comes with added power—a paycheck.

Investments

One may expect Transformers to be a little greedy (as Gordon Gekko observes in the 1987 movie *Wall Street:* "Greed is the essence of the evolutionary spirit."), but they are not likely to be gullible or graceless in the pursuit of wealth building. It is difficult to see this tactical bunch simply flinging their piggy-bank money at high-risk investments, but they already understand that market instruments have potentially much higher yields than bank deposits. Whether its T-bills, tulips, or town homes, this group is likely to do its homework, accepting advantaged information if they should luck into it, preferring the role of the lizard to that of the fly.

Material Possessions

Early evidence indicates that Transformers are avid shoppers but that their loyalties are very hard to track. Given the roles that power, chaos, and instinctive response play in their value-formation period, one may suspect that Transformers are easily rid of anything once it has yielded its finite worth and served its fleeting purpose. The insight worth exploring here is that young Transformers likely see most material goods as symbolic representations of advantage—as personal power tools rather than as "stuff."

Resources

Transformers are sharply aware that some among them have been born into better material circumstances than others. But such awareness is no more than an opening challenge to a Value Population that intuitively understands all that is out there for the taking, tangible and intangible—much of it related to the education and training that can ultimately level all sorts of playing fields. A key, again, is watching this tribe work the Internet and the free-for-all abandon with which it absorbs intellectual property.

Responsibility

With regard to their survival amidst all of the other Value Populations, the real trump card of Transformers may be their generational propensity toward maturity. Early studies are characterizing members of this Value Population as far more involved, sober, steady, and resilient than those who immediately preceded them. Revealingly, teen crime and teen pregnancy rates are now declining sharply, and teen suicide rates are falling for the first time in a decade.

Public Enemies

In most cases they are still too young to engage society's enemies, but the early signs are intense—think somewhere between Teenage Mutant Ninja Turtles and U.S. Marines. Perhaps more sad and sobering, consider the fact that many of the terrorist bombers training in the Middle East these days are reputed to be young teenage (Transformer-age) girls. Instinctive in aggression, loyal pack hunters, and far more inclined to defend than to yield, enemy and ally alike face much potential danger brewing here.

Talents

Even assuming that the universe doles out natural talent in roughly equal measure to all Value Populations, it may nevertheless be true that Transformers have some special advantage when it comes to capitalizing upon whatever gifts may have come their way. The explanation for this is simply that Transformers generally have the right supporting cast of character attributes—patience, perseverance, discipline, control, and a willingness to compete—to nurture their talent into successful manifestation. Today the news is full of artists, athletes, inventors, entrepreneurs, and scholars who are making their marks prior to their 18th birthdays. One suspects that there is much more to come.

Relaxation for Transformers

While they're still kids and watch their share of television, Transformer leisure tends more toward the dynamic; common threads are self-testing and competition against others in activities ranging from chess and soccer to video games and extreme sports—social contexts are also important for working out alliances and pecking orders.

17

THE TRANSFORMERS
History Creating Values

We venture far into the realm of the hypothetical as we attempt to analyze the Value Population that we are calling the Transformers. Here we seek to capture the mature essence of a population whose youngest members, at this time, are in grade school and whose eldest members have barely started to shave. Some pure conjecture is inescapable as we speculate about the sort of adults these young people will grow up to be.

Additionally, there is the unavoidable awareness that history tends to become clearer with the passage of time. An event or trend that still seems important 30 years after the fact likely is important. In selecting essential events and trends from the relatively recent history of Transformers, we must rely on practiced intuition rather than confirmed data (a technique, ironically, that helps to define the performance characteristics of this Value Population).

WINNERS AND LOSERS

As with the demarcation between Techticians and Believers, the difference between Transformers and Believers is greatly a matter of energy. Having endured something like social and political hibernation through the post-Vietnam era, the United States suddenly rediscovers its competitive instinct and its collective willpower (perhaps best iconically reflected in relatively easy U.S. military victories in Grenada in late 1983, and in the Persian Gulf War's Operation Desert Storm in early 1991). As will be more fully outlined in a moment, though, nowhere is this resurgence of vitality and optimism better reflected than in the economic upsurge that economic historians have labeled The Long Boom (1983–1999).

Also of symbolic importance is that the Transformer period is marked by a return to a strong presidency. While both Ronald Reagan (1980–1988) and Bill Clinton (1992–2000) arouse passionate criticism of their policies and personas, they each have many more admirers than detractors (Reagan's Gallup Poll approval rating moves as high as 65 percent; Clinton's 73 percent). Surviving particularly nasty and partisan political battles, both men parlay strong physical and oratorical presences into the perception that the country is, unlike during much of the Believer period, actually being led.

Personal energy, economic potential, and strong leadership are useful indicators of the generally optimistic tone of these times. Yet one misses an essential part of the picture if he or she fails to acknowledge the era's multilayered complexity. With Transformers, history reaches a watershed moment of nonlinear reality and a permanently fractured mass.

It is in the value-formation period of the Transformers that the proliferation of mass media, through the computerized cacophony of the information age and the emergent multicultural mash of acceptable conduct codes, creates a strong sense of instability in society's values at large. There is hardly anything, anyone, any event, any cause, or any viewpoint that does not solicit some acknowledgment of its particular worthiness amidst an increasingly chaotic and crowded cultural choir. A representative example of the kaleidoscopic energy of the times is found in the emergence of MTV, introduced in 1981 and transformed by movie-like music videos of Michael Jackson and Madonna in 1984, as arguably the most representative and influential broadcast entity of the Transformer value-formation era.

Add to this disharmony of interests and styles the realities of a world acknowledging its limited material resources as the true great prize, and the ground is clearly set for some extremely vigorous contesting of wills.

THE LONG BOOM (1983–1999)

It's the economy, stupid.

—slogan, Clinton-Gore campaign, 1992

It would be almost impossible to understate the role that financial matters play in the value-formation period of the Transformers. Please note that much of the description here is equally relevant to the period after 1995, the Transformer era cut-off date. It is the judgment here, however, that the period after 1995 represents an unmitigated economic blow-off phase that entails a set of value characteristics, in combination with other cultural factors, worthy of a separate Value Population analysis. This is not to imply that modern people haven't always been deeply attached to their wallets, but it is in this era that strategic accumulation and management of money, primarily through market investment and speculation, becomes a daily preoccupation of the common person. With the advent of financial news networks such as FNN (1984), CNBC (1989), Bloomberg (1990), and CNNfn (1995), and an amazing increase in the number of newsletters, periodicals, and newspaper pages devoted to business news—and most particularly, with the ease of access to markets and market information made possible by the proliferation of computers—Wall Street, and all it represents, ascends to the pinnacle of modern cultural concerns.

If one accepts the fact that most Americans suddenly start to feel good about themselves again because they are feeling flush (with potential if not actual profit), one gets the gist of the cultural impact of this period's economy. Emerging from a period of malaise, society becomes aware that a golden rule—*he who has the gold makes the rules*—indeed prevails.

Although there is no way to fully encompass the subject of the economic cultural impacts of this period in a few brief paragraphs, three key points regarding value formation should be made:

1. The period is one of enormous economic growth. In 1984 the gross domestic product (GDP) is $3.25 trillion; in 1995 it is $7.25 trillion. See Figure 17.1. The Dow Jones Industrial Average enters the 1984 trading year at 1220.60; it closes 1995 at 5117.10. See Figure 17.2. Coming into 1984, the national unemployment rate is 9.6 percent; by 1995 it has stabilized at around 5.6 percent. Even acknowledging a short but painful economic downturn that occurs in 1990–1991, the financial times can only be characterized as robust.

2. The personal management of wealth proves extremely treacherous. Even as they rise to unparalleled levels, the markets prove amazingly fickle. A torturous learning curve has the majority of trend followers getting beat up by the initial public offering (IPO) market, penny stocks, hot sector shifts, sudden broad market down-

FIGURE 17.1
U.S. Gross Domestic Product (GDP)

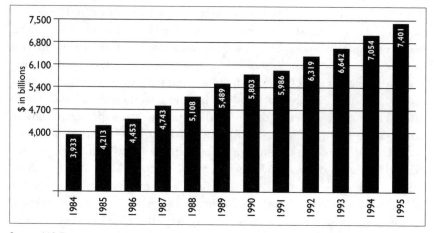

Source: U.S. Department of Commerce—Bureau of Economic Analysis

turns, and bizarrely counter-trend advice from newsletter writers and other financial gurus. Conditioned to believe that any market sell-off is a buying opportunity, and enamored of the power of computerized program trading, the average investor watches in horror as the market sells off $1 trillion of its value over a few week period in October 1989 (including a one-day 23 percent

FIGURE 17.2
Dow Jones Industrial Average

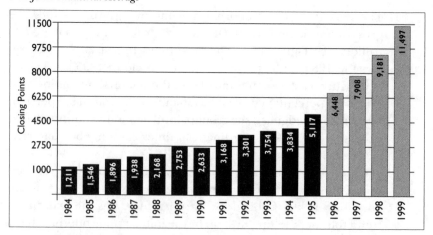

Source: MSN Money (CSNBC)—CSI

drop on the infamous October 19th). In short, as the markets create some potent winners, they create many, if not more, losers.

3. Perhaps most important in terms of value-formation, the big financial news stories of the period give legitimate rise to a suspicion that the game is rigged by insiders and can only be won by a brazen disregard of the rules. Insider trading, stock manipulation, junk bond financing, corporate raiding, and rogue speculation are the antiheroic preoccupations of the era. Backed by the deregulatory blessings of Reaganomics, the American savings and loan industry—and the American public—endure a calamitous era between 1986 and 1995 as the FSLIC fails, the Resolution Trust Corporation (RTC) is established, and 1,043 thrift institutions with combined assets of $519 billion simply disappear from the face of the earth.

In short, the Transformer value-formation era is a great period in the history of wealth creation, but equality and ethics hardly seem to tag along.

THE BLACK EXPERIENCE

In much the same way that women find themselves playing a more prominent and definitive role in the Believer value-formation period, blacks underscore the sense of the nation's emerging racial, ethnic, and sexual diversity by advancing to a position of cultural prominence in the Transformer era. This drive toward equality is still resisted by some vested interests, and the results are a mixture of the good, the bad, and the bizarre.

On the positive side, blacks make an ever-increasing contribution to the political and cultural life of the nation and the world. Among the notable events: Colin Powell is the first black man named Commander of the Joint Chiefs of Staff (1989); Clarence Thomas is confirmed as a justice of the Supreme Court (1991); South African Bishop Desmond Tutu wins a Nobel Peace Prize (1984); and in 1986, the United States celebrates the first national Martin Luther King, Jr., day. Perhaps even more significant is the rise of black heroes in popular culture, athletes and artists in particular, typified by the likes of Michael Jackson, Michael Jordan, Oprah Winfrey, Spike Lee, and Whoopi Goldberg, all of whom start their rise to international prominence in the mid-1980s.

Significantly and sadly, though, much of the black experience in the Transformer value-formation period serves as an important counterpoint to the sense of good times and recovery being proclaimed throughout society at large. While statistically there is improvement in the black economic situation (the black unemployment rate dramatically improves from 20.3 percent in 1983 to 12.0 percent in 1995), there is also much social deterioration. An enormous increase in inner-city gang-related black youth crime is recorded in the period from 1985 to 1993, and urban black families experience a correspondingly huge deterioration in quality of life. According to the Bureau of Justice Statistics, in 1985, 11.8 percent of black central-city households are greatly fearful of victimization by crime; by 1991 the figure has grown to 22.7 percent. Much of this crime and fear is linked to drug trafficking, which many black youths contend is their only conceivable route to the status and riches being pursued by the rest of society. It is worth mentioning that another significant contribution of blacks in this era is the fiercely streetwise "hip-hop" culture and rap music, with Run-DMC's *Raising Hell* becoming the first platinum-selling rap album in 1986.

Two massively publicized real-life crime dramas of this era capture the extremes of the period. In the first, black motorist Rodney King is dragged from his vehicle and beaten by four white policemen. Although the act is caught on videotape, the policemen are acquitted by an all-white jury of all but one minor count at their 1992 trail, and the city of Los Angeles subsequently erupts in racial violence that results in the death of 52 people.

In the second, black football hero and media celebrity O.J. Simpson stands trial in 1995 for the murder of his white wife, Nicole, and her white friend, Ron Goldman. Despite massive circumstantial evidence, Simpson is defended brilliantly by a black attorney, Johnny Cochran, in front of a mostly black jury and is found not guilty of the charges after only a few hours of jury deliberation. An AP poll the next day reveals that 59 percent of the white people in the United States believe Simpson to be guilty of the murders, while only 16 percent of blacks feel similarly.

But whatever the absolute truths of the respective King and Simpson events, the value-formation lesson seems profound. The poor may expect little justice, and the rich may hope to get away with murder.

CHAOS

Beginning in the mid 1980s, the worlds of academia, business, and even popular culture begin to manifest a broad fascination with *chaos theory*. Basically, this is a way of looking at the world that stipulates that change is a far more natural state than permanence and that reality is far more likely to be diverted from a straight path than to follow one. Central to this thinking is that humanity and nature are wholly vulnerable to the subtlest of external influences (the so-called *butterfly effect*), and in the information age there is no shortage of external influences.

Theory aside, the Transformer value-formation era is remarkable in the number of events that challenge deeply held assumptions about the supposed order of things. While space precludes the full analysis that many of the following events rightfully deserve, it is useful to note them and to at least mull over their potential effect on the Value Population born into a period where so much that once seemed solid suddenly seems to be something else. Ultimately, the implication may be the formation of a value system in which success depends far more on tactical skill and opportunism than on rock-hard principle—although things that actually do endure are likely to be admired for that quality alone.

GEOPOLITICAL CHANGES

For more than 50 years, the civilization-threatening antagonism between the United States and the Soviet Union is the essence of world order. Suddenly, under the Soviet administration of Mikhail Gorbachev (1985–1991), the Eastern communist bloc becomes a largely democratic and capitalistic entity, threatening military postures are essentially eradicated, and the Cold War comes to an end. That the Soviet Union, demonized by Ronald Reagan as "the evil empire," can simply cease to be is modern history's most compelling proof that nothing created by humanity is impervious to change.

During the first half of the Transformer value-formation period, the most compelling and enviable economic story belongs not to the United States but to Japan, whose favorable trade imbalance with the United States rises to an annual $50 billion (one-third of the entire U.S. trade debt) in 1985. Admired for, among other things, its rigidly structured organizational hierarchy, its cultural integrity, its long-term commitments to personnel and market development, and its tight relationship with government leaders, the Japanese business model becomes the envy of the world. Even with threats of sanction and legislative action by the United States, particularly related to Japanese below-cost dumping of semiconductors and microchips, the Japanese stock market rides a delirious rocket to just under 40,000 yen in 1991 (four times higher than in 1984).

Then, everything in the Japanese economy begins to fall apart. Much is blamed, from a recessionary world economy to political corruption to unconscionable levels of speculation, but most vehemently criticized is the closed, hierarchical, rigid system that was praised for the success in the first place.

Political and economic borders change at a furious pace. The European Common Market, 15 nations strong, institutes its "Single European Market" economy in 1993. In 1994, the North American Free Trade Agreement (NAFTA) goes into effect, creating a virtually tariff-free economic alliance between the United States, Canada, and Mexico.

Geological Curve Balls

During the Transformer value-formation period, Mother Nature in no way sat on the bench being quiet, but consistently provided examples of how the game could be changed at any time.

- The worst spring and summer drought in 50 years renders half of the nation's agricultural counties "disaster areas." (1988)
- Minutes before the start of a World Series game, the Loma Prieta earthquake shakes the San Francisco bay area, resulting in heavy damage and more than 60 deaths. (1989)
- Hurricane Andrew cuts a swath across Florida, leaving $26.5 billion in property damage in its wake. (1992)
- Mississippi River flooding inundates 8 million acres of land. Casualties include 50 dead, 70,000 homeless, and property damage estimated at $12 billion. (1993)
- The devastating early-morning Northridge earthquake in Los Angeles injures more than 9,000 and kills 51. (1994)
- A heat wave in the Northeast and Midwest results in the deaths of 800 people, many of them seniors without access to air conditioning. (1995)

Human-Made Messes

The imperfection of humankind's actions was clearly evident in the myriad disasters that occurred during this value formation period.

- A chemical leak at a Union Carbide plant in Bhopal, India kills 2,000 people and injures 150,000 more. (1984)

- The space shuttle Challenger explodes, killing seven crewmembers. (1986)
- A wayward Iraqi missile kills 37 sailors aboard the U.S.S. Stark. (1987)
- A missile mistakenly fired from the U.S.S. Vincennes kills 290 passengers aboard a commercial Iranian jetliner. (1988)
- The oil tanker *Exxon Valdez* runs aground in Alaska's Prince William Sound, spilling 11 million gallons of oil into the fragile ecosystem. (1989)
- A 51-day standoff at the Branch Davidian cult compound in Waco, Texas, ends with a government raid that results in the death of four BATF agents and a fire that kills 80 members of the cult. (1993)
- In an event that partly marks the transition from the Transformer value-formation period to the next value-formation period (one that is likely to be organized around a wide array of issues related to globalism), a terrorist bomb is exploded outside of a federal office building in Oklahoma City, resulting in the deaths of 169. (1995)

Finally, it is necessary to acknowledge that the Transformer era is the period during which AIDS permeates American social consciousness, an awareness formally accomplished in 1986 when U.S. health officials acknowledge 21,000 recorded U.S. AIDS cases and predict a tenfold increase in the year's 11,000 AIDS-related deaths over the ensuing five-year period. Fortunately, the estimate proves a bit high, although American deaths from AIDS do rise sharply, peaking at 50,280 total deaths in 1995. See Figure 17.3. It is hard to better capture a sense of the poten-

FIGURE 17.3

U.S. Deaths Due to AIDS

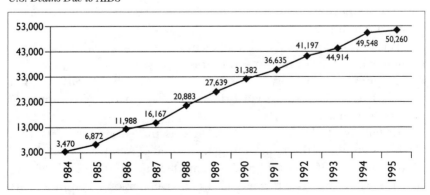

Source: U.S. Department of Health and Human Services

tial of chaos that is brewing than to consider a microscopic organism that turns the body's immune system against itself and is most often introduced through an act of consensual intimacy.

KIDS AND COMPUTERS

Relevant to an analysis of the Transformer value-formation period is an awareness that kids are very much back in vogue. U.S. births increase steadily throughout the 1980s, with a peak period between 1989 and 1993, when more than 4 million American babies are born each year. As will be seen in the subsequent "images" analysis of this Value Population, these children *generally* seem far more welcome and better integrated into society than any children since the Performers. That even "ugly" babies are beautiful is an implication of the Cabbage Patch Kids craze launched in 1986. Ditto for cars, as Chrysler rolls out the family minivan in 1984.

It is reasoned here that the circumstances surrounding this Value Population—the belief in the attainability of material prosperity, the bracing challenge of a chaotic cultural terrain, the affection and guidance of supportive parents—are uniquely arranged to create a population of highly proficient and self-confident adults. But Transformers will also live with an inborn sense that there are many inequities, inconsistencies, and injustices in the world, and so it should not be surprising to find this Value Population collectively possessed of a deliberate edginess that they will use to slice through to the heart of any demon (real or perceived) that seeks to intimidate their progress or attempts to either pull their chain or rake their pile. Born into times fraught with both promise and peril, Transformers will likely make their highest priority the attainment of personal power so as to stand among the winners when all is said and done.

Many of the potential tools and tactics of this quest will be discussed in the next chapter of the book, but it is appropriate here to make special mention of Transformers as the first from-birth *e-population*. For what early television was to Performers, the early personal computer is to Transformers.

In January 1983, *Time* magazine selects the computer as its 1982 "Man (Machine) of the Year," noting that a poll of American adults identifies "education of children" as the computer's greatest potential virtue. By 1984, when the Transformers start to arrive, personal computers are in 8 percent of U.S. homes, and a third of all American children have some access to them. By 1995, they are in 37 percent of U.S. homes, and 71 percent of U.S. children have at least some access to them at school. In recent years, computer gaming has become a bigger business than the movie industry, and polls indicate that computers are deemed more essential to this generation than television.

Time will tell what this early computer exposure will ultimately mean for this generation, but it is well worth acknowledging that, unlike 1950s television, the computer is an intensely interactive medium. Members of other event eras may cluck over violent games, pornography, and stolen intellectual property, but to many Transformers, the computer may simply be an extraordinarily powerful tool that trains both thought and perception to a level that an emergent reality, and its still unknown events, will inevitably demand. They will not let you know the truth about this until it is to their advantage to do so. It is the Transformer way.

18

THE TRANSFORMERS
Cultural Expressions of an Era

I've distilled everything to one single principle: "win or die."
—Glenn Close as Marquise de Merteuil, *Dangerous Liaisons* (1988)

100 percent pure adrenaline.
—Patrick Swayze as Bodhi, *Point Break* (1991)

LIGHTS, CAMERA, ACTION!

In a review of the thousands of movies and television shows introduced during the Transformer value-formation period, it might almost be easier to list the movies that *aren't* based on action. If nothing else is gleaned from the cinematic images of this era, we must note that we are dealing with a value-formation period in which life is a thrill ride—an intense adrenaline-rich confrontation between one's will and the wicked twists and turns of truly chaotic circumstances. This is the era of *Beverly Hills Cop* (1984), *The Terminator* (1984), *Aliens* (1986), *Lethal Weapon* (1987), *Die Hard* (1988), *Batman* (1989), *Jurassic Park* (1993), and *Speed* (1994). All so in tune with the hopped-up personality of their time, they spawn multiple sequels, most of these also released during the Transformer value-formation period.

Where analysis of this action-flick phenomenon seems so often wrongheaded is in the judgment brought by critics that this era's art is essentially "mindless and violent." Filtering through their own value systems, critics from other Value Populations fail to accept the historical rightness of the Transformers' moment in time.

After the difficult Believer era, in which energy has been depleted, and in which the reactions to confrontation have manifested in considerations of love, peace, and art, it is almost inevitable that a Value Population would come along that puts a much greater premium on action and confrontation than on reflection and passivity.

The cinematic art of the Transformer era is relentlessly devoid of the sort of philosophical inquiry that concerns itself with life's great purpose or meaning. It is about the art of stylish survival, dealing far more in preparedness, power, and proficiency, as opposed to abstract thought. The great objective here is *not* understanding nor even surviving—it is *winning.*

OPPONENTS

I want this guy dead! I want his family dead! I want his house burned to the ground! I want to go up there in the middle of the night and piss on his ashes.
—Robert DeNiro as Al Capone, The Untouchables (1987)

"You want to autopsy Lucy?"
"No, no, no, not exactly. I just want to cut off her head and take out her heart."
—Richard Grant and Anthony Hopkins as Dr. Jack Seward and Van Helsing, Bram Stoker's Dracula (1992)

"A man like Ringo has got a great big hole, right in the middle of himself. And he can never steal enough, or kill enough, or cause enough pain to fill it up. And so he walks the earth, forever seeking retribution . . ."
"For what?"
"For being born."
—Val Kilmer and Kurt Russell as Doc Holliday and Wyatt Earp, Tombstone (1993)

Nothing quite captures the intensity or indicates the personal stakes of the Transformer value-formation period like the ferocity of the opponents. In the previous Believer era, the enemy is often faceless and/or institutional, and the dramatic outcome is frequently some form of bureaucratic victimization. With Transformers, the battle between good and evil is fully engaged, and things get very grisly and personal.

On the most literal level, the films of the Transformer cinema rarely shy away from demonstrating that: 1) evil does have a face, and 2) life is painful. Some of the most powerful and frightening villains and monsters ever conceived are revealed in Transformer-era cinema. Psychotic criminals (like Hannibal Lecter in 1991's *The Silence of the Lambs*), perverted lawmen (like Little Bill Daggett in 1992's *Unforgiven*), cannibalistic aliens (like Audrey II in 1986's *Little Shop of Horrors*), killer robots (like the Terminators), immortal ghouls (like the vampires in 1992's *Dracula* and 1994's *Interview with the Vampire*), and cartoon nightmares (like Ursula in 1989's *The Little Mermaid* and Slimer in 1984's *Ghostbusters*) stalk the landscape of the Transformer cinemascape, inflicting heavy damage with the relentlessness of a biblical plague.

Even more than the exaggeration of menace, though, is the palpability of danger derived from deep insight into the complexity of evil—the awareness that it is powerful and compelling and that its face is often the face in the mirror. Much memorable drama of the Transformer era features someone who is essentially good who struggles with the seductiveness of evil. For example, consider Vinnie Terranova in the television series *Wiseguy* (1987–1990), Batman in the first three *Batman* movies (1989, 1992, 1995), Jesus Christ in *The Last Temptation of Christ* (1986), or Detective Sgt. Nick Conklin in *Black Rain* (1989).

As John Corbett's character, Chris Stevens, on TV's *Northern Exposure* (1990–1995) observes:

> There's a dark side to each and every human soul. We wish we were Obi-Wan Kenobi, and for the most part we are, but there's a little Darth Vader in all of us.

Thus, while it is tempting and uplifting to see the struggle of the Transformer Value Population as a heroic fight in a world in which the strength of the enemy and the existence of chaos virtually guarantee there will be some real pain and loss, one really should keep the above Darth Vader thought in mind. For it seems that the young Transformers are being nurtured to believe that the ability to become the enemy may somehow be part of the path to victory—an awareness that is certainly intriguing in the assessment of this Value Population's possible adult fate.

POWER PLAYS

You don't have time to think up there. If you think, you're dead.
—Tom Cruise as Lt. Pete "Maverick" Mitchell, *Top Gun* (1986)

A rifle is only a tool. It is a hard heart that kills. If your killer instincts are not clean and strong you will hesitate at the moment of truth. You will become dead marines.
—R. Lee Ermey as Gunnery Sgt. Hartman, *Full Metal Jacket* (1987)

Fear causes hesitation, and hesitation will cause your worst fears to come true.
—Patrick Swayze as Bodhi, *Point Break* (1991)

tant and popular movies as *Dances with Wolves* (1990), *Rudy* (1993), and *Forrest Gump* (1994) is that their profoundly non-super title characters each manage to develop a hero's fortitude, bravery, skill, and opportunistic instincts, each ultimately claiming a remarkable life's victory in the difficult "real" world.

    How far this mythic ethos may stretch into or mitigate the Transformer value system is yet to be known, but the far-reaching possibilities can be seen by statements made by a number of Transformer-era protagonists. For example, in *A Bronx Tale* (1993), Robert DeNiro as Lorenzo Anello, a Bronx bus driver, tries to dissuade his son from the glamour of organized crime: "You want to see a real hero? Look at a guy who gets up in the morning and goes off to work and supports his family. That's heroism."

KEEPING SCORE: MONEY, JUSTICE, AND LOVE

    There may be a mythic quality to the value system of Transformers, but there is also a strong connection to the affairs of the real world. Transformers seem particularly drawn to activities in which strong wills are pitted against one another. Among the thematic concerns that dominate the cinema of the Transformer period are money, justice, and love.

Money

"Guess what I'm going to do?"

"What?"

"I'm going to come back from the dead."

"Aaahhh. And what makes you think you can do that?"

"Because I'm rich."

—Lily Tomlin and Steve Martin as Edwina Cutwater and Roger Cobb, *All of Me* (1984)

The point is there's a gulf in this country; an ever-widening abyss between the people who have stuff and the people who don't have shit. It is like this big hole in the ground, as big as the fucking Grand Canyon, and what's coming out is an eruption of rage, and the rage creates violence, and the violence is real, Mack.

—Steve Martin as Davis, *Grand Canyon* (1991)

That watch costs more than your car. I made $970,000 last year. How much do you make? You see pal, that's who I am, and you're nothing. Nice guy,

I don't give a shit. Good father, fuck you! Go home and play with your kids!
You wanna work here, close!

—Alec Baldwin as Blake, *Glengarry Glen Ross* (1992)

One is tempted to conclude that the message of Transformer-era drama with regard to wealth is that money is essentially corrupting, and that people who renounce its influence over their lives are better off. In part, this message is communicated via a relentless dissection of the irritating, self-absorbed habits of materialistic Yuppies in movies such as *Lost in America* (1985), *The Money Pit* (1986), and *Big* (1988), and on television series such as *L.A. Law* (1986–1994), *Beverly Hills 90210* (1990–2000), and *Seinfeld* (1990–1998). Even more damning are movies such as *Wall Street* (1987), *Pretty Woman* (1990), *Other People's Money* (1991), and *Glengarry Glenn Ross* (1992) that portray the financial elite as morally ruined monsters with cruel snaky styles and insatiable mercenary appetites.

What cannot be mitigated by the easy moralism of such an outlook, however, is the breadth and passion that is brought to the consideration of wealth in the Transformer era and the fact that the relationship to wealth is far more a love-hate relationship than it is just a hate relationship. That capitalism is a great enabler of pain and injustice is part of the equation. But so is a grudging acknowledgment in this competitive era that, as Michael Douglas' character Gordon Gekko proclaims in *Wall Street* (1987), "Greed is the essence of the evolutionary spirit."

It is rightfully noted that the Transformer cinema celebrates heroes whose primary appeal is that they are possessed of a brash streetwise financial savvy. Rodney Dangerfield's Thornton Melon in *Back to School* (1986), Paul Newman's Eddie Felson in *The Color of Money* (1986), and Kevin Bacon's Jack Casey in *Quicksilver* (1986) are examples. Also to be acknowledged are sympathetic characters such as baseball phenom "Nuke" LaLoosh in *Bull Durham* (1988) and the eponymous hero of *Forrest Gump* (1994) whose natures are the epitome of naïveté, but whose lives are in part enviable and remarkable because they are rich.

Ultimately, there's little getting away from the fact that, in art and real life, the Transformer era is an intense, competitive, financially obsessed period in which power is pegged to the heft of one's wallet. The feeling harkens back to the Patriot era, in which it was valid to criticize or poke fun at the rich, but it sure would have been fun to be among them. A telling moment occurs in the film *Speed* (1994), when Keanu Reeves' character, Detective Jack Traven, confronts Dennis Hopper as psychopath Howard Payne, who has wired a hostage to a bomb in order to make his escape with millions of extorted dollars.

Says Traven: "You're crazy! You're fuckin' crazy!"
Responds Payne: "No! Poor people are crazy, Jack. I'm eccentric."

Justice

*You're not gonna learn what it means to be a cop by eating hot dogs and picking
your teeth and asking stupid questions. We live this job, it is something we are,
not something we do! Every time a cop walks up to a car and has to give a
speeding ticket, he knows he may have to kill someone or be killed himself.
That's not something you step into by strapping on a rubber gun and riding
around all day. You get to go back to your million-dollar beach house and your
bimbos and your blowjobs, and you get 17 takes to get it right. We get one take.
It lasts our whole lives. We mess it up and we're dead.*

—James Woods as Det. Lt. John Moss, *The Hard Way* (1991)

*Lawyers are like nuclear warheads. I have them because the other guy has them,
but the first time you use them it fucks everything up.*

—Danny DeVito as Larry "the Liquidator" Garfield, *Other People's Money* (1991)

"I didn't kill my wife."
"I don't care."

—Harrison Ford and Tommy Lee Jones as Dr. Richard Kimble and Deputy Marshall Samuel Gerard,

***The Fugitive* (1993)**

An enormous amount of the dramatic art of the Transformer era is
devoted to a consideration of legality. But this is not primarily a philosophical consideration of justice as it is an abstract ethical principle. For
Transformers, the legal system is something like a mix between a chess
match and a socially sanctioned street brawl in which adversaries give it
their best shot until somebody resigns or goes to prison.

This is not an entirely cynical outlook. One should keep in mind
that the Transformer worldview embraces an awareness of horrible villains operating against a backdrop of chaos. The movies and TV shows
of the Transformer era relentlessly hammer home the point that the en-
forcement of law by valiant policemen and dedicated court officers are
society's best armor against evil.

By the same token, however, there is also the awareness that life is
far too complex to fit comfortably into any one set of rules or behaviors.
Social issues are as often gray as they are black and white (the TV show
L.A. Law, which ran from 1986 through 1994, is given a lot of credit for

being among the first series to explore such thorny issues as the obligations of doctors to treat AIDS patients, the rights of the terminally ill to select death, and the social accountability of the mentally ill). Similarly, the legal system authorizes its agents to exert significant power in the affairs of society, and Transformers are deeply aware that this or any power may lead to wrongful misapplication or outright corruption.

Transformers seem to appreciate both the fierce tactical contests and the personal tests of will. Whether one sees the legal system for the issues or for the people involved, it is not really about the law—it is about the pursuit of advantage and the production of adrenaline. One may reasonably hypothesize that adult Transformers will be attracted to law, as it is a uniquely appropriate arena for their emerging values and talents, and the pay can be pretty good too.

Love

"David, may I please have some ANSWERS?"
"Delaware, all of the above, 90 degrees."
—Cybil Shepherd and Bruce Willis as Maddie Hayes and David Addison, Moonlighting (1985–1989)

Love don't make things nice. It ruins everything. It breaks your heart. It makes things a mess. We aren't here to make things perfect. The snowflakes are perfect. The stars are perfect. Not us. Not us! We are here to ruin ourselves and to break our hearts and love the wrong people and die.
—Nicholas Cage as Ronny Camereri, Moonstruck (1987)

"I just gotta know, are we going to love each other?"
"I'd like to. But he's out there right now, and I've gotta go to work."
—Kim Bassinger and Michael Keaton as Vicki Vale and Batman, Batman (1989)

The Transformer era has a split personality when it comes to affairs of the heart. The extremes are represented by the quote from *Moonstruck* cited above, which demonstrates the intense Transformer capacity for surrendering to the full power of passion. The quote from *Batman* is indicative of the other extreme—basically that love may be a distraction from more important business.

In either case, love is dangerous. It is not just emotionally risky, but more important to a Transformer, it places power over oneself in the hands of another. Some of the most famous movies of the Transformer era—*Jagged Edge* (1985), *Fatal Attraction* (1987), and *Basic Instinct* (1992), to name just a few—explore the living horror that desire may become to those who indiscriminately surrender to the wrong lover (an urgent insight in the era of AIDS).

Even in the less-homicidal love stories of the era, there is a sense of romance being measured against personal power requirements. Quite revealingly, all of the following popular movies and TV shows feature couples whose central form of relating to one another is competitive banter, a verbal sparring that simultaneously seeks to establish, albeit affectionately, both personal dominance and a safe emotional distance in a relationship: *Moonlighting* (1985–1989), *Roxanne* (1987), *Witches of East-wick* (1987), *Bull Durham* (1988), *Roseanne* (1988–1997), *When Harry Met Sally* (1989), *Northern Exposure* (1990–1995), *Pretty Woman* (1990), *The Cutting Edge* (1992), *My Cousin Vinny* (1992), *Lois & Clark* (1993–1997), *Maverick* (1994), *Clueless* (1995), and *Mad about You* (1992–1999). The implicit message is that there is something equally dangerous and dull about unqualified adoration.

If there is anything approaching an ultimate insight regarding love in the art of the Transformer era, it may be found in such "odd couple" love stories as 1988's *Rain Man* (brothers), 1990's *Pretty Woman* (corporate raider/prostitute), and 1991's *Thelma & Louise* (female best friends). The lesson in all of these is that there is a point at which one must accept certain powerlessness over other people who, even if they love you, will pretty much do what is in their nature to do. No wonder that many victory-driven Transformers, like Batman, would rather take their chances contending against pure evil.

KID STUFF

"Hey—you ever get into fights when you were a kid?"

"Huh—plenty."

"Yeah, but it wasn't like the problem I have, right?"

"Why? Fighting fighting. Same same."

"Yeah, but you knew karate."

"Someone always know more."

"You mean there were times when you were scared to fight?"

"Always scare. Miyagi hate fighting."

"Yeah, but you like karate."

"So?"

"So, karate's fighting. You train to fight."

"That's what you think?"

"No."

"Then why train?"

"So I won't have to fight?"

"Miyagi have hope for you."

—Ralph Macchio and Pat Morita as Daniel LaRusso and Mr. Miyagi, *The Karate Kid* (1984)

"Do you know what it means to have contempt for your opponent?"

"No."

"It means to hate them. You have to hate them Josh, they hate you."

"But I don't hate them."

"Well you'd better start."

—Ben Kingsley and Max Pomeranc as Bruce Pandolfini and Josh Waitzkin,
***Searching for Bobby Fischer* (1993)**

Sometimes a baby's gotta do what a baby's gotta do.

—Elizabeth Daily as the voice of Tommy Pickles, *Rugrats* (1991–1994)

The single most important child-specific value-formation focus in the Transformer era is this: the best strategy for successful existence is to quickly develop power and gain control over one's own circumstances. It is important to note that this has not always been a requirement of childhood, which at one time was culturally accepted as a grace period for innocence afforded by protective adults.

As has been made clear in the discussion of the Believer era, childhood culturally took it on the chin in the 1970s. But, by the mid-1980s, we find Transformers, well-informed and street-savvy kids who, even if in perfectly well-adjusted family circumstances, have an almost natal awareness that they are going to have to contend for their piece of the action.

This is a very broad area for discussion and illustration, and full justice to this (speculative) insight will not be accomplished here. It is worthwhile, however, to look at some of the major manifestations and implications of this power-seeking phenomenon as revealed in the movies and TV shows of the Transformer value-formation period. They give a good indication as to why this Value Population will be something special to come up against in their maturity.

SKILL ACQUISITION

Tough guys don't do math. Tough guys fry chicken for a living.

—Edward James Olmos as Jaime Escalante, *Stand and Deliver* (1987)

I've got better things to do tonight than die.
—Neilson Ross as the voice of Springer, *Transformers: The Movie* (1986)

Transformer kids seem to appreciate that desire is only half the battle in the quest for power. The far more difficult part is life-skill development that, on the most traditional level, is composed of apprenticeship and discipline. *The Karate Kid* (1984), *Back to School* (1986), *The Color of Money* (1986), *Teenage Mutant Ninja Turtles* (1987–1995), *Dirty Dancing* (1987), *Stand and Deliver* (1987), *Bull Durham* (1988), *Bill & Ted's Excellent Adventure* (1989), *Dead Poet's Society* (1989), *The Freshman* (1990), *Rising Sun* (1993), and *Mr. Holland's Opus* (1995) are just some of the Transformer-era stories in which young seekers find skilled and passionate teachers and, with the practice of proper techniques, achieve significant personal victory.

Because skilled and passionate teachers aren't always available, Transformer-era youths manage to use play as a pragmatic power-development tool. The youth culture of the Transformer era, including its movies and television shows, are filled with games and toys that involve latent powers, strategy lessons, and tactical role-playing. Robots and action figures dominate the youth shows of the era, invoking tactics of mind and muscle in the midst of mythic confrontation. For example, *Transformers*, a critically acclaimed Japanese-made cartoon series that ran in the United States from 1984 to 1987, was made into a full-length movie in 1986, and was subsequently spun off into an action figure toy line so hugely successful that its manufacturer, Hasbro, reports that it is still "one of the top ranking toys in the world today" (2004). The ultimate tactical board game, chess, is very much in vogue, and the computer as a gaming device allows aggression and response simulation unparalleled in human history. For example, as early as 1984, in *The Last Starfighter,* a bored youth in a trailer park manages to adapt a video gaming skill to saving an interstellar civilization, and by 1995, in *Hackers,* 11-year-old technology savants are realistically bringing the global economy to its knees.

NEW TRADITIONALISM

This is my house. I have to defend it.
—Macaulay Culkin as Kevin McAllister, *Home Alone* (1990)

*Heroes get remembered, but legends never die. Follow your heart, kid,
and you'll never go wrong.*
—Art LaFleur as "The Babe," *The Sandlot* (1993)

". . . and then Mommy kissed Daddy, and the angel told the stork, and the stork
flew down from heaven, and put the diamond in the cabbage patch, and the
diamond turned into a baby!"
"Our parents are having a baby too."
"They had sex."

—Micah Hata, Jimmy Workman, and Christina Ricci as Young Girl, Pugsley, and Wednesday,
Addams Family Values **(1993)**

Not only is the future-oriented power of technology exploited in the youth material of the Transformer era, but there is also a respect for the strength of much that can only be characterized as traditional. Families, social institutions, and even the game of baseball are reclaimed as worthy in this Value Population.

Of course, these foundational and sustaining essences are mostly modified by the edginess and street sophistication of the times. Cliff Huxtable, Homer Simpson, Al Bundy, and Gomez Addams are hardly traditional dads in a 1950s sense (okay, maybe Bill Cosby's Huxtable is almost there, but the fact that the Huxtables are a black family *does* make a cultural difference today versus in the 1950s), but at least they are present, fundamentally loving, and loyal. Their children are portrayed as similarly devoted and eccentric. They know, among many other things that 1950s kids didn't know, how the mortgage gets paid and where babies really come from.

As has already been indicated, social institutions and functions are far more back in vogue in this period than the previous one. While certainly not always presented as paragons of skill or virtue, countless teachers, policemen, lawyers, and soldiers in the Transformer era cinema are presented as admirable and kid-considerate. While politicians and priests are hardly popular, there seems to be far more earnest consideration of their difficult social situations and less propensity to simply slam their shortcomings.

One of the most powerful tributes to tradition in the Transformer era, one with deep roots in the realm of childhood, is an obvious thematic fascination with baseball. Little of the game's cultural significance—as a field of battle, as a test of will, as an expression of attachment, as a rite of passage, as a stage for heroes and villains, as a place of innocence lost and found, as an important commercial enterprise, as a significant global export, or as a national secular religion—is left unexplored in films that include *The Natural* (1984), *Bull Durham* (1988), *Eight Men Out* (1988), *Major League I and II* (1989; 1994), *A League of Their Own* (1992), *Mr. Baseball* (1992), *The Sandlot* (1993), *Rookie of the Year* (1993), and *Angels in the Outfield* (1994). Capturing the least cynical, most hopeful tone is *Field of Dreams* (1989), which in the following passage spoken by James Earl Jones as author Terence Mann, presents the power of the game as an enduring American myth:

> The one constant through all the years, Ray, has been baseball. America has rolled by like an army of steamrollers. It is been erased like a blackboard, rebuilt, and erased again. But baseball has marked the time. This field, this game, is a part of our past, Ray. It reminds us of all that once was good, and that could be again. Oh people will come, Ray. People will most definitely come.

KID POWER

"You think about this: when you get old, these kids—when I get old—they're going to be running the country."
"Yeah."
"Now this is the thought that wakes me up in the middle of the night. That when I get older, these kids are going to take care of me."
"I wouldn't count on it."
—Paul Gleason and John Kapelos as Richard Vernon and Carl, *The Breakfast Club* (1985)

I say we just grow up, be adults, and die.
—Winona Ryder as Veronica Sawyer, *Heathers* (1989)

My parents keep asking how school was. It's like saying "how was that drive-by shooting?" You don't care how it "was." You're lucky to get out alive.
—Claire Danes as Angela Chase, *My So-Called Life* (1994)

Despite some acknowledgment of worthy teachers and traditions, the presentation of youth themes in the Transformer era hardly dwells on the subsidiary role that children play in an adult world. There is a consistent and palpable sense of both irony and superiority in the mouths of babes in this era. Youthful protagonists act very much as if they are simply waiting their turn to be in charge—and then all bets are off.

Not everything is as grim as the quotes cited above would indicate, although the edgy character of the outlook is sincere. But the thought that kids can succeed where adults fail is also a part of such gentler entertainment as *Back to the Future* (1985), *The Goonies* (1985), *Pee Wee's Big Adventure* (1985), *Home Alone* (1990), and *Last Action Hero* (1993). Particularly insightful is the movie *Big* (1988), in which a 13-year-old, *transformed* by a wish into an adult, quickly works his way from a data-entry position to vice president of new products at a toy company, thanks to behavior that is variously judged as refreshingly honest, brilliantly creative, and ultimately "adult."

The other important power aspect of the kids of this Value Population is that they are disposed toward recognizing, in self-defense as much as anything else, each other's most powerful capabilities and qualities. Screening one another constantly for empathy, they enter into significantly loyal friendships and alliances. Some of the most engaging of these are formed by ultimately triumphant "outcasts," as happens in such movies as *The Goonies* (1985), *Real Genius* (1985), *The Breakfast Club* (1985), *Stand by Me* (1986), and *Revenge of the Nerds I, II, III, and IV* (1984, 1987, 1992, and 1994).

If they are Transformers, even the nerds know time is on their side if they just watch each other's backs.

THE TRANSFORMER IDEAL

Pain can be controlled; you just disconnect it.

—Michael Biehn as Kyle Reese, *The Terminator* (1984)

They're poor, they're the unwanted, yet they're fighting for our society and our freedom. It's weird isn't it? They're the bottoms of the barrel and they know it. Maybe that's why they call themselves grunts, cause a grunt can take it, can take anything. They're the best I've ever seen, Grandma, the heart and soul.

—Charlie Sheen as Chris Taylor, *Platoon* (1986)

You think I'm a loser? Because I have a stinking job that I hate, a family that doesn't respect me, a whole city that curses the day I was born? Well, that may mean loser to you, but let me tell you something. Every day when I wake up in the morning, I know it is not going to get any better until I go back to sleep. So I get up. I have my watered-down Tang and my still-frozen Pop Tart. I get in my car with no gas, no upholstery, and six more payments. I fight honking traffic just for the privilege of putting cheap shoes onto the cloven hooves of people like you. I'll never play football like I wanted to. I'll never know the touch of a beautiful woman. And I'll never know the joy of driving through the city without a bag over my head. But I'm not a loser. Because, despite it all, me and every other guy who'll never be what they wanted to be, is out there, being what we don't want to be,

forty hours a week for life. And the fact that I didn't put a gun in my mouth
years ago—that little fact makes me a winner, baby!
—**Ed O'Neill as Al Bundy, Married . . . with Children (1987–1997)**

Transformers, as can already be gleaned from this analysis, are more likely to celebrate the traditional mythic qualities of heroic victory than any other Value Population. This is the era of the superman: the fearless Mel Gibson, the indestructible Arnold Schwarzenegger, the indomitable Bruce Willis—all daring anything and risking everything to beat the bad guys and to keep the world, or at least their own loved ones, safe and free. Throw in some of the tangible prizes of victory—money, love, nice stuff—and you have the Transformer fairy tale *par excellence.*

The catch, though, is that Transformers are likely to be complex and far more intense than they are idealistic, really tending not to believe in fairy tales. Any appreciation of victory they have will likely be derived from an awesome respect for, and often a direct knowledge of, defeat. Transformers are learning that self-mastery is hard and that one often encounters oneself as the harshest challenge on one's path to virtuosity and virtue.

So it is that the greatest of Transformer ideals appears to be the transformative power of perseverance—whatever the odds, whatever the setbacks, whatever the opponents, whatever the risks, whatever the stakes—simply keeping one's will going when body, spirit, and common sense are trying to call it quits, is at the heart of whatever may really pass for success in the Transformer worldview.

Here at the close of this analysis, we reiterate that Transformers are only kids as this is being written. But they give every early indication of having the power to truly transform the world.

Chapter

19

LOOKING FORWARD
"Who's" Next?

The concluding iconic event of the Transformer value-formation period takes place during the early afternoon of October 3, 1995. It is on this day that an estimated 160 million Americans, the largest audience ever so assembled, pull themselves away from their ordinary workday routines to watch television. The collective gasp is almost audible as the nation learns that football hero O.J. Simpson, despite a mountain of incriminating circumstantial evidence, has been found "not guilty" of the murder of his ex-wife and her male friend.

Clearly it is not the purpose here to delve into the issue of Simpson's guilt or innocence, but to acknowledge the depth of cultural preoccupation and passion stirred up by this verdict. Specifically, in a Value Population context, why does this event mark a boundary between the Transformer period and the one we are living through now?

In its broadest sense, the "not guilty" verdict is a fitting encapsulation of the Transformer value-formation period that so highly esteems winning—with any forces at one's disposal, and at all costs. Here, in a single event, is the fruition of the Transformer period themes of power, influence, street smarts, sexual politics, confrontation, malleable justice, the black experience and, certainly not least, the power of wealth. A now-famous Gallup/CNN–*USA Today* poll taken right after the Simpson verdict found that while 34 percent of Americans thought the largely black jury's racial composition determined the "not guilty" verdict, fully

73 percent of all Americans believed Simpson would have been found guilty if he were "not rich."

This astonishing public regard for the power of exceptional wealth is compounded in 1995 by financial markets that suddenly transition from steadily rising to near verticality. While there are many qualifications to the story, the fact remains that the Dow Jones Industrial Average rises a staggering 35 percent in one year (and 26 percent the next), fostering widespread hopes, particularly among middle class investors, of becoming wealthy. One of the earliest value themes to arise out of this new value-formation period is the grandly optimistic and ideology-enabled expectation that "we're *all* going to get rich and powerful because we are fortunate enough to live in the greatest capitalist democracy in the world."

The value-formation proposition is complicated, however, when the skyrocketing four–year bull market comes to a rather abrupt end with the crash of speculative technology stocks in 2000. This gives a broad hint of the complex tensions that will beset both wealth creation and values formation in the coming period. Transposed to the notion of great and inevitable growth in U.S. wealth and prestige is an increasingly populous world whose resources are shrinking, whose ideologies are in conflict, and whose borders are rapidly disappearing. In terms of value formation, it is in 1995 that the United States wakes up to the imminent demands and dangers, and not just the economic opportunities, of globalization.

History will likely record 1995 as the year that the Internet becomes a reality for the average citizen; and in fact, the very term "Internet" is first formally defined by a resolution passed by the U.S. Federal Networking Council just three weeks after the Simpson verdict. This is also the year that AOL, CompuServe, and Prodigy first become competitive Internet service providers, MSN is launched, and Netscape goes public. From this historical point onward a "connected world" is neither a metaphor nor an abstraction, and the aptly named "World Wide Web" starts to weave itself, part temptation and part trap, into the fabric of civilization and value formation.

The 1995 bombing of the Murrah Federal Building in downtown Oklahoma City, the deadliest act of terrorism ever perpetrated on America soil prior to the 2001 bombing of New York's World Trade Center is an even more profound indication of what post-Transformer youth are likely to confront. This act, even though perpetrated by Americans, opens the era up to the most frightening value-formation themes and repercussions of globalization. In the most horrific way imaginable, the bombing of the Federal Building delivers a message that American social, economic, and political institutions have their zealous detractors, and that these institutions are vulnerable to attack on a very broad scale— and no longer only on foreign ground.

Despite the unsettling implications of these events, the task of assessing the value set of the individuals being value formed in this era is not necessarily grim. One is well reminded to consider the Performers, a Value Population formed in the constant shadow of a nuclear tipped Cold War, who ended up as perhaps the most affirmative and life-embracing of all the Value Populations. This cohort group may conceivably prop itself up on a platform of optimism, recognizing that some sort of universally coherent and socially beneficial ideology, and not just "raw" power, is the key to a worthy and desirable life—for themselves and all of mankind.

On a final note, in 1995 Mr. Potato Head returns! Voiced by comedian Don Rickles in the year's biggest box office hit, Pixar's breakthrough animated tale *Toy Story*, Mr. Potato Head is now projected onto the silver screen and into the consciousness of post-Transformers. Although the durable "Mr. P" is portrayed as a character who badly misjudges the motives of the film's cowboy doll hero, he does play a meaningful role in the film's exotic toy culture that learns to embrace the considerable differences and various skills of its members. Viewed from the perspective of value formation, the toys, some of them quite deformed and "foreign," successfully and unselfishly unite in a common cause to vanquish a pernicious youngster of Transformer age. *Toy Story* may well be the first great values parable of the post-Transformer era.

While we can't possibly yet know how this will all turn out, we can acknowledge that in 1995 the value formation emphasis shifts from the cultivation of personal power to the identification of sustainable ideological values in an unstable era of cultural confrontation. In the Transformer value system, power wins. In the next Value Population, the spoils may well go to the philosophers—who understand that nobody wins if "might" is all that "right" has to offer.

So "who" is this new Value Population? Perhaps we should call them the Owls.

MARKETING TO VALUE POPULATIONS

In this third part of *The Consistent Consumer,* specific marketing implications and business applications of the Value Population material will be addressed and anchored in examples drawn from direct work with clients.

The first three chapters of Part Three cover selected consumer-focused research projects and presentations created for Near Bridge, Inc., clients. Chapter 20, "Core Customer Migration," looks into the world of upscale home improvement service providers through the eyes of California Closets and The Franchise Group. Chapter 21, "Reaching an Audience," outlines how understanding Value Population research helps clients such as major entertainment providers like the National Basketball Association and the Miami Heat better communicate and advertise to target audiences. Chapter 22, "Social Marketing," shows how organizations, like Vegan Outreach, can effectively use Value Population findings to create powerful and targeted collateral material that will have the largest impact on influencing behavioral change in specific target audiences.

Finally, Chapter 23 offers the highlights of an article that initially appeared in *QSR Magazine,* the leading trade publication of the American quick-serve restaurant industry. The chapter analyzes the impact that historical icons and consumer trends have on the quick-serve (fast food) restaurant industry and serves to illustrate the applications of Value Population insight to real marketplace issues.

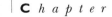

20

CORE CUSTOMER
MIGRATION

Not all consumer goods and services companies attempt to derive their mission from behavioral research data. Some are concerned with an aspect of the consumer that cannot be readily reduced to keystroke counts or computer-aided analysis. Such companies believe the mystery of the consumer is to be unlocked in the areas of deeply held attitudes and values—that it is neither silly nor superficial to consider that every shopper has a soul.

In 1978, California Closets invented the upscale residential customized storage industry. Today the company is a nationally-franchised $200 million unit of a billion-dollar Canadian consortium called The Franchise Company, and it remains the customized storage segment's sales leader. According to Edward Leaman, who serves as the company's Executive Vice President as well as President of The Franchise Company's Nomads and Growers marketing arm, California Closets' brand development was, has been, and will continue to be intuitive rather than research led.

According to Leaman, California Closets' positioning as an "attitudinal brand" stems from an appreciation of the role that the home plays for today's consumer. In a world where individuality and personal expression are increasingly thwarted in the public domain, the home becomes the place where the consumer can most comfortably and effectively express his or her identity, thereby making it an arena in which a service company must endeavor to connect by "substantiating customers' feelings about themselves." In such a paradigm, explains Leaman, "one must market to the meaning a customized closet may have for someone—whether it's for life simplification or to create a sense of order or to enhance a feeling of personal security or to experience pride of possession—far more than one must dwell on the purely functional material and manpower considerations of building a closet."

In this context, what attracted Leaman and California Closets to the Near Bridge Value Population research was the fact that the material dealt in the identification and explanation of attitudes, or *values* in the Near Bridge lexicon. By emphasizing values migration—the phenomenon of cohort groups retaining their values throughout their collective lifespan and carrying them with them as they pass through different life phases—the Near Bridge material also promised some extremely useful insight into why today's core California Closet customer, a Techtician woman in her 40s with an annual household income in excess of $75,000, did not appear to have the same values as the Performer customer with the same demographic description from only a decade or two earlier. What adjustments in the marketing, sales, and installation processes, California Closets wondered, were thereby warranted?

Compounding and qualifying the urgency of this inquiry were the size and structural changes in the home improvement industry itself. No longer a "bijou business," to use Leaman's term, customized storage has become a $2 billion category in the still rapidly expanding $300 billion home improvement industry. In a brave new world of big-box do-it-yourself retailers and in an era of burgeoning internet sales, was it prudent to confine one's marketing efforts to positive word-of-mouth and the pages of *Architectural Digest*?

The analysis performed by Near Bridge on behalf of California Closets concentrated on identifying the discrete set of values that differentiate Techticians, the "new" core California Closets customer, from Performers, the "original" core customer. See Figure 20.1. Unlike other generational analyses that lump the mid-1940s and 1950s post-WW II babies with children born from the late 1950s through the early 1960s (although finally suspecting there may be some lack of consistency, one now increasingly encounters the terms "late" and "early" applied to Baby Boomers), the Near Bridge matrix defines a rather sharp values break between the children of the 1950s and those of the 1960s. Under California Closets' direction, Near Bridge endeavored to identify how each of these groups approaches a luxury purchase, emphasizing such issues as the collection of information, feelings about what constitutes status, desirable retail environments, effective sales approaches, and, in the broadest pos-

FIGURE 20.1

California Closets' Migrating Customer Base

	PERFORMERS	TECHTICIANS
Population	66 million	63 million
% of U.S. Population	23	22
Median Age (1978)	30.5	13.5
Median Age (2003)	55.5	38.5
Total Expenditures (2000)	$1.32 million	$1.45 million

sible sense, what each of these value populations is looking for in a premium brand. See Figure 20.2.

Among the findings identified as particularly valuable by California Closets is the practical, heavily analytical, information-rich orientation of Techticians toward significant purchases. While scrutinized from a number of perspectives, this point is particularly well driven home by a comparison of shelter magazines and median readership ages. A Performer-oriented magazine, such as *Architectural Digest,* that clearly positions itself as an aspirational lifestyle journal, is certainly appealing to a different set of values than the Techtician-oriented *Home* magazine, which pragmatically describes itself in terms of its contribution to asset investment and project utility, and tends to run articles on dozens or even hundreds of ways of accomplishing a home improvement objective.

This insight similarly helps to explain, at least in part, the allure of the Internet and the importance of multichannel marketing to the Techtician shopper, whose luxury purchases often begin with extensive data collection relating to features. This infatuation with information often transpires before an appreciation of benefits and, only then, concludes with the satisfaction that a "smart" choice has been made. While time and stress factors can force a Techtician to make a decision before all the

FIGURE 20.2

VP Shopper Value Matrix

ATTRIBUTE	PERFORMERS	TECHTICIANS
Communication	Dramatic	Information Rich
Environment	Stimulative	Orderly/Efficient
Proposition	Self-Referential	Analytical
Time Sense	Distracted/Involved	Methodical/Starved
Variety	Form	Function
Luxury	Exclusive	Consensual
Brand	Image	Promise Delivery

facts are in, this is hardly the normal course of affairs when a significant outlay of cash is involved—these people generally being the antithesis of the one-stop, one-source shoppers.

It is this realization, says Leaman, that has helped him to understand the appeal to Techticians of "ugly" big box stores such as Costco and Home Depot, in terms of their broad product inventory rather than the niceties of the shopping environment that Performers prefer. He now acknowledges that information-seeking Techticians love such places as they simultaneously offer a large breadth of inventory and clearly defined product features. He further acknowledges that possession of this insight will be top of mind as California Closets for the first time contemplates a variety of strategic alliances and licensing agreements with retailers—appreciating more than ever that an approach to the Techtician consumer means being involved at as many relevant information intercept points as possible, whether there is an obvious traditional "quality" connection or not.

"When it comes to brand building, very few companies have real faith in their customers," observes Leaman. "They treat their brand as a little statue that you polish, rather than as a response to a living and evolving set of circumstances. Brands don't matter to the customer with anywhere near the intensity that most companies think.

"I trust the customer more than anyone," says Leaman, "but you need to understand them and connect with them. It's not just about measurement."

21

REACHING
AN AUDIENCE

What is bought before it is produced, cannot be touched or wrapped, and requires the consumer to go to the factory to get and use it—and once purchased, leaves nothing tangible to take home but memories? The answer? A sports or entertainment experience—and promoting it is one of the toughest challenges any marketing team can face.

No other industry has to so deeply and consistently resonate with a "consumer's soul" as does the sports and entertainment industry. Building a lasting brand around a living and continually changing product is difficult. If that is not challenging enough, the product has to be created and simultaneously consumed by a broad and demographically diverse audience, while meeting the needs of each demographic group and not offending the others.

Professional sports organizations are very familiar with these challenges. Leaders in these organizations are increasingly aware of the significant shifts in the values of their core audience and are now seeking new ways to more effectively understand, reach, and retain their target markets.

In an effort to counter flat or lagging season ticket sales, a tarnished public image of some players, diminishing corporate sponsorship, and a narrow retail product strategy, Bernie Mullin, the Vice President of Marketing for The National Basketball Association (NBA), invited Near Bridge to address these issues based on Value Population research. He was interested in knowing how he, the League presidents, and all the team marketers could better use this information to more effectively target the core values of the NBA's current and potential customer base.

Near Bridge presented its findings at the NBA's annual spring presidents' meeting. To better enable the attendees to quickly relate to the research, Near Bridge offered examples of legendary players whose personalities exemplified the emerging value set of each Value Population expressed in a sports context. These players personified the values of an emerging Value Population and became cultural icons of the era in which they played.

- *Performers: Bob Cousy, 1950–1963.* Bob Cousy was the heart and soul of six Boston Celtic championship teams, and his fans loved his zeal for the spotlight. He played the game of basketball with flare and passion and was flashy before flashy was cool (once famously being benched in college for showboating), constantly diving for loose balls and perfecting the showy behind-the-back pass. Cousy played basketball as if it was more than just a game and as if he was more than just a player. He was, rather, perhaps the first basketball player who appreciated that he was a prominent star in a hit show—and thereby a significant Performer icon.
- *Techticians: Wilt Chamberlain, 1959–1973.* Wilt Chamberlain personified skill under control and is arguably the most dominant player ever in NBA history. A marvel of statistical accomplishments, Wilt walked the talk and held many incredible NBA records such as: scoring 100 points in a single NBA game; averaging 50 points a game for an entire season; and, most incredibly considering his role as a silent but deadly intimidator, never fouling out in over 1,200 games. Unlike many of today's athletes who lose control and act out emotionally on the court, Chamberlain kept his mind in control of his actions and foreshadowed true Techtician values by always giving his best, measuring the results, and constantly improving. But what about winning? Merely icing on the cake.
- *Believers: Ervin "Magic" Johnson, 1979–1991.* Magic Johnson brought "vibe" to the game of basketball. The ultimate team player, he believed that personal passion for the game was best revealed by helping one's teammates perform better. In an era of weakening traditional aggressive male values and a growing mistrust for overtly "macho" leadership, Magic focused on group dynamics and personal relationships with his peers to win games. (Interestingly and

representatively, this value did not always include his boss, as the concept of loyalty to the boss was "bogus"—and he proved this by getting one of his coaches, Paul Westhead, fired.) Above all else, Magic's selfless style and contagious smile reinforced the emerging Believer message to fans, teammates, and opponents everywhere that even when championships are at stake, there is still room for looking good and having fun.

- *Transformers: Michael Jordan, 1984–1994.* The ascent of Michael Jordan to basketball prominence is a testimony to what power, skill, talent, and the desire to win can accomplish. Jordan demonstrated that institutions that survive and win (and that collect championships as regularly as clocks tell time) must be vested with endurance and an edge. Consistently rising to any challenge, Jordan was the chief sports icon in an era that brought black culture into mainstream American, and he will always be remembered for "effortlessly" flying through the air and into the country's TV sets and living rooms. Interestingly, as powerful a figure as he was, he still believed that tradition, with a little luck, was important too, as he always wore his college basketball shorts under his NBA shorts. Jordan knew that winning required a strong team made up of competent players, but like Transformers today, he realized that sometimes, when times get tough, one cannot hesitate to drive the key and "take it to the hoop" all by oneself.

Early research for this NBA project revealed that ticket sales, corporate sponsorships, and retail strategy were each dominated by a single, but different, Value Population. The bulk of individual season ticket sales fell to the Techticians, the seven-figure corporate sponsorship decisions were made primarily by Performers, and a high percentage of sales of merchandise, video games, and apparel were being sold to Transformers. With this information, and a newfound understanding of each of the Value Populations and their link to more effectively generating revenue, the NBA and its teams were shown how it is possible to focus marketing dollars more effectively on target audiences with values-based advertising campaigns.

As in any business, some of the key challenges the NBA teams face are continued revenue growth and profitability. In the context of this book, understanding Value Populations research allows the NBA to focus on this by including and specifically targeting multiple Value Populations in their ticket sales, sponsorship, and merchandising campaigns. For example, instead of relying heavily on season ticket sales to come mainly from Techticians, it can refine its marketing aim to include more emphasis on attracting Believers and Performers—significantly reducing single-source revenue exposure, upping attendance, and ultimately increasing profits.

A marketing campaign, run by the Miami Heat, targeting season ticket sales illustrates the effectiveness of this method. Like many other NBA teams, Heat ticket sales had been flat for three years as the market for sports and entertainment dollars in its trade area was highly competitive. Eric Woolworth, president of the Miami Heat, contacted Near Bridge and asked that his entire organization be trained on the concept of Value Populations. He wanted to use the resourcefulness of the entire organization to develop a highly targeted season ticket radio campaign suited to each Value Population.

Up to this point, the Heat strategy was heavily weighted toward a single, blanket campaign aimed at numerous local radio stations—a scattergun, one-ad-fits-all approach with little attention paid to segmenting their diversified audience. In other words, the same sales pitch went out to all the stations, regardless of the audience's demographic breakout. Because radio, unlike TV, allows for nearly instant and inexpensive modification of advertising, Woolworth wanted to change this strategy and use a targeted Value Population approach. With this strategy in mind, Near Bridge helped the Heat create new radio spots targeted at the different Value Populations.

In order to accomplish this, Near Bridge requested the Heat's marketing department to identify key area radio stations based on the specific age parameters of each Value Population. In order to increase the creative value of this material, the Heat's 160-person staff was first trained in the basics of the Value Population research and then divided into breakout groups with the instruction to create a 60-second radio spot directed at a specific radio station with a targeted Value Population audience.

An easy listening station with a Performer audience, for example, had an ad created for it that focused on the customer as king and emphasized personal service in Club Chivas—an exclusive place to watch the game. A rap station, with a primarily Believer audience, promoted a laidback, cool, and "chic" atmosphere where the "gang could hang."

As a result of this guided exercise, according to Kim Stone, Vice President of the Heat, "Not only did the breakout teams use the information to work together effectively, they developed spots that were so creative that they were used in our fall advertising campaign . . . We also saved money because we did not need to hire an expensive advertising company to create our spots that year. And, at the end of that campaign, and after working with Near Bridge, we had definitely sold more tickets."

More importantly, Stone said, "Looking at core values is way outside the box and makes immediate sense. Because of our new understanding of Value Populations, we now have a powerful way to more effectively reach our fan base."

22

SOCIAL MARKETING

Social marketing, although similar
to cause marketing, is not quite the same. *Cause marketing* is a commercial activity by which businesses and charities or causes form a partnership with each other to market an image, product, or service for mutual benefit. Examples include such partnerships as: Avon Cosmetics and the Avon Breast Cancer Crusade; American Airlines—Miles for Kids in Need; and Barnes & Noble and the Anti-Defamation League "Close the Book on Hate" campaign.

Social marketing, on the other hand, is the use of commercial marketing techniques to influence behavioral change that will improve the well-being of a specific target audience or society as a whole. Examples include such issues as smoking cessation, recycling, sober driving, and eating a plant-based diet. What separates social marketing from commercial marketing is its fundamental motivation—to strictly benefit an individual or society rather than a marketer's organization.

Some examples of organizations that employ social marketing techniques include: The Centers for Disease Control and Prevention; local, state, and federal health agencies; The U.S. Environmental Protection Agency; nonprofit organizations, and in the case of this discussion, specifically Vegan Outreach, a 501(c)(3) nonprofit educational organization.

Vegan Outreach is "dedicated to reducing animal suffering by promoting a vegan (pronounced VEE-gun) lifestyle." Vegans do not purchase or consume products that contribute to that suffering. By not buying or using items such as meat, eggs, dairy, and leather, vegans are, in effect, economically boycotting animal-based products.

In her book, *Hands-On Social Marketing: A Step-by-Step Guide,* Nedra Kiline Weinreich points out, "The first lesson in social marketing is there is no such thing as targeting the general public. To be most effective, specify the audience for your program as precisely as possible." It is in this vein that Near Bridge assisted Vegan Outreach in redesigning their *Why Vegan?* promotional booklet.

Vegan Outreach believes that their message is best received and acted upon by young people. So, through widespread distribution of full-color illustrated booklets, titled *Why Vegan?* and *Try Vegetarian,* they aim their message at adolescents and college-aged youth. These booklets are handed out by many volunteers, from students to animal advocacy organizations such as, Farm Animal Reform Movement (FARM), Farm Sanctuary, In Defense of Animals, The Fund for Animals, People for the Ethical Treatment of Animals (PETA), and Viva!USA.

Because social marketers usually have a very strong personal connection with the issue they are promoting, they often create promotional material that resonates more with their own core values than those of their target audience. This was the case with *Why Vegan?* While the main targeted audience for Vegan Outreach is college students, which up until 2003 were primarily made up of Believers, the majority of the members of Vegan outreach responsible for writing, compiling, and formatting the *Why Vegan?* booklet were Techticians. The booklet strongly reflected a Techtician slant—it was heavy on detailed information at the expense of being inviting—and for Believers, being inviting is not an option, but a requirement.

Figure 22.1 shows the original "Techtician" booklet cover on the left. It is loaded with text, has a strong sense of knowledge signaling, and a heavy emphasis on detail is apparent. Techticians, who are more pragmatic than idealistic, operate from a place of intellect rather than emotion—and data and information sells.

Believers, on the other hand, whose values were developed during a time of social dysfunction and economic malaise, and who are much more oriented toward empathy and welcoming assistance, respond favorably to relationships, love, and harmony, and are much more apt to resonate with peaceful and inviting advertising rather than a "data download."

In the revised cover of the *Why Vegan?* booklet shown in Figure 22.1, the heavy data-rich overtones are gone and have been replaced with an inviting and friendly look. The font has been rounded and is less "ag-

23

AN INDUSTRY OVERVIEW
Quick-Serve Restaurants

This chapter offers highlights from an article that initially appeared in *QSR Magazine*, the leading trade publication of the American quick-serve restaurant industry. The intent of this chapter is to review the five Value Populations, offer a glimpse of how historic icons and consumer trends specifically impact an industry, and illustrate the applications of the Value Populations insight to real marketplace issues faced by the quick-serve industry.

PATRIOTS STAND ON TRADITION

Value Population Overview

Born:	**1920–1937**
Size:	**12% of U.S. Population**

With the Patriots one encounters a Value Population "forced" to accept a uniquely complex, unknown, and dangerous future. Life is somehow more consistent, measured, local, and experientially familiar prior to the advent of mass industrialization and modern media, not to mention global depression, despotism, and war. While mass prosperity and personal freedom beckon in this new age, it is the collective pain that fate inflicts via global calamity, economic disappointment, and a rending of the established social fabric that most clearly leaves a mark. Subjected to the grim residue of war and want, the Patriots, more than any other Value Population, are about exercising caution; are about mistrusting the motives of others, keeping their hands on their wallets, and, most of all, attending to the rules and rituals of the families, friends, and social equals who validate and protect the Patriots' physical, psychological, and financial well-being.

Cultural Menu. The Complex and Sobering Aftermath of WW I, Prohibition, The Roaring 20s, The Jazz Age and The Age of Radio, Stock Market Collapse, The Great Depression, FDR's New Deal, The Rise of Foreign Dictatorships, and The Gathering Clouds of WW II.

Some Key Personalities. Woodrow Wilson, Al Capone, Babe Ruth, Louis Armstrong, Mae West, King Kong, Franklin Delano Roosevelt.

Primary Population Values (Partial List). Familiarity, Security, Affection, Abundance.

Quick-Serve Restaurant History

Although most contemporary quick-serve-restaurant chains do little active courtship of Patriot customers, the birth of the fast-food industry is actually simultaneous with the start of the Patriot value formation period. The nation's first drive-in restaurant, The Pig Stand, opens in Texas in 1921. Featuring a menu comprised entirely of a "Tennessee" BBQ Pork Sandwich and drinks, and offering carhop service, the chain expands to 120 units nationwide by 1934.

Even more noteworthy, because it still remains very much in existence, is the White Castle hamburger chain, founded in Kansas, also in 1921. Patriot values are plentiful in the brand new White Castle, whose *institutionalization* of the hamburger sandwich as America's chief culinary icon is built upon a creed of *uniformity*, ranging from product specifications to cooking to pricing to building construction to employee apparel. (White Castle is given credit for the creation of the military-looking paper hat.) Particularly indicative of Patriot values is that the chain has always remained a closely held family business.

Besieged by war, economic turmoil, and modernism, and subsequently devoted to the self-protective strategies of group survival, Patriots put a very high value on loyalty, consistency, and the comfort of familiar surroundings. Their own moods may change but they do not readily accept external variations that are thrust upon them. They are certain about what belongs where.

Todd Coerver, group director of operation services for Whataburger, offers a revealing glimpse of the Patriots' worldview. Whataburger, he explains, skews towards younger customers but does have "a great relationship with older loyal customers." He says that a number of Whataburger units are late-morning gathering places for local seniors, which he refers to as Coffee Clubs that have grown out of a long-ago free-refill coffee mug promotion.

"We have a restaurant across the street from headquarters that really needs to be rebuilt," says Coerver. "But the Coffee Club heard we were thinking about remodeling, and one day I get a package in the mail that turns out to be a formally produced report. Basically it says don't even think about remodeling until you meet with us, and it has 60 Coffee Club signatures followed by the number of years they've been coming to the restaurant—up to 40 years. The best part is that our tag is 'Whataburger . . . Just Like You Like It'. But printed on the cover of their report is 'Whataburger . . . Just Like *We* Like It.' I guess they were letting us know who really shepherds the brand."

Quick-Serve Restaurant Issues

Menu. The typical fast-food menu suits this group that is inclined towards sweetness, saltiness, and deep-fat frying as well as soft and thick textures; aggressively demand appropriate food temperatures; looking for comfort foods, but a lifetime of experience makes them finicky about perceived quality.

Service and Atmosphere. Easily scared into defensive posture by the unusual; crave familiarity and consistency in everything.

Price/Value. Money has always been of massive importance to this group, and its cautious retention and investment is largely characteristic of this group; senior discounts essential.

Nutrition. There are clearly health-based concerns in this age group, but there is also a strong sense of "treat"; born in an era of global plague and depression, this is perhaps the last modern generation that at least subconsciously links girth with health and happiness.

Marketing. Much mass retail image marketing to seniors includes grandchildren, but this is a generation that also values its place among its own contemporaries; images and messages should stress inclusion and safety; age-based off-hours promos have appeal.

Employees. As the population skews older, the concept of the Wal-Mart greeter should be kept in mind; peer presence works with this group as it establishes both a level of respect and a sense of cultural security.

Patriot Notables

1920. National prohibition of alcohol goes into effect. Speakeasies, commercial moonshine, and bootlegging come into existence. Alcohol becomes key icon of generational rebellion. Ice cream parlors are designed to mimic saloon experience.

1931. Irma S. Rombauer's *The Joy of Cooking* is published; conscientious home cooking is codified as the book's sales eventually top 15 million.

1933. Wheaties, first introduced in 1924, invents the slogan "Breakfast of Champions" and becomes a national pioneer in the radio broadcast and promotion of baseball and other sports. Cereal company also introduces a popular radio serial, "Jack Armstrong—All American Boy."

PERFORMERS COURT THE WORLD'S FARE

Value Population Overview

Born:	**1938–1957**
Size:	**22% of U.S. Population**

Performers sometimes seem unduly self-involved, but perhaps they've earned the right. Born during and just after global war, heirs to the advent of "we will bury you" Communism and its attendant threat of nuclear annihilation, offspring of a Value Population [the Patriots] most notably characterized by caution and an obsessive allegiance to the prevailing practices of the clan, the Performer generation might well have emerged as a tribe of crushed gray spirits quivering in the darkest corners of their own repressive nightmares. But be it a matter of fate or fortune or their own sheer numbers, the Performers take the exact opposite group tack . . . that of lighting their own inner flames rather than cursing the darkness. No other Value Population quite compares with their lust after life's sheer drama; for the belongings, feelings, and events that make an individual feel unique and very much alive.

Cultural Menu. The 1939 New York World's Fair Foreshadows The Future; The Wizard of Oz "Techni" colors the World; World War II, Cold War, and The Atomic Age; The Baby Boom; A National Highway System; The Creation of Suburbia; and Television Arrives.

Some Key Personalities. Adolph Hitler, John Wayne, Nikita Khrushchev, Senator Joe McCarthy, Walt Disney, Marilyn Monroe, Elvis Presley.

Primary Population Values (Partial List). Freedom, Adventure, Creativity, Romance.

Quick-Serve Restaurant History

It is not often that a discussion of the Baby Boomers, who begin to arrive *en masse* after WW II, looks back to the years just before the war. Socio-cultural analysis reveals, however, that the years 1938 and 1939 are a treasure trove of foreshadowing regarding the cultural blueprint of this vast population. The war is a grim interruption, but the key to the Performers is keeping in mind that their essence is a passion for beating back the grim reaper through taking delight in being alive.

Dairy Queen, which is born in 1938 and grows to more than 2,500 units before Ray Kroc opens his first McDonald's in 1955, tells part of the tale. Far more than dessert destinations, Dairy Queens become the community theatres of the heartland, the place where a car takes you so you can fraternize, flaunt, flirt, and fight about football. To understand the deep connection that the Performer Value Population has to dining out, even at quick-serve restaurants, is to keep in mind all of the books (Larry McMurtry's *Walter Benjamin at the Dairy Queen;* Bob Greene's *Chevrolet Days, Dairy Queen Nights*) and movies *(Texasville; Adventures in Babysitting)* that nostalgically evoke Dairy Queen as the place, as opposed to the family dinner table, where life's best stories unfold.

Away from the heartland, likely the most formative food event of 1938–1939 is the New York World's Fair, whose central exhibit is General Motors' Futurama. Beyond giving a prescient insight into the suburban/

consumer/car-oriented/television society that will appear after the war, the fair captures the international cultural eclecticism that will eventually become a prized part of the American social fabric. More than 20 foreign restaurants are featured at the fair, and trend-setting New Yorkers open their hearts, minds, and mouths to the possibilities.

All these years later, Performers remain a population that seeks both culinary eclecticism and personal passion in their dining out experiences. Age and society have placed issues such as nutrition, speed, and convenience on the plate, but Wallace Doolin, president of la Madeleine, probably gets closer to the truth when he speaks of "quick casual" as a great segmentation opportunity with this group because of its broad culinary experience and sophistication, or when Jim Adams, the Chipotle spokesperson, acknowledges that today's 50-year-old customer is still looking for "fun, discovery, and adventure."

"A company like Panera understands that these are the perfect people to spend $8 for a 30-minute trip to Tuscany," observes David Groll, a veteran research and development chef who has worked on many national chain menus. "This group wants great breads, and veggie pestos, and high flavor profiles that are truly unique. They are looking for things that are *interesting*."

Quick-Serve Restaurant Issues

Menu. Knowledgeable and experienced diners; quality, variety, and personal choice must figure into the menu mix; they savor the high-flavor profiles of international cuisines; open-minded but rarely fooled by pretentiousness.

Service and Atmosphere. This group grew up with a love for the restaurant experience; those quick-serve restaurants who can create comfortable and gregarious in-store environments may yet do well with a group that expects more from dining than the efficiency of a drive-thru.

Price/Value. In broad terms, this is a population of shoppers rather than savers; the current economic downturn coupled with the ambitious upscaling efforts of fast casuals may prove a financially, as well as gastronomically, happy match.

Nutrition. Aging, they are clearly interested in nutrition, especially with regard to heart health and youthfulness; this card can be over-played, however, as many Performers were the guinea pigs for the early low fat/low salt days that generally meant terrible taste; want it on the menu, may not eat it.

Marketing. More into the story than the icon; like things to proceed at a pace rather than e-fast; they can be accessed through flattering images of themselves and affectionate portrayals of (their own) children.

Employees. Their personality-plus approach to doing business can be very effective around clients and customers (if not always coworkers); worldly, warm, and courageous they are often excellent in life-mentoring roles.

Performer Notables

1938. Lawry's Seasoned Salt is introduced. The colorful flavor-enhancing mixture is a perfect taste (and visual) icon for the Performer population.

1941. M&Ms are created. This value population truly presides in the change from black and white to Technicolor.

1950. The first credit card appears. Appropriately enough, it is the card that eventually becomes the Diners Club card.

TECHTICIANS SAVOR THE SYSTEM

Value Population Overview

Born:	**1958–1971**
Size:	**23% of U.S. Population**

Techtician values derive from a complex mix of scientific rationalism, social idealism, and world-weary cynicism. Born into a world flush with scientific, social, economic and personal opportunity, the Techticians are ultimately subjected to a degradation of events. JFK invokes outer space as a metaphor for man's unlimited potential, but even a moon landing can't mask an era of political assassination, violent generational confrontation, self-serving economic and social proselytizing, and the ethical calamities of Vietnam and Watergate. Hoping for the best and prepared for the worst, Techticians now seem to be marked by nothing so much as their pragmatism and the belief that we all need to try just a little bit harder.

Cultural Menu. Mass Media—Commercial Jet Travel—Dawn of the Computer Age; JFK's "Camelot" Years Usher in Broadly Hopeful Social and Scientific Agendas; Americans Land on the Moon; Vietnam War Divides Nation; Assassination of Key Political Figures; Strong Economy Ultimately Sours.

Some Key Personalities. John, Jackie, and Robert Kennedy; Martin Luther King, Jr.; The Beatles; Capt. James T. Kirk; Muhammad Ali; Lyndon Johnson; Richard Nixon.

Primary Population Values (Partial List). Self-reliance, Pragmatism, Skill, Efficiency.

Quick-Serve Restaurant History

Glen Bell, the founder of Taco Bell, freely borrows. So do Carl Karcher and John Gallardi, the founders respectively of Carl's Jr. and Der Weinerschnitzel. In the late 1950s, Southern California is fairly awash with soon-to-be-household-name fast-food entrepreneurs who recognize that Ray Kroc has latched onto something important. That something is a *system* comprised of a limited menu, uniform pricing, assembly line production, and self-service, all ultimately codified in McDonald's first ever system-wide operations manual ("the Bible") introduced in 1958.

The modern quick-service restaurant industry is itself a key icon of the Techtician value-formation period. Built upon such factors as: an emerging cultural fascination with speed; a belief in the consumer benefits of technology; the proliferation of suburban shopping; the growth of a youthful population out on its own with limited financial resources; the dynamics of national brand television advertising; the rapid conviction of Wall Street investors in the vast replicability of fast-food-restaurant systems; the proliferation of the national quick-serve-restaurant industry as the first modern "meal solution." To this day Techticians prize efficient systems that resolve the requirements of a complex state of cultural affairs.

Significantly, advertising historians identify the year 1958 as the moment when women's magazines begin to tout the virtues of convenience products such as frozen vegetables and cake mixes in efficiently putting an attractive and wholesome meal on the family table. The issues of convenience and quality are both juxtaposed and intertwined in the value-formation period, with Techticians growing up to understand the difference between convenience and scratch cooking, accepting both for what they are and appreciating the role that each plays in a busy lifetime (explaining, perhaps, why so-called speed-scratch cookery is popular with chefs of this Value Population today). It is in the Techtician era that American regional cooking is first placed on a culinary pedestal, albeit at the unfortunately named Festival of Gas Pavilion at the 1964 World's Fair.

To appreciate the mature fruition of the Techticians, one needs only to connect the dots between the original Taco Bell (with no slight meant toward the ambitious company of today) and a company like Chipotle. Like the former was in its earliest days, the latter is a hip testament to functionality and minimalism, a model of operational efficiency deftly straddling the divide between mass production and attractive product. All of the creators and executives of Chipotle are in the Techticians Value Population, and they are fully aware, according to spokesperson Jim Adams, that the core values of the chain "reflect our values."

"We're selling burritos," says Adams, "so civilization is not riding or falling on what we do. But on the day when you are looking for something that tastes good, we want you to think of us. And on the days when speed is important, well, that's us too."

Quick-Serve Restaurant Issues

Menu. Gravitate towards upscale versions of regional and ethnic comfort food; seek authenticity in flavor profiles; understand superior ingredients and preparation; like to construct their personal version of perfection from cooking-style and garnish choices.

Service and Atmosphere. Speed and orderliness are essential here; particularly require efficiency and accuracy in the drive-through; expect minimally invasive but informed and well-trained service; value cleanliness and properly functioning equipment.

Price/Value. Human calculators; sometimes looking to make life a little simpler when they buy quick-serve food and therefore appreciate combo meals and simple uniform pricing policies; deeply experienced and informed as to what your competitors charge.

Nutrition. Very often a major preoccupation for both social cause and personal health reasons; fascinated by scientific details, they can rarely get enough information; "natural" and "organic" have significant appeal but so does premium chocolate.

Marketing. Many who market to this group allow edgy technical effects and cynical humor to take precedence over the product message; these have their place but so do the facts.

Employees. Detail and service oriented; far more hardworking than they are usually given credit for in generational analysis; powerfully competent with computers, they can be a little impatient with people who think at less than warp speed.

Techtician Notables

1963. The introduction of the self-cleaning oven, the birth of Weight Watchers, and the television debut of Julia Child capture many of the culinary crosscurrents of the time.

1966. Ronald McDonald airs in his first national television commercial, and McDonald's stock splits for the very first time. Fast food is vested as an industry of national importance.

1971. Starbuck's opens in Seattle's Pike Place Market, and Chez Panisse opens in Berkely, California. The sincere and intelligent upscaling of the basic American food experience is on, although, soon afterwards, the chic inherit the earth.

BELIEVERS ESCAPE TO HAPPY MEALS

Value Population Overview

Born:	**1972–1983**
Size:	**17% of U.S. Population**

It is tempting to dismiss the Believers as victims of a bad patch of history. Their value formation takes place in an era of broad political, economic, and social distress, with the term "power outage" best describing the tone of the times. What makes the Believers vital, though, are the values they develop to cope with the issues posed by a time of such cultural malaise and distress. These qualities include empathy, forbearance, and, perhaps most importantly, a real faith that rescue is always a possibility. The essence of the Believer value-formation period is that at its darkest hour the Ronald Reagan administration comes along and things just get better. Grace, Believers seem to inherently know, can only arrive if one makes room in the spirit for its possibility.

Cultural Menu. Vietnam War Ends With U.S. Troops Withdrawal; Watergate Ushers In Period of Weak Political Leadership; Oil Embargo and Energy Crisis; Inflation and Recession; Broad Social Dysfunction; Iranian Hostage Crisis; Feminist Culture Ascends.

Some Key Personalities. Gerald Ford, Jimmy Carter, John Travolta, Helen Reddy, Patty Hearst, Ayatollah Khomeini, Darth Vader.

Primary Population Values (Partial List). Affinity, Patience, Diplomacy, Faith.

Quick-Serve Restaurant History

They may seem impossibly quaint and goofy these days, but the Hamburglar, Grimace, and Mayor McCheese are originally born, in the early 1970's, out of a sort of historical necessity. The same holds true for McDonald's national roll out of the Happy Meal in 1979. Be it a brilliant marketing insight or an act of corporate philanthropy, the folks at McDonald's seem to understand that society has at least temporarily moved its children to a low rung on the social totem pole and that these children are very hungry for some consideration and a little escapist fun.

Whether it is such social problems as broken homes and the excesses of the disco era, or economic problems such as energy shortages and high unemployment, or political problems such as Watergate and the Iranian hostage crisis, one quickly comes to realize that the Believer value-formation period is dominated by physical, spiritual, and cultural exhaustion. It is useful to recall "Fred the Baker," the Dunkin' Donuts advertising pitchman introduced in 1981, who wearily sleepwalks back and forth to work intoning the litany "time to make the doughnuts." In such a milieu, simple pleasures come to matter a lot.

Menu changes and innovations throughout the period are instructive. Runaway inflation drives the cost of premium protein to untenable heights, and the restaurant world is suddenly flooded with "gourmet" hamburgers (instead of prime rib), fried veggie appetizers (instead of shrimp cocktails), salad bars, and the minimalist high-style offerings of nouvelle cuisine. Positioning dwells on freshness, fun, and garnish aesthetics that make life seem just a little less oppressive and colorless.

While quick-serve restaurants are certainly an everyday-since-birth fact of life for Believers, as much convenience as destination, the key to this Value Population is that they are still after that sense of escape. Tim Hackbardt, Vice President of Marketing for Del Taco, shares a relevant insight as he discusses the chain's key 18- to 34-year-old male demographic: "(Our key demographic) is looking for very large portions at very inexpensive prices. But when you sit down and ask them what they like about Del Taco, every one of them has a story about something cool that has happened in their lives at a Del Taco at 2 AM in the morning. They are still creating those memories."

Quick-Serve Restaurant Issues

Menu. Not much big meat focus (with the exception of steak house celebrations); into appetizers, fruits, veggies, and foods served with some artistic flourish; often happily fad-oriented yet gravitate towards the social security of brands; many are without even rudimentary home cooking skills.

Service and Atmosphere. Require a total lack of discomfort and hostility in the "vibe"; respond well to contemporary aesthetics and empathic service; like friendly social scenes.

Price/Value. Born into real economic duress one might expect price to be everything, but this is a group that can be up sold with literal and conceptual "freshness"; group-oriented and comfortable with taking on debt, they somewhat easily share money with peers.

Nutrition. Significant body consciousness here, and dietary sensitivity is high; nevertheless, there is also a tendency to try out different behaviors, and one might well think of the Believers as "cigarette smoking vegetarians."

Marketing. Many marketers have appropriately fixed on the strong social orientation of this population; nevertheless, frequent emphasis upon gross humor may not be as effective as an emphasis on kindness and empathy; orientation to children will prove important (painful memories versus wanting to do better).

Employees. Tricky; Believer women formed their values during an era of feminist empowerment and seem generally both capable and ambitious; young men of the era had less effective role models and often seem to equate diligent commitment with the life of Fred the Baker; "luck" is sometimes the plan.

Believer Notables

1973. Miller Lite is born to the slogan: "Everything you always wanted in a beer. And less." Company begins long campaign to put macho spin on feminist-era product.

1979. Coke airs the legendary Mean Joe Green ad in which the fierce Pittsburgh Steeler tosses his game jersey to a kid in thanks for a Coke. It is a totally on-target tearjerker.

1982. Wolfgang Puck opens Spago. Little pizzas are made available in designer flavors.

TRANSFORMERS: "WHERE'S THE BEEF?"

Value Population Overview

Born:	**1984–1995**
Size:	**16% of U.S. Population**

Although still in their childhood and adolescence, one may safely assume that this Value Population will aggressively lay claim to a share of the world's wealth and power. Whereas the Believers who preceded them appear to have accepted peace as a path through turmoil, the Transformers have received their value conditioning in an era that endorses a far more energetic, bold, and competitive approach towards personal survival and self-satisfaction. Created in a complex time of personal and economic power resurgence amidst dangerous chaos, built by the speed and perception-bending qualities of the computer age, and fraught with streetwise intelligence about what separates winners and losers, the fate of the already exquisitely adept and savvy Transformers is very likely to be written on their terms.

Cultural Menu. Return To Strong U.S. Political Leadership; Economic Boom; Cold War Ends—USSR Dissolves; Wall Street Rules; Black Culture Ascends; Geological and Humanmade Disasters; Chaos Theory; Aids Epidemic; Personal Computer Proliferation.

Some Key Personalities. Ronald Reagan, Bill Clinton, Michael Jordan, Arnold Schwarzenegger, Oprah, Ivan Boesky.

Primary Population Values (Partial List). Power, Clarity, Perseverance, Fidelity.

Quick-Serve Restaurant History

Transformers will simply not be victimized. Even if the oldest of them is now merely 20 (2005), there is broad spiritual kinship with Clara Peller, the aged actress who first famously stood at the order counter of a Wendy's competitor, in 1984, stared at a miniscule beef patty on an oversized bun and demanded to know "where's the beef?" Peller's plea captured the historical moment to perfection, as the resurgent Reagan era bred a new sort of red meat mentality in a nation that had become gastronomically distracted by exotic fruits, tiny vegetables, and the effete preciousness of nouvelle cuisine.

The key here is more towards attitude than menu. Not long after the Wendy's campaign launched, Burger King brought in "Herb the Nerd," a poor nebbishy soul who had never eaten a Whopper, to pitch its corporate wares. The campaign was a monumental failure as the era of pulling for, or identifying with, the underdog was quite simply over.

Ultimately, the Transformers are about obtaining and exercising power. While there are many implications for quick-service restaurants in this observation, chief among them may be that this is a generation of kids who, if not ready to be perceived as adults, will just not tolerate the condescension and manipulation frequently aimed at children. They may accept the bribe of a free toy with their meal, but they also are quite aware that dad's getting a bigger burger.

"I actually do believe that today's ten-year-old is a lot more sophisticated," offers Joe Adney, Senior Director of Marketing for Baskin-Robbins. "It is amazing how much they tend to mirror adult tastes versus kids of 20 or 30 years ago. I'd definitely say that the current group of 12-and-ups tends to brand emulate their parents."

Scott McCullough, Director of Marketing for Fuddruckers, takes it even a step further. His observation is that the Fuddruckers produce and toppings bar concept appeals to today's adolescents because it confers control of the dining experience to them.

"What a wonderful thing it is for a teen to order a 2/3-pound burger and pile on the toppings," says McCullough. "It is a huge thing to them to have authority over these decisions. They love affirming their identity."

Quick-Serve Restaurant Issues

Menu. An expanded concept of "traditional" foods includes the likes of focaccia, fajitas, and noodle bowls, but Transformers favor the familiar and seem generationally indisposed to the purely avant-garde; early signs point to adult tastes in spices, dipping sauces, and portion sizes; "new traditionalist" label fits.

Service and Atmosphere. Advantage to quick-serve restaurant is that this group pretty much expects food to be ready when they want it; disadvantage is that they will not accept being faceless patron fodder for "the system."

Price/Value. Born into the era of the value meal and preternaturally savvy about money, this group is being programmed to expect a bargain.

Nutrition. The jury is still out; this is the first generation to receive comprehensive education regarding the personal and social benefits of proper nutrition, but they are suspicious of nutritional authority being wielded as a political and economic power.

Marketing. They frequently respond to the bold, sexy, and sometimes violently competitive icons of their generation; must not be talked down to or suspect that they are being "handled."

Employees. Seriously ambitious, they fully intend to work their way to the top and will employ practice, perseverance, and cunning to get there; they will respect authority only if it is competent and willing to coach.

Transformer Notables

1987. The California Raisin Board introduces the claymation raisins. Black culture goes mainstream on the sports pages, the stage, and the street.

1990. The first Jamba Juice opens. A nation begins turning towards energy additives and nutriceuticals to help produce an edge.

1993. The Food Network premiers. Simultaneously, the culinary mano a mano that is to become the network's biggest phenomenon, *Iron Chef,* premiers in Japan.

Part Four

OPENING NEW AVENUES: MANAGING TALENT AND FINDING TRENDS

While the first three parts of this book focused on describing and applying Value Population research to better understand and connect with customers, Part 4 broadens this approach and opens new avenues from which the reader can additionally benefit: internally, toward workforce management, and externally, toward the early identification of trends.

In Chapter 24, "Attitudes at Work," the benefits of lasting values will be discussed as an effective tool for attracting, training, motivating, coordinating, compensating, and retaining a strong workforce. Furthermore, the recognition of the "intergenerational mix" of Value Populations *within* the workforce provides a constant object lesson as to how the corresponding Value Populations *outside* an organization, i.e., the customers, may be best understood and conceptually approached on a values basis.

In Chapter 25, "Attracting Trends," a proprietary method developed by Near Bridge, Inc., that uses cutting edge thinking in regard to chaos theory to uncover and predict trends is discussed and an example of its use with two Near Bridge clients, the United States Potato Board and the Foodservice and Packaging Industry is presented.

The final chapter of this book, Chapter 26, "The Age of Meaning," offers executives and entrepreneurs additional ways to use Value Population research to increase their market penetration and financial profitability.

24

ATTITUDES AT WORK

With a broadly reported decline in job loyalty and a projected decrease in skilled workers creating a dangerous double whammy for business, it is particularly important that business professionals pay close attention to what motivates, grows, and retains workers. Because of this, more and more companies today understand that they are not only marketing to external customers, but to internal ones as well.

Current demographic trends confirm that we are entering into an era that will be characterized by the most generationally and ethnically diverse workforce in American history. Value Population research is of enormous value in identifying the natural team players (Believers), the personality marketers (Performers), the efficiency experts (Techticians), and the population that may well be coming along to eat everyone's lunch (Transformers).

Motivation and collaboration are the keys to a well-oiled workforce, and Near Bridge Value Population insights will certainly help anyone who has to negotiate the human resources "minefield."

In the following pages we explore the attitudes of the Value Populations with regard to their orientation toward work, including such areas as: styles, motivation, talent, relationships, and rewards. At the end of each section is a set of key workplace attributes intended to provide the reader an overview of the Value Populations attitudes within the work environment.

PATRIOTS: THE PLEDGE OF ALLEGIANCE

Now in their 60s and 70s, Patriots are quickly fading from the employment ranks. Yet, many businesses still act as if the work-related values of the Patriots are the values of more contemporary groups, and, therefore, it is important to at least briefly consider their orientation to work and the workplace because theirs is the lingering paradigm.

As a result of a confluence of factors—the First World War and its attendant manufacturing requirements; large-scale immigration; and the emergent mass popularization of such consumer goods as the automobile, the radio, and the telephone—the Patriots are the first truly modern and mass industrialized population. It is in the Patriot value-formation period when broad society encounters the struggle between the dehumanizing requirements of assembly line work and the emotional needs of human beings. Due to value formation during a Global Depression, the fierce motivational force of money and general material security is also never far from conscious consideration.

As has already been suggested throughout this book, the resolution of Patriot needs lies in the cultivation of material rewards and the establishment of a useful personal role within a group definition. Fear of want, an understanding that life is hard, a shared bearing of burdens, and the security of "creed-based collectivism" are rolled up in this population. In this group there is an especially strong gravitation to the one-man-in-charge, drill sergeant archetype—strong and blustery leaders whose mission is to vigilantly protect the well-being and the creed of the group, gregariousness and graciousness be damned.

Not surprisingly, much of the business theory that emerges in the Patriot value formation era pertains to mass production, from quality control to social implications. Notions of "scientific management" begin to proliferate, extolling such virtues as efficiency, trained skills, and sacrifice of the individuality to the system—a workplace philosophy with profit benefits to the owners and overtones of dependability, and therefore security, to the workers. The problem here, as eloquently pointed out in the classic Charlie Chaplin movie *Modern Times* (1936) and referenced earlier in this book, is that a workplace based solely upon "scientific principles" is quite capable of beating the humanity right out of you.

Along these lines, perhaps the most useful theorist when it comes to an appreciation of Patriot workplace values is George Elton Mayo, a Harvard Business School professor, who between the years 1927 and 1932 conducted a series of studies at the Western Electric Hawthorne Works in Chicago. His research involved isolating teams of assembly line workers and monitoring their productivity as they were subjected to variables relating to the fatigue and monotony of their work. These isolated teams were monitored by an observer who explained to the groups what was transpiring and solicited their input and reactions regarding the particulars of the study.

What Mayo discovered, in a series of conclusions that have collectively come to be known as The Hawthorne Effect, is that the specific study variables (break periods, working hours, work weeks, work techniques, and environments, etc.) had far less a predictable impact on productivity than the simple fact that the groups were being formed, observed, and consulted. What apparently motivated the groups (and productivity did rise in almost every case regardless of variables) was observation by a superior and the bonding dynamics of the group itself.

While the privations of the Depression era witnessed a corresponding rise in fear-based workplace motivation, there is little denying that a group ethos, coupled with meaningful personal stature within the group, is the key principle of productivity.

The security orientation of the Patriots may be amply evidenced in their present day concern with retirement plans and Social Security, but the Patriot value keynote has been and always will be group participation, group loyalty, and group approval. Patriots are very loyal workers and do well in positions that work to serve the organization as a whole. When marketing work to Patriots, security of their job must not be breached. In the end, the best way to motivate Patriots is through clear direction, strong leadership, safety for the group, and a pledge of, "one Nation under God, indivisible, with liberty and justice for all." See Figure 24.1.

FIGURE 24.1
Key Patriot Workplace Attributes

The big metaphor	→	Military
Work nature	→	Defensive
The leader is	→	A drill sergeant
The follower is	→	A soldier
Key strength	→	Loyalty
Fear/Vulnerability	→	Loss of security
Conflict technique	→	Defensiveness
Resolution technique	→	Assurance
Tends to avoid	→	Innovation
Training	→	Group instruction
Rejuvenation	→	Rest
Reward beside dollars	→	Security
Coin of the realm	→	Money

PERFORMERS: I'VE GOTTA BE ME!

The landmark insight for anyone who wants to understand a Performer boss, colleague, or employee is contained in the work of Abraham Maslow, a founder of the field of humanistic psychology. It is in Maslow's article, *A Theory of Motivation* (1943), that he first introduces the notion of a "hierarchy of human needs." In it Maslow sets forth the premise that after a human being satisfies basic survival needs such as food and shelter, and after addressing such security needs as group belonging, and even after experiencing love, a human being can find greatest fulfillment in the exaltation of his or her individuality through "peak experiences" leading to self-actualization and personal transcendence.

To the Patriots, such a worldview flies in the face of the centrality of the collective and to the Techticians, who will be considered next, humanistic psychology is plainly self-indulgent, unscientific, and inefficient. Yet to accept the Performers on their own terms is to accept the fact that to them direct personal experience is a great, maybe the greatest, good. Noisy, restless, profligate, pontificating, overly-dramatic, and self-referential though they may sometimes be, at this point in their advanced career lives, Performers are becoming increasingly more prized for the real wisdom that has accrued through lives that have been far more active than passive, and far more bravely intuitive than safely tactical.

A December 2003 *USA Today* article reported, "In the battle for jobs during this jobless expansion, workplace veterans over 50 have caught up to and may soon surpass their younger rivals when it comes to finding new positions in the shortest amount of time. The median search time for unemployed executive-level staffers 50 and older has dropped 10 times faster than that of younger job seekers." While Performers are easily bored and demand considerable attention, their breadth of experience translates into very attractive big picture capabilities. Particularly, a lifelong interest regarding what others outside "the tribe" think and do is paying dividends for smart companies in a global environment. Naturally gifted in such interpersonal disciplines as sales and marketing, enthusiastically oriented toward consideration of foreign cultures, and generally able to go with the flow when the unexpected occurs, this group may find mentoring, of both younger colleagues and consumers, a perfect marriage of personal needs and the needs of the American economy.

In a February 6, 2004, press release, The Home Depot, the world's largest home improvement retailer, and AARP, the leading membership organization for the 50+ population with over 35 million members, announced a national partnership to attract, motivate, and retain eligible older workers as part-time and full-time associates in new and existing stores across the country.

"This hiring partnership with AARP is a great opportunity for The Home Depot to attract qualified, knowledgeable, and skilled individuals to work as associates in our stores," said Bob Nardelli, Chairman, President and CEO of The Home Depot. "AARP has a broad national reach with the mature workforce making it a powerful resource and an ideal organization for Home Depot to partner with for a national hiring initiative. At The Home Depot, we believe knowledge, experience, and passion never retire."

Bob Nardelli is on to something with both his description of key Performer qualities and his "never retire" observation. When one considers the broad financial ramifications of downturns in the economy coupled with the Performers' sense of material entitlement, and when one acknowledges that the prevailing Performer sense of "retirement" is one of active engagement rather than restful retreat, it becomes clear that Performers have every intention of working later into life than any previous population.

A 2003 Towers Perrin study, "Redefining Retirement in the 21st Century," provides additional insight into this phenomenon. Although retirement has traditionally involved a period of leisure following a 30-year to 40-year career, 78 percent of employee respondents said they expect to continue working in some capacity well into their retirement years. Of these respondents, 64 percent expect to work part time, while 57 percent plan to change occupations. Significantly, 35 percent of those employees who expect to continue working into their retirement years said they would continue working for financial reasons, while more respondents—43 percent—said they would work chiefly to stay involved and active.

Ultimately the Performers are a group that will continue working because of material needs but also, and far more importantly, because of the continued possibilities for personal discovery and fulfillment. Performers are terrific leaders of a cause and do well in positions requiring strategic thinking and enthusiasm. They are very well-suited for sales and marketing positions and make excellent recruiters and human resource managers. When marketing work to Performers, *personal dignity* must not be compromised. Sincere praise and appreciation goes a long way here as well. See Figure 24.2.

FIGURE 24.2
Key Performer Workplace Attributes

The big metaphor	→	Theatre
Work nature	→	Strategic
The leader is	→	A star
The follower is	→	An actor
Key strength	→	Curiosity
Fear/Vulnerability	→	Personal disrespect
Conflict technique	→	Self-importance
Resolution technique	→	Concern
Tends to avoid	→	Detail work
Training	→	Bells and whistles
Rejuvenation	→	Travel and adventure
Reward beside dollars	→	Status
Coin of the realm	→	Enthusiasm

TECHTICIANS: IT ALL ADDS UP

No less of a shift in workplace consciousness than that from the Patriots to the Performers takes place when one moves from the Performers to the Techticians. The most obvious dividing line here is information technology. The average Techtician worker has more faith in the abilities of his computer to rationally and efficiently model reality than in the insights and agendas of his human colleagues to create a rational and efficient reality—particularly the non-Techtician ones.

As discussed in the previous section of this book, Techticians formed their values in a hopeful era characterized by vast scientific advances and a belief in mankind's ability to adapt this science to the broad political, economic, social, and environmental benefit of mankind. Sadly, due to the Vietnam War era and its society wrenching value conflicts between Patriots and Performers, Techticians have apparently come to the somewhat cynical conclusion that only the science, and not the big picture social agendas, has any real clarity and objective truth.

At the risk of oversimplification, Techticians are really "skeptical pragmatists" at heart. They are Dilberts to the pointy-haired bosses, Mr. Spocks to the Captain Kirks. Mistrustful of abstraction, particularly in such attitudinal business areas as marketing, these are the individuals who deify data and measurement. What matters most are circuitry and task, the efficient organization and flow of information for the solution of specific issues, not ruminations regarding the greater society or the corporate master plan.

A key to understanding the Techtician value system is their belief that most any business issue can and should be addressed with a spreadsheet, a flow chart, or a formula. For example, Greg Diamond, Techtician, founder, and managing partner of Clovis, a staffing firm in Gaithersburg, Maryland, uses a formula to decide whether it is more cost-effective to hire an employee or hire a temp as was pointed out by Chris Pentilla in *Entrepreneur Magazine,* July 2004.

Even in sports such as baseball, as Michael Lewis adeptly describes in his book, *Moneyball,* professional scouts increasingly rely on the laptop over the clipboard with legal pad to do their jobs. *PC Magazine* has identified a segment of largely Techtician-age knowledge workers that they call "The New Geeks." Basically, these workers are bringing their computer-based statistical backgrounds into fields other than traditional IT. Steve Lohr wrote the following in the July 2004 *PC Magazine:*

> Andrew Davenport, a 36-year-old researcher at IBM, has a background that is both deeply technical and academically rigorous. His field of expertise is mathematical optimization, and his Ph.D. in computer science was in optimization constraint programming, followed by postdoctoral research . . . Davenport is one of the New Geeks, people who are technically trained but also have the ability and inclination to work comfortably in other disciplines like business, the sciences, and the social sciences. They personify the future of computing as its impact spreads further. Computing has already helped transform everything from the way scientists plumb the mysteries of biology, chemistry, and physics to the way Detroit designs cars and Hollywood makes movies. As it moves increasingly beyond traditional calculation, computer science is inevitably becoming more interdisciplinary, introducing the computing arts to a wider circle of people.

The downside to the Techtician approach to work, at least in the eyes of other Value Populations, is that Techticians most often would rather be correct than useful. People skills and relationships tend to suffer when data is made king, as data-based conclusions foster rigid attitudes about objective truths and right or wrong answers. An example of the attitude and tone many Techticians bring to work is found in the title of a recent book by organizational consultant John Hoover, *How to Work for an Idiot.* This title clearly articulates the frustration Techticians feel when confronting Performer bosses—who may be more dramatic, self-referential, and intuitive rather than practical, self-effacing, and logical.

FIGURE 24.3

Key Techtician Workplace Attitudes

The big metaphor	→	Laboratory
Work nature	→	Tactical
The leader is	→	A tactician
The follower is	→	A service provider
Key strength	→	Industriousness
Fear/Vulnerability	→	Outdated skills
Conflict technique	→	Sabotage
Resolution technique	→	Interest
Tends to avoid	→	Conceptual work
Training	→	Self-administered
Rejuvenation	→	Continuing education
Reward beside dollars	→	Personal development
Coin of the realm	→	Information

When in the service of a leader who has a coherent vision, Techticians can be remarkably swift and capable in realizing and appreciating the specifics of a strategy or plan. What is particularly interesting, though, is that Techticians are now becoming the corporate leaders, the culture creators, and the visionaries of workplace organizations. When one considers the Techtician predilection toward micromanaging, and a worldview in which data collection is never quite complete, it does not necessarily add up that members of this group, whose loyalties are task oriented, will be able to effectively set strategy over the long haul.

Ultimately, Techticians tend to stay around as long as their jobs make not just dollars, but *personal sense*. Work that is well-defined on a task level, where new career-enhancing skills may be acquired, and loyalty is defined by contribution rather than longevity, is the motivational ticket for this group. Techticians often handle pressure well, although, often with cynicism, and have a cultural-biased disposition for positions requiring analysis such as engineering, manufacturing, material control, accounting, and program management—and when working with Techticians, for God's sake (and yours), keep your meetings short and your technology up to date! See Figure 24.3.

BELIEVERS: THE CULTURE CLUB

Much about the Believer Value Population is frustrating to those who subscribe to the protestant ethic that "life's rewards come from hard work." Unlike the Techticians, Believers do not easily resonate with the merits of duty, details, and discipline. Believers are convinced that objectives have an inconsistent relationship with outcomes and often avoid stress by assuming that "grace" will prevail.

Considering the various traumas of the Believer value-formation period—energy shortages, economic malaise, challenges to family morals, weak leadership—history has taught this group that the most important thing they can do in life is to pick their friends, associates, and significant others well. Then, even in the most oppressive of environments, one will have like-spirited allies to make the hard times seem easier. Beyond that, all one really needs is faith that "the ship" is eventually going to come in.

As a group that defines itself through peer relationships, there is at first glance something vaguely reminiscent of the Patriots here. However, Believers are far less willing to go along with authority just because of a title on the door and far less likely to accept relentless pain as the price of a paycheck. They are also far less accepting of oppressive cultures that are imposed upon them by "accidents" of tradition or birth. Yet, ironically, participation in a coherent culture *is* of the essence.

A fertile area for studying Believer work-related values is the retail industry, whose store-level jobs are for the most part presently held by Believers. Despite enormous general turnover rates (close to 50 percent per year), some companies such as Starbucks and Petco are doing an exceptional job of worker retention. These companies understand that workers of Believer age are adamant about work being an extension of personal values.

In the May, 2004 issue of *California Jobs Journal,* Michael Kinsman writes that Petco, with more than 650 stores and more than 15,000 employees, retains employees by viscerally engaging them in their work at the value level. "Turnover is all about the right hire," declares spokesman Don Cowan. "It really begins for us in function and fit. Do they have the skill sets we need and how do they fit in. The fit here is about how they fit in the culture." Consequently, Petco seeks to hire people who like animals and relate to them well. "We have living, breathing animals," Cowan stresses. "We want to keep people engaged by hiring the kind of people that will relate to them."

John Izzo, author of *Values-Shift: The New Work Ethic and What It Means for Business,* does an excellent job of addressing some of the realities and implications of the Believer-age population in the workplace. He notes that this is an age group that expects to find social fulfillment at work, with spontaneous celebrations, job-related friendships, and even marriages rapidly proliferating at this time. A study of recent college graduates, reports Izzo, reveals that for two-thirds of this group, "work life will never be more important than personal life." This suggests that wise employers will recognize this attitude about timely recognition, relationships, and fun, and will build it into the corporate culture.

An unusual corporate freebie that some companies have adopted for their single employees is dating agency membership. Rachel Basger, business development director at the dating agency Club Sirius, explains in a May 2004 *Managing Information Strategies Magazine* article, "Some people have the view that people in a relationship are happier, more productive, and easier to retain. As a result, some companies have membership as a perk for staff who are relocating, as otherwise they can get lonely in the evenings. They want them to have a good balance between work and life."

Similarly, one catches an interesting glimpse of a Believer value manifestation in the *blogging* phenomenon. Blogging, the creation of personality-intensive online diaries, is a business communications strategy with great appeal for Believers—who need to feel a human connection with others about their work.

A June 2004 *Business Week Online* article reported that executives are increasingly encouraging employee blogs as a way to personalize customer transactions with an otherwise faceless behemoth. Microsoft has been one of the biggest evangelists. A year ago, it had about 100 corporate bloggers. Today there are 800. They post pictures of company refrigerators—there's one that has all Coke and one that has all Pepsi—and spout off on everything from the death of Boots the cat to renaming Longhorn, Microsoft's long-anticipated new operating system, "Longwait." Furthermore, says *Business Week Online,* Microsoft Chairman William H. Gates III is so certain that corporate blogging is the next gold rush in communications that, "he's practically handing out the pails and shovels by enabling any employee to create a blog within two seconds." Microsoft does not teach employees to blog, but it does allow employees to hold meetings to talk about them. The blogs carry disclaimers, but other than that, "our unspoken policy on blogging is: Don't be stupid," says Microsoft product manager Adam Sohn.

It is interesting to contemplate how members of this group will eventually fair as leaders. While there is definitely some aversion to conflict and distaste for exercising authority that is often integral to action, the members of this Value Population may accomplish much through peer consensus building in a generally supportive culture.

As followers, Believers are in a very difficult position. While Techticians struggle with Performer bosses who don't seem to care about the details and seem to focus too much on the drama of the situation, there is a natural order in a boss who is strategic and a subordinate who is tactical.

Unfortunately for business, no such natural order is found as Techticians, who just want to get things done, tend to be unemotionally direct in their management style, and now manage Believers who want to build consensus among all of the players before a decision is made.

Fortunately, for the Techtician manager who understands this issue, there is a solution—consultative management. Unlike consensus management, which is often slow because it seeks complete group approval to resolve issues, consultative management, a more efficient and often a more effective process, encourages the voices of all to be heard, but gives final authority of the decision to the manager. Consultative management meets the needs of both Value Populations as Believers get to be heard and Techticians get abundant information and the ability to move forward quickly.

Because Believers are truly team players, they do well in positions requiring strong emotional support and interaction such as human resources, training, customer support, and call center operation. Never motivated by fear, Believers prefer flight to fight in difficult situations; and in the Believer world, the quality of the work will always be linked to the quality of the relationships. See Figure 24.4.

FIGURE 24.4
Key Believer Workplace Attributes

The big metaphor	→	Social club
Work nature	→	Communal
The leader is	→	A consensus developer
The follower is	→	A team player
Key strength	→	Charm
Fear/Vulnerability	→	Peer conflict
Conflict technique	→	Passive resistance
Resolution technique	→	Appreciation
Tends to avoid	→	Conflict
Training	→	Group participation
Rejuvenation	→	Socializing
Reward beside dollars	→	Inclusion
Coin of the realm	→	Relationships

TRANSFORMERS: THE ART OF WAR

Although they have yet to enter the workforce in a meaningful way, Transformers are bound to take their work lives very seriously. As has been discussed earlier in this book, Transformers already tend to see life as a competition for increasingly limited resources. For Transformers, the business avatars are likely to be individuals such as Lee Iaccoca, who in his 1984 autobiography writes that the most important qualities in a job candidate are "fire in the belly" and "street smarts," and the Sun-Tzu quoting fictional capitalist Gordon Gecko, who in the 1987 movie *Wall Street* puts forth the proposition that "greed captures the essence of the evolutionary spirit."

One of the great misperceptions in today's marketplace is that today's Transformer teens are essentially like the social, flirty, financially blithe, trend-following Believer teens who have just vacated their adolescent years. While some life-phase echoes of Believers do linger, Transformers are infinitely more particular when it comes to statements of personal style, group dynamics, price/value relationships, and the perception of what matters in securing a successful future. Most importantly, to consumer marketers and future employers alike, the Transformers are fierce rejecters of manipulation.

It is worth noting that Believers spent their teen years in the boom economy of the 1990s, attending high school and college during a period of robust employment opportunities and apparently stress-free career paths. No such illusions exist for the Transformers, who are now battling to obtain the entry-level retail jobs and largely menial summer employment positions that are now increasingly occupied by older workers pushed down the employment ladder.

According to an analysis by the Center for Labor Market Studies at Northeastern University in Boston, as reported in *USA Today,* May 3, 2004, the annual teen employment rate tumbled from 45 percent in 2000 to 37 percent in 2003—the lowest since the figure was first tracked in 1948.

"Kids are doing worse this year than last," says Andrew Sum, the center's director. "The job growth hasn't filtered down. If anything like this happened to the adult workforce, you'd call it a depression. It's that severe."

The implications of this state of affairs are intriguing. On one hand, Transformers are likely to acknowledge that entering the employment arena is going to be difficult, requiring the cultivation of skill, courage, foresight, persistence, responsibility, useful contacts, and the ability to endure tradition and authority as a right of passage. On the other hand, this situation is making them more astute, avaricious, and angry, such that given their value predispositions they may well come to regard business as a battlefield in a way that is only slightly metaphorical—making them the perfect "corporate soldiers." Transformers will bring training, concentration, generally solid instincts, a bias for taking action, and easily identifiable motivations regarding money and power into the work arena. More and more reports speak to what may well be a rare cohort confluence of skill, savvy, and ambition. The best and brightest of them will have a lifelong appreciation for the twin virtues of preparation and patience—and an innate grasp of technology that has been developing from birth.

According to the results from Junior Achievement's 2003 JA Enterprise Poll of more than 1,100 teens, reported in *Better Homes and Gardens,* February 2004, while teens find the idea of starting their own business alluring, such dreams appear to be firmly grounded in reality. The teens also showed that they were aware of the challenges and risks involved in a start-up, the necessary preparation to be successful, and trade-offs between working for others and being self-employed. Of the students surveyed, 88 percent also acknowledged a college education would be a factor contributing to their ultimate success

Indeed, some companies are already starting to transform*er* themselves. For example, per *QSR Magazine,* July 2004, Dan Cathy, CEO of Chick-fil-A, volunteered during an executive roundtable that his company is now doing more and more management-track recruitment of "mission capable" teens, some as young as age 15 and 16. Parents are involved in the interview process, and grades, as well as character, must be exemplary. "They bring competence, character, and chemistry," says Cathy, "and they put passion into it."

Transformers understand that apprenticeship is part of the game—but not forever, and they will quickly expect to move up in the organization, or even run it, once they have mastered the required skills. They will do well in almost any position that requires savvy thinking, heightened competition, and winning results such as legal, sales, and product design. Transformers are motivated by responsibility and power, and ultimately, may prove to be the most business-oriented of all the Value Populations. See Figure 24.5.

Understanding, anticipating, and meeting the needs of current and potential customers is the fundamental role of marketing, but to be successful in this quest requires many people working in unison. Understanding the workplace attitudes of different Value Populations gives

FIGURE 24.5
Key Transformer Workplace Attributes

The big metaphor	→	Street gang
Work nature	→	Assured
The leader is	→	A champion
The follower is	→	A challenger
Key strength	→	Courage
Fear/Vulnerability	→	Marginalization
Conflict technique	→	Engagement
Resolution technique	→	Compromise
Tends to avoid	→	The weak
Training	→	Competency-based
Rejuvenation	→	Competition
Reward beside dollars	→	Responsibility
Coin of the realm	→	Power

marketing executives a competitive advantage in that it allows them to create stronger and more balanced marketing organizations, effectively recruit and retain good employees, reduce the friction between team members, and better motivate their teams. So in the end, they can spend less time managing their people and more time searching for ways to uncover or, better yet, attract trends.

25

ATTRACTING TRENDS

By now it should be clear that Value Population analysis focuses on consistent *lifelong* values rather than *transitory* mass behaviors—or trends. As temporary and conditional as trends may sometimes be, however, they are certainly the stuff of which opportunities are made, and forecasting, or better yet attracting trends, is a profitable marketing strategy.

While many consulting groups and advertising agencies are in the business of forecasting trends, most of this "trend prediction" is not so much predictive as it is an early recognition of already observed behaviors. Generally, there is little acknowledgment that in our very complex and kaleidoscopic world, trends most often just emerge randomly and spontaneously. Value Population analysis contends that a systematic approach to evaluating change in terms of consistent values is of much greater worth to marketers than simply capturing random events that are already sliding into the past.

CHAOS THEORY

Chaos Theory helps to explain this systematic approach with its notion of the *strange attractor.* Not as well known as the "butterfly effect," i.e., the power of the tiniest force to elicit extraordinarily profound and random disruptions in a system over time, the somewhat diametrically

opposed "strange attractor" principle deals with the tendency of a chaotic system to spontaneously organize itself around what are at first seemingly random and arbitrary points within the system.

Why, it is reasonable for professional marketers to ask, do consumers become so suddenly and passionately, albeit temporarily, enamored
with oddities? Why are boy bands and Britney Spears the center of the
cultural universe for a season and then old news? What makes carbohy-
drates such a pillar of healthy living one year and such a pillory the next?

Near Bridge addresses this phenomenon of the random and spontaneous emergence of short-term trends through an understanding of
macro value factors we term *Trend Attractors*™.

UNIVERSAL TREND ATTRACTORS™

Issues such as globalization, security, technology, education, poverty,
and the environment are all examples of *Universal Trend Attractors*. Despite the daily random chaos of life on our planet, these are some of the
issues around which we all form our *present* basic understanding of civilization and through which we express some of our deepest values.
While each Value Population is predisposed toward certain and unique
valuations of these issues, every one of these issues touches the value ma-
trices of every Value Population.

Thus, the first principle in Trend Attractor analysis is to identify how
the apparently spontaneous emergence of trends may or may not be integrated with each Value Population's relationship to Universal Trend
Attractors. Is a given new product merely stylish, or does it address in
some fashion the primal value structure of the group(s)? Does a particular pitch merely call for a passing glance, or does it subliminally connect with consumers at their greatest depth of understanding regarding
the way society itself must be perceived and understood?

Trend power and longevity are largely related to how deeply ingrained a phenomenon is with the individual value interpretations that
the Value Populations make with the Universal Trend Attractors.

SITUATIONAL TREND ATTRACTORS™

A subsequent Trend Attractor phenomenon occurs in the valuation of
specific trend phenomena. Whenever a company or an industry addresses
the development of a strategic response to a trend, they are actually con-

fronting a set of *Situational Trend Attractors*. As will be illustrated in the project example that shortly follows, Situational Trend Attractors are the macro factors around which we presently form our basic understanding of a particular industry, product, service, or cultural phenomenon.

Thus, for example, if we are looking at an increase in wine consumption among American consumers, we are considering all of the Situational Trend Attractors surrounding wine. These may range from issues of connoisseurship to issues of health to issues of social responsibility to issues of leisure, etc. In most cases, the closer the relationship a Situational Trend Attractor has with a variety of Universal Trend Attractors, the more powerful factor it will be in qualifying the importance of a trend.

In the Near Bridge system, identifying Situational Trend Attractors and putting them through the filters of the various Value Populations yields practical insights into the market forms that messages, products, and services should take with each Value Population in the successful capitalization of a trend. Intriguingly, a company or an industry may well define a set of Situational Trend Attractors independent of a specific trend phenomenon, and by pushing these Situational Trend Attractors through the Value Population lenses, can identify and quantify, or more powerfully, create likely trends!

WORKING WITH TRENDS

A pair of projects undertaken by Near Bridge for nonaffiliated trade organizations, the United States Potato Board and the Foodservice and Packaging Institute, helps to clarify this Trend Attractor approach. Both of these organizations directed Near Bridge to consider their primary products in a specific context. For the United States Potato Board, it was potential at-home potato usage in the context of a growing number of smaller one-person and two-person households. For the Foodservice and Packaging Institute, it was the role of single-serve disposable packaging in the context of a rapidly burgeoning take-home meal phenomenon.

In both instances, it became clear that there were some significant overlapping issues. For example, in the broadest sense of "trend," both assignments entailed an evaluation of a consumer's decision to dine at home rather than to eat in a restaurant; and that being the case, there is an inherently similar set of Trend Attractors, both Universal and Situational, brought to bear on the diverse particulars of the assignments.

While the significance and strength of a particular Trend Attractor is not always of equal importance in the separate projects, nor do they necessarily figure with equal prominence in the values of the various Value Populations, here is a list of some of the Trend Attractors and some of the questions that were raised during these projects.

- *Time and convenience.* In this case, this Trend Attractor is Situational as well as Universal. Nearly everyone reports time stress these days. But given some discretionary recuperation time, is the member of a particular Value Population likely to fill it up with chores or to pursue pleasurable activities—or to just "give it a rest?"
- *Menu entitlement.* Today's consumers are exposed to an enormous amount of culinary variety and choice including, cuisines, cook styles, customized ingredients, garnishes, and price points. When dining at home, which of these are likely to be more important? Is variety itself a two-edged sword to some Value Populations?
- *Social situation.* The United States Potato Board project stipulated one-person and two-person households, but is this meal part of an evening of work, an evening of romance, or an evening of collapsing in front of the television set—and are these activities looked at similarly by each Value Population?
- *Health and nutrition.* No dining occasion is devoid of dietary bird-dogging these days. Being healthy and staying healthy, or at least staying thin, is a top priority. But how does nutritional prudence and sound dietary practice vary between the Value Populations?
- *Safety.* Admittedly, this is more of an issue to the membership of the Foodservice and Packaging Institute than to the United States Potato Board. But, in either case, how differently does each Value Population define and understand safe practices regarding food transit, storage, and preparation?
- *Environmental impact.* To companies that manufacture single-serve disposables the issue of environmental impact looms large. But are there Value Populations so cause-oriented toward this issue that they even wonder if a potato peel is bad for the environment?
- *Brands.* Such a big buzzword these days! But what does a brand or label portend for different Value Populations—a guarantee of quality and timesaving convenience, or the feeling of romance and escape?
- *Fun factors.* Current "trends'" in the home improvement industry suggest that more and more people regard their homes as the one place left where they can have fun and still safely pursue creative personal expression. How does this figure into the Value Populations view of at-home dining?

- *Service.* Surveys indicate that service is still the number one area of concern for retail customers. As a packaging issue, the implications are multiple, including speed of service, materials dependability, and information labeling. Regarding at-home dining, does the perception of poor service in restaurants encourage greater eating-in frequency consistently in all Value Populations?
- *Fuel gauging.* Here is a good example of a Situational Trend Attractor that "suddenly" emerges. Until it becomes empirically clear that a rise in fuel costs depresses an industry's sales, insiders pooh-pooh the impact of an extra few dollars worth of gasoline on consumer discretionary spending. Aided by a burst of media attention, however, the twin issues of price and perception are suddenly on everyone's mind. How do the different Value Populations deal with the economic impact of a ride to the store?
- *Price/Value.* Arguably, this issue is, and will always be, the key to a consumer's soul. The less obvious questions are, how do the Value Populations differ in their orientation toward money and how does this affect their purchasing decisions?

"VALUING" TREND ATTRACTORS

While confidentiality and space requirements must limit the discussions of all the findings and recommendations associated with these two projects, here is an overview of some of the findings related to the previously mentioned Situational Trend Attractors in regard to Value Population values.

Performers

This Value Population strongly resonates with the Situational Trend Attractors of *Menu Entitlement* and *Fun Factors*. There is an expectation that dinner will have entertainment value, even if that entertainment is provided by the television. Performers gravitate to food that is internationally inspired, uniquely seasoned, colorful, and novel. They are often talkers and flirts, and they tend to value the social content of a meal as much as the sauce.

Recommendations:

- Recipes that can be described as "romantic" and "sexy" are top shelf with Performers.

- Performers, as the Value Population first exposed to TV Dinners, have some desire that food be packaged and presented as a novelty.

Techticians

Techticians have an inordinate sensitivity to the Situational Trend Attractor of *Time and Convenience,* having little patience for things that are unnecessarily complicated or take longer than seems reasonable. Dining experiences are, for the most part, vested with a desire for intelligence . . . stretching beyond efficiency to such Situational Trend Attractors as *Health, Environmental Impact,* and most certainly *Price/Value.*

Recommendations:

- At home, Techticians are particularly comfortable with healthy side dishes served alongside grilled items—enjoying the opportunity to master this relatively straightforward and expeditious cooking technique that also lends itself to further personal "perfecting" through discretionary seasoning and sauces.
- Regarding take-out packaging, Techticians expect spill-proof and sanitary materials—up to the task of temperature and texture retention.

Believers

Social Situation and *Brand* are two of the Situational Trend Attractors that loom large in the Believer worldview. If it looks good, it must be good. To Believers, a desirable brand, be it restaurant or packaged goods, is one that guarantees the delivery of "edible chic." It is important to keep in mind that this Value Population collectively has little culinary training, so *Safety* and *Convenience* and *Time* will always be part of the equation—even if they do not realize it.

Recommendations:

- Socially, Believers tend to be far more concerned with "trendy" aesthetics than tasty dishes and expect to look at something stylish on their plates.
- When Believers are by themselves, they are very likely to pursue some extremely easy and personally restorative indulgence—with

take-out and/or a microwave oven featuring prominently in their choices.

Patriots and Transformers

The scope of work undertaken for the United States Potato Board was confined to the three Value Populations listed above. Similarly, the Foodservice and Packaging Institute project acknowledged that the Patriots are not a key consumer group driving the take-home restaurant meal trend. However, it is interesting to consider some similarities between Patriots and the Transformers.

Although widely separated by age, these two Value Populations share a child-centric theme and certain culinary echoes—related to a similarity in attitude regarding the selection of what is personally pleasing and plentiful versus any marketing concept of what one "should" like. Thanks to life-phase considerations, while Patriots may always ask for their food to be hotter and Transformers never think their food is "cool" enough, both of these groups share a primal appreciation for food as emotional sustenance.

In the end, the age-segmentation process inherent to Value Population analysis is only one set of lenses appropriate to the discussion of Trend Attractors. Clearly, an analysis of Trend Attractors can also benefit from traditional demographic breakouts such as consumers' income, gender, education, ethnicity, location, and life phase. However, the Trend Attractor/Value Population approach is of particular benefit, in that it simultaneously embraces a consistent set of values while allowing for life to unfold in its often unpredictable ways.

To observant marketers, that concept is universally attractive—and highly profitable.

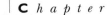

26

THE AGE OF MEANING

In the early 1980s, John Naisbitt's classic work *Megatrends* proclaimed that a profound shift had occurred in the nature of human affairs. According to Naisbitt, the world had demonstrably shifted from an Industrial Age to an Age of Information. Global society had become a realm in which "we now mass-produce information the way we used to mass-produce cars" and in which "everything comes in thirty-one flavors."

What is sometimes overlooked in Naisbitt's seminal work is that he also foresaw the negative as well as the positive implications of this new information age. Indeed, there is certainly both awe and appreciation expressed regarding the data-driven society exploding around him. But Naisbitt also astutely observed that, "we are drowning in information but starved for knowledge."

The concepts expressed in *The Consistent Consumer* are driven by the desire for data to evolve into something more cohesive and sustaining than "fact candy." While marketing may yet have much to derive from quantitative techniques, the beauty of addressing lasting values versus episodic behaviors is that values speak to clarity and longevity, and thereby offer real knowledge and the ability to apply it to daily business situations.

Proceeding from this knowledge of values, it becomes feasible to develop products and services, write marketing campaigns, institute hiring and training strategies, and create corporate cultures that partner with the future rather than simply pass through it. So many industries might benefit from this broad-perspective values-based approach. Consider the following.

Apparel Industry

Styles seem to always change from generation to generation. Today, for example, the clothing tastes of Believers, the group just leaving its teenage years, are radically different from today's teenagers, the Transformers. Transformer girls are far less into the flirtatious, skimpy, "Britney Spears" look and very much want the discrete option of dressing conservatively and not to be so overtly sexually objectified. A lot of apparel manufacturers and retailers haven't caught on to this yet. There's still a remarkable opportunity in this regard, and there will be for another decade.

Service Businesses

In service businesses, there is generally high personal contact with the individual customer. To "get the contract," it is important to quickly understand how to meet the customer's needs and how to interact with the customer appropriately. Whether you're running a cleaning firm or a repair business or a travel agency or a network marketing company, it's important to know, for example, that Techticians will generally go over your work with a fine-toothed comb and Patriots will be very upset if you overrun the price estimate or threaten their private physical or emotional environments. Performers, on the other hand, are less sensitive to these issues and generally like it when service people have entertaining personalities and show some true personal passion for their jobs.

Restaurant Management

Value Population research can address many issues in the restaurant management industry. Consider menu development, where Value Population principles can literally be applied to the subject of taste. With Performers, whose sense of self-determination is large, one has to include opportunities for personalized ingredient and topping options. Techticians will "grill" you if something represented as "authentic" is anything but authentic. Believers tend to opt for pleasing visual aesthetics and anything that the "in-crowd" has elevated to cult status this month.

Financial Products and Services

Anyone who sells a financial product or service can use Value Populations information to effectively improve their customer service and their close rate. Think about all the financial instruments available to an investor, ranging from stocks and bonds to hard assets to savings accounts to aggressive derivative products, and so on. Generational insight into risk tolerance and financial sophistication is of incredible value to someone doing financial planning. It's not just a matter of older individuals being more conservative because a monetary mindset is also based on the core values created in one's youth.

Real Estate Agents

It's common sense that homebuyers are looking for value and the potential for resale profit, but residential real estate brokers need to understand that most people looking for a home are also looking for something to love. For Techticians, who generally like to stay busy around the house, home offices, sophisticated kitchens, and landscape gardens are desirable features. Believers are more interested in balancing community life with a sense of sanctuary. Also essential to real estate agents is an understanding of the Transformers, who expect to be consulted in major family transactions and will have real influence over their parents in the home-buying "deed being done."

Strategic Planning

It used to be a popular workplace practice, whether one was talking about products or personal career paths, to seriously address five-, ten-, or even fifteen-year road maps. While some organizations still do strategic long-range planning, there is increasing cynicism about the usefulness of these "guestimated" timelines. Values, as has been seen in this book, are a way of readdressing long-range issues within a context of consistency and durability over long periods of time. Rather than asking the consumer, the client, or the colleague, what they will be doing in ten years, Value Population demography suggests that a more useful question is, "In ten years, what will you value?" The answer is likely to be, "Pretty much the same thing I value today."

In Part One of this book, our attention was on the reasoning behind values-based demographic profiling and the method used to identify Value Populations. In Part Two, we introduced the Value Populations and outlined the significant events, cultural artifacts, and lasting icons associated with each. We also provided a glimpse of "who" might be the next Value Population. Part Three moved into the direct application of this material with real businesses that have successfully used Value Population research to increase their marketing impact and business profitability. Finally, in Part Four we outlined how values can and should be an important part of any business strategy—from organizational structure to personnel management to employee motivation to trend identification and creation.

To this end, the authors hope that the reader accepts *The Consistent Consumer* on its intended terms—not as a mature work of the Age of Information but as an earnest early contribution to the Age of Meaning.

DISCARD

NORTH CAMPUS
MIAMI-DADE COLLEGE
MIAMI, FL